JINXED

How Not To Rock 'N' Roll

To Lizzie
Be warned, no ~~sex~~,
but lots of drugs 'n rock 'n'
roll.

Love
Del x

DEL GREENING

ISBN: 978-1-8380116-4-2

First Published 2022 by Tome & Metre Books
Revised Edition Published 2023 by Tome & Metre Books
© Tome & Metre Publishing
Photographs (unless stated) Copyright © Derek Greening
Back cover photograph: Steve Potts

Printed by Stephens & George Print Group
Goat Mill Road, Dowlais, Merthyr Tydfil, CF48 3TD.

T&M Books Artwork Editor: Rob Cook
Book Cover Design: Viki Vortex
T&M Books Text Editor: Mark Chadderton
Assistant Editor: Martin Cooper
Tome & Metre Books Draft Readers Club: Nathan Jessup, Mark Kite

Tome & Metre Books and Tome & Metre Publishing
are wholly owned subsidiaries of Time & Matter Recordings.
Tome & Metre Publishing, P.O. Box 5261, CV37 1JR.

www.timematterrecordings.bigcartel.com
www.timematterrecordings.bandcamp.com

T&M 049-2

This volume is dedicated to

Steven Greening
Tracy O'Brien
Callum Henderson
Nick Marsh

I would like to thank the following people for putting up with my constant harassment to contribute to this book:

Dave O'Brien, Tim Dawes, Smelly, Nick Loizides, Marcus Myers, Sue Wade, Ogs, Peter TT, Trapper, Guy Gillam, Doume Septier, Nick Linazasoro, Carmen Myers, Kev Mills, Rocco Barker, Henry Klaere, Arcturus Greening, Rachael Greening, AD Harris, Walnut Greening, Rum Philp, Christophe Saunière, Dr Nigel Hindley, Paul H, Jimmy Skurvi, Sam Fuller, James Mitchell and Nick Abnett.

In addition, I would also like to acknowledge the following people for their help in providing photos and filling the gaps in my memory:

Mark Chadderton, Rob Cook, Viki Vortex, Martin Cooper, Simon Hall, Lolly Dobrijevic, Gill Carpenter, Tony Mottram, Luc Carson, Gavin Watson, Graham Trott, Lee Strickland, Damir Thomas, Pete Jones, Steve Potts, Tracy O' Brien, John Delf, Michelle Knox-Brown, Mark Richards, Andy Aggro, Mark Kite, Dod Morrison, Steve Drewett and John 'Welshy' Welsh.

CONTENTS

FOREWORD

INTRODUCTION

01	Growing Pains	3
02	Lucky Bastards	9
03	Here Comes The New Punk	17
04	Ogs' Bollocks	25
05	Bonksville, USA	33
06	Peeling Carrots	43
07	That's The Way To Do It	49
08	The Cringe Club	57
09	Duncoke Spirit	63
10	The Hand Of God	71
11	Mustn't Grumble	79
12	Banana Shoot Pussy	87
13	Ich Bin Ein Frankfurter	93
14	Blue Shark Attack	101
15	Blue Shark Attack 2: The Revenge	111
16	Berserkers	117
17	While My Guitar Gently Slurs	125
18	Headlock Holiday	131
19	Dancing With Squirrels	137
20	36 Arseholes	143
21	A Tale Of Two Dinners	151
22	Die Again Tomorrow	157
23	Land Of The Rising Pie	167
24	Some Turtles Never Make It	175
25	Gimme A Dollar	183
26	Mid-Tour Madness	191
27	Reasons To Be Cheerful	199
28	Drum And Drummer	209
29	Sheep Worrying	215

30	A Foot Full Of Bullets	223
31	Tombola Time	231
32	The Shite-Inery	239
33	Alright 'Lil	247
34	Touring's Boring	257
35	The Del Strangefish Show	265
36	Prima Donna Bermuda Triangle	275
37	Comments Of Mass Destruction	283
38	Billy Bunter's Free Holiday	293
39	Giving Up Drinking	305
40	New Found Freedoms	309
	AFTERWORD	319
	Appendix 1: Del Greening Discography	321
	Appendix 2: Del Greening Filmography	324

The thoughts, views and opinions expressed in this book are my personal, drunken memories. Some names and circumstances have been changed out of respect for the victims and their families.

FOREWORD

Much prose has been devoted to the subject of rock 'n' roll and many are the performers who have swaggered and boasted their megacephalus way through turgid and tedious autobiographies in conceited attempts to boost their egos and convince readers of their importance, but this volume, like its author, does not conform to that hackneyed stereotype. 'Dodgy' Del Strangefish is not only a lazy and selfish purveyor of punk rock, but he is also a literary kleptomaniac and here, for the delight and amusement of the reader, he purloins extracts from various journals and diaries, pinches ideas and plagiarises purposefully for your personal pleasure.

[Good luck saying that after 12 pints of Strongbow! – Del.]

The world of rock 'n' roll is, most of the time, far from the glamorous and decadent lifestyle that the egotists would have their audience imagine, it can be gruelling, sometimes boring and, at times, utterly hilarious as well as degrading and embarrassing. I have had the pleasure (and sometimes misery) of sharing stages, dressing rooms, hotel rooms, vans, tour buses and more with Mr Strangefish and have seldom met a character with a more engaging way of telling a tour tale.

As you read these entertaining pages your time will not be wasted with lengthy descriptive passages or flowery adjectives, just good entertaining storytelling dishing the dirt on the realities of life on the road.

(Caveman) DAVE O'BRIEN - March 2022

INTRODUCTION

Do you wanna rock?
Do you wanna roll?
Do you wanna take a ride on a journey from humble beginnings to the
top of the world charts?
Yes?

Well fuck off and buy someone else's book then!

Once upon a time, I worked as a tour manager in a faraway land.
Two of the travelling show's headline acts had temporarily left us to do
some radio and TV promotion. So, over the next couple of days, the rest
of the remaining crew got together to drink the tour bus dry.

The subsequent party was filled with hilarious rock 'n' roll stories of
cock-ups, self-inflicted calamities and disgusting rock-star behaviour.
As we took turns to retell those unbelievable but true tales, we laughed
until we were rolling around in tears. That's when it struck me. Why not
write all this down?

So, if you're ready, strap yourself in, and let's take it from the top…

…a one, a two, a one, two, three, four.

DEL GREENING - August 2022

CHAPTER 1 - GROWING PAINS

Hello, cruel world.

As the prophecy foretold, on the three hundredth day of the year of our Lord, nineteen hundred and sixty, at London's Queen Charlotte's Hospital, I burst forth from the dark warm security of the backstage area, into the blinding cold stage lights of reality as I was abruptly expelled from the comfort of the womb.

Two years earlier in October 1958 at St Augustine's Roman Catholic Church on the Fulham Palace Road, Mary Johanna Brady, an unassuming Irish Catholic girl, from Crumlin, a suburb of Dublin, had married Leslie Geoffrey Greening, a born and bred London lad.

A brief encounter at Euston Station had brought them together. Les, a London transport police officer, used to take his tea breaks in the station's refreshment room where Mary served him coffee. As part of a large family, she had grown up living next door to Phil Lynott, later to become the frontman of Thin Lizzy, who would sit on her garden wall playing his acoustic guitar. Upon arriving in the UK, Mary changed her name to Maureen to avoid any anti-Irish prejudice that was prevalent at the time.

My father was law-abiding, honest, and hardworking, and lived his life by the book. A man who couldn't open a packet of instant custard without taking the time to sit down and thoroughly read the instructions. He would store his impressive record collection alphabetically, so if my brothers or I messed with them, we would instantly be rumbled by the way we had put back the vinyl and inner sleeve. Nowadays that sort of behaviour would be attributed to OCD, ADHD, AC/DC or some other misdiagnosed dyslexic initials that 'experts' now invent to describe anything slightly less than normal human behaviour.

My parents were simple folk; they didn't drink or smoke and hardly ever ventured out to socialise. Mum loved to read, and Dad liked to listen to music and watch TV. Every week he would buy the Radio Times and circle the programmes he intended to watch in Biro. No fluorescent highlighter pens back then, they would have blown his mind.
Dad would follow us around the house switching off the lights, closing windows and turning down the heating. A trait that I myself would later develop, once I had joined the bill payers' club and assumed the role of 'guardian of the thermostat'. I also later inherited his 'Mr Pedantic Pants' gene and became the crazed creator of over-detailed 'to do' lists.

Breathe In ✓
Breathe Out ✓
Go on shit tour.

When I was three, Dad brought home The Beatles' 'A Hard Day's Night'
LP. I still have an early memory of staring at the front cover, intrigued
by the fact that one of the band pictures was of the back of George
Harrison's head. Alternative, I liked it.

In 1966, along with my two younger brothers Steven and Warren, we
relocated from our London flat at 12 Ravenscourt Road, Hammersmith
to a brand-new bungalow with a small front and back garden at 113
Edith Avenue in Peacehaven, East Sussex.

Peacehaven was an undeveloped shithole located above the chalk cliffs
of the South Downs, approximately six miles east of Brighton. At first,
there wasn't even a road outside our new house, as Mum remembered
scraping the thick mud from the pram's wheels after a trip to the only
shop. Its geographical claim to fame was that it coincided with the point
where the Greenwich meridian timeline crossed the English south coast.

   Timelinetastic!

Peacehaven has featured in a couple of books and films, such as Graham
Greene's 1938 classic novel Brighton Rock, where the central character,
Pinkie Brown drives there with his new wife, Rose, intending to
persuade her to kill herself, but instead, ends up falling over the cliff to
meet his own death. The 1979 film 'Quadrophenia' starring Phil Daniels
as a mod named Jimmy also ends in Peacehaven, when he finds out his
idol, the suave mod Ace Face (played by Sting) is, in reality, a bellboy.
He steals Sting's scooter and heads out to the Peacehaven Cliffs.

During the filming, 'The Who Films Ltd', were offering £10 per day plus
a free lunch to be a mod or a rocker extra. Peter Bywaters, my soon-to-
be bandmate in Peter and the Test Tube Babies, actually made the cut in
a few scenes.

After they settled in East Sussex, Dad took on a travelling sales job while
Mum took up a position on an assembly line at 'Vacco'; a factory in the
neighbouring port town of Newhaven which produced thermos flasks.
Occasionally, the hot glass tubes would explode on touch and Mum,
after returning home, would spend the rest of the evening picking glass
pieces from her hand with a sewing needle.

My first school was Roderick Avenue Infants. In our art class, Mick Troak was about to sit down when I yanked his chair away. As he crashed to the floor, the whole class burst into laughter, but the teacher didn't see the funny side, and I was reported and heavily reprimanded. Mrs Randall the headmistress decided to make an example of me, so in front of the whole school, she slowly took her rings off one by one, bent me over her knee and gave me a damn good arse thrashing during the school assembly.

Like 'Operation Yewtree' never 'appened.

On to primary school and every day my old mate, skinny ginger tearaway Tim Dawes, and I would kick a tennis ball a couple of miles to attend Telscombe Cliffs School. We invented a game where you would score a point if you hit the ball against the next lamp post, but if it missed or didn't quite reach, it was the other player's turn. A bit like golf, but without the clubs or the silly trousers.

Tim reminisced about some of our early school days...

"I remember at Telscombe Cliffs, Del and I were in the school chess team and qualified for the regional playoffs. Del got to the final and was one move away from winning the whole tournament. He made the wrong decision and his game ended as a stalemate, which gave the other school just enough points to win the tournament for themselves.
On the school minibus, we cried all the way home.
Another day after lessons, we stole the key to the tuck shop from the teacher's drawer, got into the cupboard, and pinched a couple of boxes of Tomato Puffs, each containing 24 bags. We then put the key back in the drawer, so no one would know there had been a break-in. We sat by a trough in a farmer's field at 'Pigs Hill' and made ourselves sick trying to scoff the lot."

On weekends, after breakfast, I would disappear off into the countryside on my pushbike, returning at tea-time once hunger struck and then clear off again until nightfall. In those days there was no need to worry about being bundled into the back of a van and snatched away onto the dark web. The family home didn't even have a telephone so people would have to call around on the off chance that you might be home. Simpler times.

I moved on to Tideway Comprehensive in Newhaven, which must have had one of the most garish-coloured uniforms in the entire English school penal system. Bright orange jumper and tie or 'tangerine' as the school called it, and grey trousers. I hated secondary school and had no interest in anything I was being taught, spending most of my time devising ways to skip classes and bunk off which resulted in failing all my exams. While taking my English test, I was about halfway through the creative writing section when I looked around and saw all my mates preparing to go to the pub. I quickly cut short my essay by writing... 'and then I woke up.'

When I spoke to the careers officer, I described my dream of becoming a rock star.

"Army or Navy?" was the reply.

Right, I need to get this sad part out of the way so we can quickly get back to defying punk rock gravity. While on his paper round, my 13-year-old brother Steven's push bike was hit by a bus, and he was killed. They kept him in intensive care for a while before eventually turning off his life-support. During that time, our family went through hell and we were all profoundly affected, I believe still to this day. Steven was learning the guitar before he died and Warren and I would make fun of him the whole time. After he left us, both of us took up playing the guitar ourselves, so that his spirit could live on. Throughout my life, I've felt as if he has been watching over me, steering me past danger, offering guidance and grabbing me by the collar at the last minute to yank me out of life-threatening situations.

Now, back to the fun and games. My earliest encounter with Peter Test Tube was a joint nicking operation, stealing cans of coke and confectionery from the Tideway School tuck shop. One of us would distract the seller, while the other one leant over and helped themself. One afternoon after lunch, we offered to help carry the stock back to the storeroom and made a detour off with a couple of crates of Coca-Cola. We had pushed it too far this time, and the police were called to the school. After several interviews, we confessed to stealing one can of coke and a packet of peanuts. We got away with a police caution and were ordered to repay 26p between us, even though our continuous crime spree had been in operation throughout the summer term.

We both had paper rounds at Barrett's Newsagents, a small shop at the bottom of Roderick Avenue. We'd collect orders from our schoolmates so that when old Mr Barrett was out the back marking out the papers, we would shoplift and sell the stuff at a reduced price.

At the age of 13, I saved up my paper round money and walked three miles to Newhaven to go and buy The Sweet's brand-new single 'Ballroom Blitz'. I had some money left over, so on the way back, I plucked up the courage to go and see if I could get served in the Castle Hotel on the A259 in Peacehaven...

"Pint. Please?"
"How old are you son?"
"It's OK. I'm in the corner."
"OK. Just the one, then on your way."

At that moment, as I sat there with my new Sweet 7" and my first pint, guitar-based rock music and alcohol had already begun to misshape my life.

As the only one out of the gang with some bum fluff around the facial area, I remember shaping it into sideburns and a moustache, after being assigned the duty of going to the off-licence at the bottom of Roderick Avenue to get the Friday night supplies in. I waited outside until there were no other customers and entered as the door creaked open and the old sprung doorbell rang loudly...

"Please can I have twenty cans of Ruddles, two bottles of VP Sherry, some Babycham for the ladies and a quarter bottle of vodka?"

Aware that I was not yet 18 years old, eager for the money yet cautious to avoid having any teenage deaths on his hands, the elderly shopkeeper sighed.

"You can have the twenty cans of Ruddles, the two bottles of sherry and the Babycham but I'm not selling you any vodka."

I got bored of Peacehaven, hanging out with the same people in the same places, so, even though I was still underage, I began frequenting a heavy rock club on Brighton seafront called 'The Hungry Years'. It was a dark, dingy venue where the carpet was filthy and soaked in beer, but the atmosphere was always great. A typical Hungry Years DJ set would consist of 'Free Bird' by Lynyrd Skynyrd, 'More Than A Feeling' by Boston, '(Don't Fear) The Reaper' by Blue Öyster Cult, 'Reeling In The Years' by Steely Dan and of course, 'Stairway To Heaven'. I used to look forward to headbanging to 'Rock And Roll' by Led Zeppelin, 'Paranoid' by Black Sabbath and anything by AC/DC. They were all a bit faster and shorter than the usual tripe.

One rainy Wednesday, I went to the 'Years' but soon regretted it when I discovered it was Steve Hillage appreciation night. Some sort of backwards sounding, keyboard, headfuck guitar nonsense. I managed to avoid slipping into a coma and trudged out early. While making my way to the bus stop outside I heard shouting, swearing and guitars being tuned up. Intrigued and strangely drawn towards it, I made my way around the corner and down some stairs into a hot, dark, dingy room, where I discovered Brighton punk band, The Piranhas dressed as policemen. There was no stage, so the band stood on chairs, except for the drummer. Swearing into a microphone is pretty acceptable nowadays, but not back then, so I was shocked to hear someone doing it loudly through a PA system. There was an electric atmosphere in the air and all the songs were short, funny, frantic, and out of tune.

Perfect! I had discovered punk rock.

I loved T.Rex, Slade, David Bowie and my Mum's old next-door neighbour, Phil Lynott's Thin Lizzy, as they could all write classic three-minute singles. I started to eagerly watch out for any punk or new wave bands on Top of the Pops and bought the first Clash album. It sounded so exciting to me, like a chainsaw grinding its way through the rotten old prog-rock plank, plus their songs only lasted a minute or two. Even better!

Peter and I lived around the corner from each other and took the same bus to school. He had the first Ramones album, and I had the first Clash album, so I used to visit his house where we'd sit on the bed in his room and listen to them both from start to finish. One night Peter turned up at 'The Joff', which was our local youth club, dressed as a 'punk' with a picture of a woman's breast safety-pinned to his ripped-up jumper. My teammates from the club football team locked him in a cupboard and pushed it down the stairs.

Almost every Saturday, Mum would go to Brighton to do the big shop, and I would hand her my comprehensive list of all the latest punk and independent singles to order. The simplicity of punk rock had inspired me to get on with learning the guitar, so for my birthday, Mum bought me some lessons. Unfortunately, my first lesson was with some horrendous petunia-stinking hippie, who kept showing me how good he was at playing Wishbone Ash riffs. We spent the first lesson learning how to tune-up. I didn't want to tune-up. I just wanted to play.

I never went back.

CHAPTER 2 – LUCKY BASTARDS

I left school and lied my way into a crappy office job as a trainee draughtsman at Ranalah Steel Moulds in Newhaven, a dismal concrete building on a soulless trading estate. As a kid, I always enjoyed sketching and art, so I picked it up pretty easily and even started doing the other apprentice's work for him. The money was crap, £20 a week, less tax. In my pokey little office, I managed to train myself to be able to sleep with my head resting against the drawing board, so if the door handle creaked, I would wake up and look as if I was working before anyone entered the room.

One afternoon, I was summoned upstairs to see Mr Smithard, the weasel-faced managing director in his dusky office. While staring at me inquisitively from behind his desk with his half-moon shaped glasses balanced on the end of his long nose, he asked when he could expect to receive my exam results. In my initial interview, I had exaggerated my possible qualification chances in order to secure the position and had managed to hogwash him for about six months with a catalogue of flimsy excuses as to why my certificates had not yet arrived. He thus ordered me up to the school to go and retrieve them. Sometimes, after a pack of lies, the best card to play is the truth, so I confessed on the spot and nervously stood there waiting to be fired. He shook his head, scratched his chin, pondered the situation and then announced...

"Well, to be honest, you're pretty good at your job, so get back to work and we'll say no more about it."

Some weeks later, while sitting in my office with the sun beating down on my back, a group of friends strolled past the window, laughing and joking, with rolled-up towels under their arms on their way to the beach. I had an epiphany, there must be more to life than this.

I wished I were unemployed. Lucky bastards.

Nevertheless, having a job had helped me save up enough money to buy my first guitar amplifier - a Carlsbro Stingray, which led me to start up my first band with a group of like-minded ex-school friends. They were Simon 'young gifted and black' Hall (guitar and vocals), Kim 'Jim Lad' Burfield (drums), who had starred as a child alongside Orson Welles in the film Treasure Island, and housewives' favourite, Christopher 'Trapper' Marchant, a tall bespectacled, bumbling streak of piss (bass). In the beginning, we called ourselves Restriction, then The Restrictors, which later became, The Cornflakes, a slightly less 'metal' sounding name which we hoped would fit in with the quirkiness of the 'Brighton Beat' scene.

We would practise in Simon's bedroom, whenever Simon's Mum was out, rigging up my new amp so all the instruments and vocal mics could go through it. Kim had just passed his driving test, so he bought a Triumph Herald convertible to drive his drum kit and our amplifiers around. Young and inexperienced, we were yet to realise that the world of rock 'n' roll was soon to be filled with loneliness and pain, hidden beneath a haze of drink and drugs. But that's enough optimism for now.

We argued a lot in the band, and one of the biggest bones of contention was whether or not to include some of my freshly written punk rock songs in the set.

In 1977, punk had already made its way to Brighton from London, where it took hold in the local scene. Peter, now dubbed the 'first punk in Peacehaven', had managed to land us a few support slots in Brighton, so he temporarily became our manager. A job, which mainly entailed coming to band practice, getting pissed and falling asleep in the corner. There was unease within the band concerning the future musical direction and things came to a head when Phil, our supposed 'new manager', began showing up at rehearsals. I overheard whispers of matching suits and wedding receptions, plus local guitar virtuoso, John 'never out of tune' Hogben, had been waiting in the wings to take my place. So, when my Carlsbro Stingray amplifier overloaded and blew up, I was chucked out along with my new punk songs.

Peter and I had started hitchhiking into Brighton to attend gigs and one night we were excited to be going to see The Stranglers in the basement of the Buccaneer on Brighton seafront. We paid at the door and hurried downstairs but soon realised we had got the dates mixed up as the place was heaving with Teddy Boys. The band started…

"Well, it's a one for the money…
Two for the show…
Three to get ready…"

It was Shakin' Stevens and the Sunsets. We felt like a couple of vegetarians at a meat raffle as a sea of greasy quiffs turned to stare daggers in our direction.

It was time to go, cat, go. Immediately.

We made our way along the seafront and found another venue where a drummer was playing in a bay window with his back to the street. It was a dark dingy pub named the Alhambra, now demolished to make way for The Jurys Inn, Waterfront. We wandered in, bought a couple of pints, and stood in the half-empty bar watching some shitty local band called 'High Flying Clive' playing turgid blues covers. The two of us looked at each other and had the same thought, we could do better than this lot on attitude alone...

Why not start a punk band?

Subsequently, Peter and I got together in his old man's garage and cobbled together our first few songs. 'Elvis Is Dead' (three chords) and then we went all progressive with 'The Queen Gives Good Blowjobs' (four chords) plus a couple of other tasteless 'classics' such as 'Being Sick', a 10-minute, walking bass, 12-bar jam where Peter made up the lyrics as he went along. Pretty soon we had what appeared to be 'a set', so we borrowed Trapper from The Cornflakes, who were now called Marrakech or something equally shit, and enticed drummer Trevor Rutherford with a promise of actual gigs instead of endless practising with no endgame. Trevor's Dad owned a factory in Newhaven, so we got to practise as loud as we liked at weekends. We also had a few 'The Queen Gives Good Blowjobs' T-shirts made, leading to Trapper taking a few blows at his job when he proudly wore one to work and got attacked by some royalists.

In the summer of 1978, Peter, Trapper and I took a trip up to London to take part in the Rock Against Racism march in Victoria Park. After tumbling out of an East London pub we spotted reggae-influenced London punk rock band The Ruts playing on the back of a flatbed truck. We then bumped into long-haired Brighton punk legend Hugh, aka Smelly, and we all climbed on board.

Smelly remembered that day vividly...

"We climbed aboard The Ruts' lorry where I remember Peter singing his new song to me 'The Queen Gives Good Blowjobs'. He also told me that he was forming a new band. Then he gave Malcolm Owen from The Ruts his card and said - 'We've got a band as well; you can support us if you want?' We were then promptly kicked off the back of The Ruts' truck by the Rutettes, a gang of South London punk girls wearing tampons as earrings."

Peter continued to blag his way backstage and hassle for support slots in Brighton, and within a week, we had secured our first two gigs. Tuesday night at the Alhambra with Fan Club (featuring future drummer 'Ogs') and Thursday at The Richmond Hotel with Nicky and the Dots. About a year later, for some bizarre reason, we swapped bass players with Nicky and the Dots for six months. Trapper went to them and Blotto came to play with us. Look at us - we were ahead of our time. 'Bass Player Swap', a predecessor to the reality show 'Wife Swap' - where two wives change their environments by swapping houses.

After a few barrels of Dutch courage, we stumbled up onto the small stage and for some odd reason, the crowd seemed to enjoy whatever it was we were supposed to be doing. We only had four or five songs, so we did each song twice. Since we had no name at that point, we made up names on the spot, such as Peter and the Pints of Beer, Peter and the Packets of Peanuts, Peter and the Testicles, and so on.

One night we were on our way to a gig when we saw a newspaper headline 'WORLD'S FIRST TEST-TUBE BABY BORN' and that one seemed to stick. From then on, promoters started advertising us as Peter and the Test Tube Babies. I guess we were just in the right place at the right time because punk rock and its subcultures were spreading fast across the UK and the fact that we were rude, obnoxious, and could barely play, meant we fitted right in.

Our second ever show was attended by Rick and Julie Blair, who were starting a new independent record label, Attrix Records, operated out of a shop located in Sydney Street in Brighton's North Laine.
A compilation LP of local bands currently playing the alternative circuit was in the works. Rick thought we were so hilariously bad, that we'd be perfect for their new project. After just two gigs that week, we were already in the studio (well, someone's living room) making our first record. We recorded 'Maniac', one of the first punk songs I had ever written, that had been rejected by The Cornflakes, and at the end of the session, with about half an hour left we quickly bunged down 'Elvis Is Dead' as well. As so often happens, the afterthought was selected for the final record.

Chris Marchant, Peter, myself, and Simon Gaul, a curly-haired Newhaven hard nut with a soft centre, started hanging out together. Simon loved a good fight and guarded the stage like his life depended on it and was soon our unofficial security guard. We all liked punk music, going to gigs, and getting drunk, so we became a band of brothers looking out for each other.

One afternoon, after a heavy lunchtime session, we were wandering along a track out in the backwoods of Peacehaven when Chris got down on all fours and put his ear to the ground.

"I can hear horses coming…"

Several horses galloped into view around the corner, of course, we'd already seen them, well everyone except 'four eyes' as Peter called him... and so the nickname 'Trapper' was born. Simon was good at coming up with nicknames, mine was 'Uncle Del' and my brother Warren's became 'Walnut' after he shaved his head, and you could see all his lumps and scars. After Peter had his first skinhead haircut, most of his head appeared to be a chin. Simon began calling him 'Chinhead', 'Chin and Tonic', 'Chinzano', and 'Funghibum' (trust me, you don't wanna know!), but eventually it became shortened to just 'Chin'.

Simon also used to be able to get hold of drugs. We used to do blues, which were massive throughout the 60s and 70s with the mods. If only taken occasionally, one would see you through a night out, but your body would become resistant, so we'd be popping as many as three or four a night, which caused us to drink three times as fast, so most upcoming gigs were now spent paralytically drunk and speeding out of our heads. Then we managed to get hold of Tuinal, buying it from the old tramps who used to hang out in the bus shelter at Steine Gardens near the Buccaneer pub. Tuinal was a sedative-hypnotic (sleeping pill) which came in a brightly coloured half-reddish orange and half-turquoise blue gelatine bullet-shaped capsule. Without the addition of alcohol, it would put users to sleep quickly, so you'd have to wait until your fourth pint to drop one and then you'd be flying. After the alcohol starts to leave your body, you lose it very quickly and often wake up in someone's front garden with the sun coming up, tangled up in a rose bush, missing a shoe.

One night on the way back from a gig, as Simon was dishing them out in the back of the van, Trapper tried to convince him that he was 'used to two'. Later that night, while carrying the drum kit, he fell face-first down the concrete steps of the rehearsal rooms. Trapper also admitted...

"I remember chatting up a girl in the early days when I'd had about four of them, she said, 'Do you mind not spitting in my face and fuck off!'"

A few of the younger and trendier teachers from my old secondary school began showing up at our gigs in Brighton, including my old geography teacher, Mr Sandford. After one show, we were having a drink at the bar when Sandford suggested that we should play at Tideway School's end-of-term party in the assembly hall. A huge red flag went unnoticed, and a date was set. Little did he know his teaching career was about to be left hanging by a thread…

We were the first band to ever play at Tideway School, if you discount The Wombles' guest appearance at the Christmas disco, who were subsequently attacked, resulting in Tim Dawes pulling off and keeping Great Uncle Bulgaria's nose.

Our crew for that school show was the Piranhas' singer 'Boring' Bob Grover and their road manager, loveable Dave Bullock, RIP. Dave was tragically killed, and several other band members were badly injured after the Piranhas' bus was struck by another vehicle on the way back from a show. Dave and Bob picked us up in the Piranhas' van and we headed to the school for a 10am soundcheck. As we arrived, we couldn't pull in because there was a poor man's impression of Beatlemania going on. Mr Sandford and Mr Marsh dispersed the crowd and we met up with unofficial security guard, Simon, who helped us load in. Trapper couldn't make the soundcheck as he was putting up a TV aerial, so Bob stood in on bass. After a trip to the pub in Newhaven town centre, we headed back to the school to prepare for the show. A live rock band playing at a school meant that the place was buzzing, and the hall was packed. Before the show, Mr Sandford pleaded with Peter not to use any foul language, for the whole event was his idea and if Peter failed to follow the school's no swearing policy it would be him that would suffer the consequences. It was like asking your new puppy to guard the sausages. As we entered the last chorus of 'Elvis Is Dead,' Peter yelled…

"WHAT A FAT CUNT HE WAS!"

The plug was pulled and a girl in the front row wearing an 'Elvis is King' T-Shirt burst into tears, as did poor old Mr Sandford.

Amazingly, we were also booked to play the Peacehaven family carnival - do these people never learn? A local plant hire company loaned us a flatbed truck, but we were again without a drummer, so we enlisted the help of a guy called Cat, who was playing with The Chefs and Rick Blair's band, The Parrots. He'd also been in a punk band called Smak with big-nosed rock god Rocco Barker, who was later to become my future bandmate in goth/pop rockers Flesh for Lulu.

On the day of the carnival, Cat was feeling sick and had been throwing up all day but soldiered on regardless. We managed to get hold of a generator, set up the equipment and pulled into our position on the procession, between Peacehaven Boy Scouts and an infant school dressed as fairies. Imagine that friendly carnival scene as we passed Roderick Avenue in Peacehaven with 'The Queen Gives Good Blowjobs' blasting out of the PA system to a sea of astonished faces. A police panda car appeared alongside the truck and a two-miles-per-hour police chase ensued as they signalled for the driver to pull out of the procession at the next junction. In fear of arrest, the driver immediately put his foot down and sped off back to the plant hire depot. As Cat began to throw up again, guitars and amps flew around on the back of the truck whilst we all clung to whatever was bolted down. Today, there is a new roundabout at the bottom of Sutton Avenue on the A259 where we were diverted away from that infamous parade. Now, every time I drive past, I chuckle to myself and consider starting a petition to erect a statue or at least install some sort of commemorative plaque reading…

TEST TUBES BOOTED OUT OF PEACEHAVEN CARNIVAL HERE

One night, I took my 14-year-old little brother Warren (soon to become Walnut), into town to witness his first punk gig, The Ruts again, this time at Brighton Art College. We used to bunk in over the back fence by climbing up a tree and then holding onto a branch until our body weight lowered us down far enough for our feet to touch the ground inside the backyard. Sadly, Walnut only weighed about eight stone, so he had to let go 10 feet from the ground, ending up in a heap below. We arrived home drunk and covered in mud at two in the morning. Mum was furious and chased me up the driveway for keeping him out so late.

After that night, and in order to avoid the tedious late-night bus ride back to Peacehaven, I left home and moved into a bedsit in St Michael's Place, in the centre of Brighton.

"I thought you would wait until you had a wife and a child of your own before you left home."

"It's not the bloody Waltons, Mum."

I lived in one room with a bed, a single-ring electric cooker, and a tiny fridge the size of a pint of milk (the fridge, not the room), as well as a small communal toilet at the bottom of the stairs. The landlord had given me a spare key, but I couldn't find a place to hide it inside the building, so I stashed it between two bricks on a vacant plot of land on the corner of the street. One morning, I woke up with a flashing temporary traffic light and a shopping trolley in the room. God only knows how I got those up the stairs? I was still half cut and bursting for a piss, so I made a dash for the toilet downstairs and as I was standing there naked, doing my business, I heard the flat door slam shut in the wind. OK, now where was that spare key?

In the aftermath of my epiphany, I was now no longer interested in the tedium of 9-5 work and decided to live an alternative lifestyle. I had no intention of spending my life filling someone else's pockets, only to be handed a crappy gold watch by some stuck-up faceless billionaire after 60 years of hard labour. So, for these reasons, I started not showing up.

One Monday morning, I was lying in bed with a hangover, pondering what delights my job-free day would bring, when I heard a loud knocking at the front door. I tiptoed my way downstairs and slowly lifted the letterbox flap. Standing outside were Ranalah Steel Moulds' managing directors, Mr Smithard and Mr Pope. As quietly as I could, and without answering the door, I crept back up the stairs and went back to bed.

At Ranalah, there was a charming old gentleman named Charlie who worked in the storeroom. He was in his 80s, well past retirement age and had worked there all his life since he'd left school aged 13. He was familiar with every tool and piece of machinery in the building and could vividly recall every previous job in great detail. If you had a question, Charlie would be the man to see. I sometimes wondered why he hadn't retired so one day I asked him and he told me that it was his life and he didn't want to retire because he had little else to do. Shortly after that, word came down from head office that he had now been deemed 'too old' to work and they intended to force him into retirement. After he'd been made to leave, we regularly saw Charlie standing outside the factory gates in his raincoat and trilby hat with his hands firmly behind his back, gazing longingly through the window. A few weeks later we heard he'd passed away.

Later that day, I got up as I had arranged to meet some mates at the pub. When I got to the bottom of the stairs, there was a piece of paper on the doormat. I picked it up and read it...

Dear Derek,
We hope you are okay. Please come back to work as you are a valued member of our team.
Please take as much time as you need and when you return, we will be happy to discuss your salary and job security.
We hope to see you back soon.
Kind Regards
The Directors
RSM

Two chances - slim and fat.

CHAPTER 3 – HERE COMES THE NEW PUNK

Ever since I first picked up a guitar, the thought of being in a touring band always felt like an unachievable dream. A privilege reserved for bloated mega-groups such as Camel, Tangerine Dream or ELP. You had to be able to sing like Bob Dildo or play the guitar like Eric Clappedout. If you attended one of their gigs, you would watch the band like tiny ants on a postage-stamp-sized stage from a mile away. Then, as they walked off stage, security would whisk them away into a waiting limousine. Punk rock doesn't work in arenas, as the fast beats blend into an inaudible echoey blur. Small, sweaty clubs and pubs are the best places to watch live music, where the band and audience both become part of the show and you can enjoy drinks and a chat before, after, and during the gig.

In 1978, 'Vaultage 78', featuring our track 'Elvis Is Dead' was released and upon hearing the album BBC Radio 1 DJ John Peel gave The Piranhas a coveted 'Peel Session'.

Coincidently, it was at a Piranhas gig upstairs at the Alhambra, when Peter spotted John Peel next to him at the urinals.

"Oi Mate. When are you gonna give us a session then?"

Peel mustn't have thought that Peter was taking the piss in 'the John' because just a few days later John Walters, Peel's long-time producer, invited us up to the BBC where we recorded four tracks: 'Elvis Is Dead', 'Beat Up The Mods', 'Moped Lads' and 'Porno Queen'. I remember being thrilled with them at the time but on recent listens, through gritted teeth, not so much now.

We had now acquired a permanent drummer, Nick Loizides, who we had stolen from Lewes punk band Chaos, and as a result of our 'progress', a draft record contract from No Future Records had arrived in the mail. Peter wiped his arse with it and posted it back. An improved offer followed and while we were waiting for them to get their shit together and send us some money, we got a call from Garry Bushell, a journalist from one of the influential music papers of the time, Sounds. He had heard our 'Peel Session' and asked if he could come down to Brighton to write an article. We invited him along to a rehearsal at the Vault, an underground crypt with a series of tombs and arches which had been turned into rehearsal rooms. Situated beneath an old Presbyterian Church near Brighton Station, sometimes the coffins were smashed open by glue-sniffing punks with nothing better to do. The skull of a child was once found in a nearby phone box.

Bushell sat amongst the graves and watched us rehearse with his fingers in his ears, making notes between songs, and afterwards, we went on an obligatory pub crawl to take some pictures with him and his photographer, Tony Mottram. We made the front cover and centre spread of Sounds and a few weeks later we got another phone call from Bushell telling us that he was putting together a compilation album entitled 'Here Comes The New Punk'. He asked if we would like to record a couple of tracks as it was to feature many of our contemporaries, such as Slaughter and the Dogs, The Exploited and the Angelic Upstarts. We liked the idea, gave it the green light and were invited up to EMI's Manchester Square Studios. This was the site of the cover photo for the first Beatles LP 'Please Please Me', which shows the group looking down over the stairwell.

We recorded our proposed duo of tracks 'Rob A Bank (Wanna)' and 'Intensive Care' but shortly before the release of 'Here Comes The New Punk' we were told that it was now going to be called 'Oi! The Album'. What? What a stupid title we thought as we joked about it and imagined a scenario of a skinhead entering a record shop in an attempt to buy it.

> *"Oi!"*
> *"Yes, Can I help you?"*
> *"Oi!"*
> *"Yes?"*
> *"Oi!"*
> *"You have my attention, sir."*
> *"Oi! the album..."*
> *"Yes. We have albums. Which one would you like to purchase?"*
> *"Oi!"*

To start with, the idea was probably a bit of a wind up by Bushell, but following its release, the joke soon backfired and began to take on working-class political overtones. Whenever we played in London, a coachload of boneheads would show up from Leicester, King's Lynn or wherever, but soon left disappointed, as they'd paid to see some kind of powerful, rage-filled protest band but all they got instead was four drunk idiots bumbling around on stage and shouting jokes down the microphone. Luckily for us, they stopped coming to our shows and started following some other poor sods.

In 1982, Nick Loizides left the band due to the violence that had begun to surface...

"The straw that broke the camel's back for me was when my friend Neil

Poste got beaten up in the toilets at The Crypt in Hastings.
I also remember I was driving and forgot to pick Del up in the van.
Don't know how he made it to the gig?

At another gig, two busloads of punks came up from Brighton and were attacked by the National Front. At another London show, at the Bridgehouse in East London, I was threatened backstage in my own dressing room by the other band. I lunged at their singer and had my hands around his neck but got pulled off by his mates. After that, what seemed like hours (probably 15 minutes), Peter came by and managed to talk them into letting me go. One night, we played at the Presbyterian Church above the Vault and the NF allegedly burnt it down afterwards. It was a Rock Against Sexism gig and Peter shouted over the mic, 'Dance you cunts.' Then they cut the power, so we carried on with just the drums and the crowd singing along. At another show, Peter shouted 'It's Trapper's turn to be spat at', I think I hid behind my drums wearing a crash helmet.

In the end, all the chaos was too much for me, so I left the band."

Shortly after Nick's departure, we added the final piece to the classic Test Tube Babies line-up, drummer Mark Andrew Storr Hoggins aka 'Ogs'. A big jovial chap who loved a laugh and was at his happiest cracking ridiculous jokes with a drink in his hand. Ogs had been a member of a band called Plastix who had appeared on 'Farewell To The Roxy' LP with the track, 'Tough On You,' which was recorded live at The Roxy on New Year's Eve 1977. Nick Sayer, the guitarist from Plastix, later went on to form Transvision Vamp with Wendy James. Ogs and Nick used to live in one of the arches in the vault and when drummerless bands would turn up to rehearse, Ogs would be raised from his tomb and asked to fill in for the price of breakfast and a pint. There was a large space near the entrance where anyone could put on a DIY gig using a makeshift stage in the corner and I remember going to a punk festival down there and Ogs was playing for every band on the bill: Fan Club, The Accents and The Chefs amongst others. In 1980, the Test Tubes played the final show there, upstairs at the Resource Centre, which was then destroyed by an arson attack, allegedly by the National Front. In its place now stands the Brighthelm Centre.

Ogs was also currently part of a band called Midnight and the Lemon Boys at that time which featured Marcus Myers (who would later become the Test Tubes' fifth Beatle, Marcus 'Mystery'). Nick Sayer was again on guitar with Chris Anderson completing the line-up on bass. They were on the verge of something 'big', so CBS Records and a bunch of other record companies came and watched them play at Dingwalls in North London.

Marcus later recalled that moment of reckoning:

"We were headlining at Dingwalls and Altered Images were supporting. It was the Lemon Boys' big break and all the record companies were there. CBS signed Altered Images instead. We were all heartbroken and it was basically the end of the band. Our roadie, Big Mark Anderson, nicked Claire Grogan's Glasgow bus pass, then we all got drunk."

In the interim between Nick and Ogs we had a stand-in drummer for a while called Danny. As we were preparing to embark on our UK tour, we called around for him, but his landlady told us he had moved to America.

Nice to have been informed.

Midnight and the Lemon Boys' guitarist Nick had hurt his back, so they were on hiatus when I met Ogs at the Inn Place, a seedy disco under the Alhambra on Brighton seafront. In those days pubs and clubs weren't allowed to serve alcohol after 11pm unless they had a restaurant licence. Ahmed, the landlord, used to get around this by giving you a raffle ticket for a crappy burger and coleslaw on a paper plate. The dance floor soon became a coleslaw ice rink as everyone threw their food on the ground. Ogs and I, more than worse for wear, were holding each other up at the bar when I offered him all the free beer he could drink if he did the one tour for us.

He stayed with us for nearly 10 years and during that time, he never once admitted to actually being in the band, openly auditioning for other groups. Ogs surely deserves a place in the Guinness Book Of World Records as the longest stand-in drummer in rock history. Every time I see him now, he still demands...

"Oi! Greenin'! Where's all that free beer you promised me?"

I recently caught up with Ogs again, when he reflected on his time in the band in his own words…

"I was helping a Brighton sound company set up a PA when I saw the Test Tubes for the first time. I watched from the side of the stage and thought to myself 'who are these four little pissed up idiots?' Then I ran into Del on a night out at the Inn Place underneath the Alhambra where he asked me if I wanted to do a tour, drumming for them. I was in a band called Midnight and the Lemon Boys at the time and our guitarist Nick Sayer had done his back in. I was pissed, so I said yes.

Ten years later I woke up to find myself still in it.

   At the rehearsal, Peter kept looking around every time I made a mistake or forgot to stop. He was warned in advance...

   'Look around at me like that while we're playing live, and I'll shove these two drumsticks in your nostrils!'

   Also, I tried to change my name from Ogs to Jimmy Jambo to avoid embarrassment. We had some great laughs over the years, made some records, travelled the world and all that sort of hoo-hah.

The majority of my time in the band was a blur, but I became close friends with Del and visited him at his home in Spain.

   A few years later in 2022, I actually bought a ticket to see them again in Brighton. Nothing much had changed except Charlie Chinhead (Peter) had tripled in size!"

While he was playing for us, Ogs' girlfriend, Sue Wade, began running our fan club. Here, she explains how she first got involved with the band and ended up joining us on the road…

   "Being Ogs' girlfriend meant I was soon inveigled into Test Tube life. This generally involved helping out with whatever was needed, regardless of experience. It proved to be quite the music business education, albeit an alternative one. Aside from running the fan club and producing the odd copy of a fanzine called 'Rip It Up', I was soon driving the van when they were stuck for a roadie, as none of them could drive. I think Del actually could, but he'd cannily put off taking his test as he didn't want to get lumbered with driving duties, which would have interfered with the necessary drinking; before, during and after the gigs.

My rosy-coloured ideas of demurely sipping my bottle of Merrydown silver label in the wings as the guys played up a storm, never seemed to materialise as I manned the merchandise table while they were on stage, on one occasion jumping up on the stand to put a lanky skinhead in a headlock and wrestle a T-shirt back from his light-fingered grasp.

Similarly, 'lighting technician' was not on my CV, but one night at a show in Germany, in Osnabrück I believe, we learned that the PA company had turned up a man short and it was either me or nobody if we wanted a light show. The problem was the lighting console was ancient and, in my determination to put on a good show for the band, I pushed the box to its limits, pounding away on the controls in time with the big riffs until about three-quarters of the way through the set when smoke started pouring out of the desk. The lights blowing up was not an option, I prayed to the Punk Gods and kept going, my fingers starting to burn with the heat from the smouldering controls. A miracle - the band played their final song, and I was able to peel my fingers off the console. My only comment afterwards was from Del who said... 'You did quite well, you were only about a second behind the beat!'"

The word had got around that Test Tube Babies gigs were strictly fun-filled affairs and that anyone with any violent intent would not be welcome. We were having to choose our shows carefully but occasionally a dodgy one would slip through the net.

Sue goes on to describe a nightmare trip to Feltham Football Club...

"On a trip to the West London suburb of Feltham, we knew the gig might be a tad tricky. The atmosphere was tense, and the place was packed with skins with not a punk in sight. The crowd were definitely looking to kick off at the slightest opportunity, so we holed up in the dressing room. Through the wall, we could hear the support band as the lyrics of a klan-inspired crowd-pleaser floated through the wall and into our backstage dressing room, clearly, the punters were going to feel very let down by our good-humoured set. Nobody fancied braving the crowd to visit the toilets, so someone had the bright idea of digging a hole out of the plasterboard wall - Hey Presto! - an impromptu urinal. The most desperate band members christened the cavity wall as only they knew how. We then devised an exit strategy to get the equipment off stage and out of the venue as fast as possible. The gear was packed away at lightning speed. I sat behind the wheel of the transit, getaway-driver-style and as soon as the rear doors were slammed shut, with the jeers still ringing in our ears, I hit the gas. I don't think I took a breath until we were safely back on the A23 with the incentive of a 'gutbuster' at Brighton's all-night Market Diner cafe, where we always used to celebrate our safe return from an out-of-town show."

On one Sunday, we were scheduled to play Skunx in Angel Islington. I was still in bed after a late night when the van arrived in the afternoon. I got up as soon as possible, grabbed the nearest article of clothing, rushed downstairs and got into the van.

That night I played to 200 angry skinheads in my girlfriend's pink dressing gown!

I decided to move from my bedsit in St Michael's Place to Brighton's notorious Anarchy Ranch. Among the ranch hands were Peter Test Tube, Neil Poste from Chaos, myself, and a bug-eyed loon named Danny Bell, a sort of punk/hippie hybrid who wore a Gestapo-style long leather coat. He was the frontman of punk band Probe and went on to sing with Brighton 'out of tune' glam rockers, The Defectors.

We had many visitors, so most mornings, you would wake up to find people asleep everywhere, in the kitchen, on the landing, or in the hallway. Among those regular visitors were schoolkids Mark Verrion, later gloriously nicknamed 'Skweeech' for giving speeches in a loud, high-pitched voice, and his best friend Andy. They had formed a punk band called 'Andy Aggro and the Plastic Bodies', but before they had a chance to play a gig they had split up, when Andy shagged Skweeech's mum.

The Anarchy Ranch itself was actually an impressive five-bedroom Victorian townhouse at 6 Chesham Street, owned by the Invisible Man… or an actor who once played him. He lived next door and we could tell he was an actor by his bellowing theatrical voice that often came vibrating loudly through the wall…

"SHUT THE FUCK UP.
DON'T YOU ANIMALS EVER SLEEP?"

Peter was recently recognised in the street by the current owner, who told him he wanted to put up a blue plaque - a permanent sign installed in a public place of interest, to commemorate the site of the famous Anarchy Ranch… but his wife wouldn't let him!

The money from No Future eventually arrived, so we headed off to record Peter and the Test Tube Babies' first stand-alone 45 rpm single. We'd booked Oakwood Studios in Herne Bay but on the day, we got a call from John Boyer, our then driver, who said he was too ill (or hungover) to drive but we were still welcome to use his van. None of us had passed our driving tests but Trapper had just got his licence to operate a forklift. That'll do for us. We stocked up on beer and hit the M23, at one point taking a bend on two wheels before Trapper discovered the availability of four other gears.

Incredibly, we made it to the recording studio in one piece. The night before, Peter and I had gone to the Clyde Arms in Bristol Gardens, around the corner from the Anarchy Ranch, with a hidden cassette player to record the locals at closing time. This recording is included at the start of the track 'Banned From The Pubs'. In the studio, we also recorded 'Moped Lads' and 'Peacehaven Wild Kids', a story about a gang of my brother Walnut's mates, based on the headline in a local paper which warned: 'BOOT THREAT by WILD KIDS', after a minor skirmish was reported. One-man law enforcement officer PC Campbell considered the Wild Kids to be Peacehaven's public enemy number one.

After the release of the single, rival gangs of hooligans would make their way down from around the country to The Joff (Peacehaven Youth

Club) to attack the Wild Kids. At Test Tube gigs, they would get pointed out with a shout of "*That's them, get 'em!*"

Eventually, in 1979, the Wild Kids formed their own band 'Gatecrash' with Anarchy Ranch hand and lead singer of Lewes punk band Chaos, the legendary late Neil Poste.

More recently, in 2018 during the Test Tubes' 40th anniversary year, I received a message on Twitter from Dan Palmer, the club secretary of Peacehaven Football Club.

> *"Could you make a song for us to play when the team runs out?"*
> *"Yes. Would love to…"*
> *"Amazing. That will keep the Wild Kids happy."*
> *"OK great. When can we come to a game? Spruce up the royal box…"*
> *"OK. We'll knock up a VIP area. Keep the riff-raff away."*

Ha!

I went for a pint at The Black Horse in Rottingdean with their commercial manager Mike Bradbury, where he told me we could use their clubhouse to raise the money to record the track. He put me in contact with media marketer Phil Merry and we devised a plan to raise the money to record the new Peacehaven F.C. anthem.

People travelled from all over Europe to attend the show, and we easily raised enough money to record the new ten-minute version of the track. Peacehaven F.C. players now enter the pitch to our song 'Peacehaven Wild Kids' blaring out across the fields of Sussex.

A small victory at last!

CHAPTER 4 – OGS' BOLLOCKS

Every year, when September arrived at the Anarchy Ranch, we became the magic mushroom kings. We would drive to Blackboys near Heathfield where Simon Gaul worked, pick them, bring them home and then stay up for days tripping our bollocks off without sleep. Hence, the classic Test Tubes tracks '(I Can't Wait Until) September'. Parts 1 & 2.

An old Spanish friend of mine, Juan, once told me that a popular Spanish band had covered the song and during an interview on MTV explained that the song was about waiting for their exam results!

On our first time harvesting, we used the pick one, eat one, pick one, eat one, a method that failed miserably as no one was in a fit state to drive home. Peter's then-girlfriend, Julie, tried to give us a lift back in her mini, but was so out of it that she kept going through red lights and driving on the wrong side of the road. God only knows how we made it back to Brighton unscathed. Once back at the Ranch, we'd dry them out by the fire and then in the evening, make a delightful magic mushroom omelette or a nice cup of psychedelic tea.

Dan would bake the freshly picked mushrooms with his homegrown weed to make his infamous 'Dan's Cake', which, once digested, would render you a dumb, incompetent dribbling fool.

One afternoon, Walnut, local drinking buddy Paul 'H' from post-punk/gothic rock band 'Bone Orchard', and I went out to Blackboys in my car and harvested a bumper crop, a whole carrier bag each. We went for a few pints in The Blackboys Inn, then I dropped H off at his flat and told him we'd be back later for a mushroom brew before we hit the town that night.

On the way back to the Anarchy Ranch, Walnut said he needed some cash and asked if I could stop at the cashpoint on London Road. I pulled up opposite the Abbey National and Walnut got out and went across and joined the queue. In my rear-view mirror, I noticed a young bobby on the beat approaching. He walked around the back of the vehicle and tapped on the window, so I rolled it down.

"Good afternoon sir, do you realise you've stopped in a no-parking zone?"

As he leant through the car window his eyes widened as they wandered to the back seat and spotted the three carrier bags full to the brim with magic mushrooms.

"Is that alcohol I can smell, sir?
Been drinking today, have we?

Would you mind pulling around the corner, please?"

He then proceeded to stand in front of the car with his arms outstretched waving me around the corner into a side street.

My dream of a fantastic evening out on the 'shrooms' with my mates was now turning into a nightmare, with the prospect of spending the night stone-cold sober, alone in a police cell.

Being half-Irish and born under a four-leaf clover, a series of fortunate events began to unfold. An old guy in the cashpoint queue in front of Walnut fell to the pavement clutching his chest. A concerned crowd gathered around him, and an irate woman started yelling across the street.

"Officer... Officer, over here... quick... we need help... radio for an ambulance!"

I could see the anguish etched across his face as his chances of a promotion were about to be destroyed quicker than my brain cells during my planned night out.

The crowd continued waving and beckoning to him.
In the end, he had to go across.

"YOU, wait here."

Walnut withdrew his money, dashed across the street and jumped into the passenger seat. I was still in shock trying to think of some flimsy excuses I could employ once I'd had my collar felt.

Walnut screamed.

"JUST DRIVE, PUT YOUR FUCKING FOOT DOWN!"

As we screeched away up the road, I hoped Inspector Clueless hadn't had time to write down my registration but just in case, we went straight back round to Paul H's flat, had a glug of nerve-calming whiskey and told him to get the brew going. Aaah!

Back in the real world, our first two singles, 'Banned From The Pubs' and 'Run Like Hell' had both made 'single of the week' in the popular music papers, Melody Maker and Sounds. We were approached by a man named Nick McGerr, who had worked as an artist rep for the infamous London promoter John Curd. We'd played a few of John's big Sunday night shows at the London Lyceum and after one show Nick offered to help us get more gigs and on doing so, ended up becoming our manager.

Our first album 'Pissed And Proud' was released in 1982. Originally it was going to be called 'Tubular Balls Up', a parody of Mike Oldfield's million-selling LP 'Tubular Bells'. We even had a glassblower make a test tube the same shape as the bent tubular bell on Oldfield's cover. Ogs suggested calling the debut album 'Ogs' Bollocks' with a close-up of his hairy testicles on the cover. Unsurprisingly, that got rejected.

At that time, whenever Ogs was asked why he had acted so irresponsibly the night before, his comeback would be...

"Pissed and proud, mate!"

So we used that. I always preferred 'Ogs' Bollocks'!

The majority of our set had already been featured on singles and compilation albums so there was no point in re-recording them all, so we made the unusual decision to record our debut LP live. The album was captured at two separate venues, Blackpool Tower Ballroom at the 'Up Yer Tower' festival and the Klub Foot at the Clarendon in Hammersmith. We were supposed to record the whole thing in one go in Blackpool, but the festival, unfortunately, turned into a riot as glass bottles smashed against the back wall and rained down on us until eventually, we had to leave the stage when someone in the crowd threw a lump of wood which tore all the strings from my guitar. In order to fill in the gaps left in the set caused by the Blackpool riot, we decided to keep all the recording equipment for the next show at the Clarendon.

Barry Sage, who had 'worked with the Stones' and had a 'logbook' credit on 'Some Girls' mixed and produced it. Peter recalled the drunken photo sessions during which the record sleeve was created...

"I hate live albums (except for these three: 'Space Ritual' by Hawkwind, 'Made In Japan' by Deep Purple and 'Live & Dangerous' by Thin Lizzy), which explains why I never listen to it. However, it allegedly captures us at our best and many fans still rate it as one of their favourites. The cover photo was taken on Brighton Nudist Beach - you should see the uncensored pictures! As we crossed the road I got hit by a car and the bottle of Merrydown I was holding exploded, so if you look at my hand closely you will notice it's a bit bloody. The other photos on the sleeve contain some interesting personalities. Ogs is pictured in one photo with his then-girlfriend Sue, who for a while ran our fan club. He's also pictured

with Andrew 'Toot' Carmen, who at that time was our roadie, he went on to become the drum roadie (sorry, 'drum tec' as they say in the business) for Status Quo. There's also a picture of Del's brother Walnut cuddling up to my then girlfriend - Julie. Walnut must have been about 14 and looks it! Oh, by the way, that picture of Ogs lying down on the beach? Yes, he is having a piss! All the other photos were taken at the Anarchy Ranch. All the lyrics are in my crap handwriting."

On the LP's release, Sounds' John Opposition gave it 4.5 out of 5 stars…

'The long-awaited Peter and the Test Tube Babies' debut album comes as a live set, and that's how it should be: Never in the history of Merrydown Cider was so much consumed by so few in front of so many, and a Testies gig was the place to be in a lacklustre 1982. Despite their awesome consumption rate, the band are nearly always rock solid on stage and pretty versatile with it. They're not just terminal piss artists but bloody good on their instruments as well (the musical sort, I mean) so a live album is definitely the order of the day. Here you have the stage set more or less in the order they play it. The recording is excellent and it has the raw feel of a truly live album rather than one that has been endlessly overdubbed in the studio.
It's a fine debut album and I for one am very pleased that after all this time, Peter and the boys have finally got it together. There's just one snag though.
They'll have to write some new material 'cos they can't play the same songs for the next four years! Lock yourselves in your rehearsal studio with seventeen crates of Merrydown lads, and I'm sure you'll be ok…'

After its release, new manager Nick soon developed a hate/hate relationship with Chris Berry from our label No Future Records and decided he couldn't work with him any longer, at one point threatening to go down to Malvern where Berry lived and hang him out the window, Don Arden style.

Nick then helped us set up our own record label 'Trapper Records' – obviously named after our bassist. I suggested a possible label design could feature a picture of a penis wearing a pair of glasses with the record company tagline… 'Trapper, the Head of the Record Company'. This was also somehow rejected.

Back in Brighton Ogs and Toot had introduced us to Merrydown Dry Cider which became synonymous with the Test Tubes over the coming years, almost resulting in a sponsorship deal with the makers based nearby at Horam Manor in Horsham, East Sussex.

The local paper The Evening Argus reported on the association:

'Brighton band Peter and the Test Tube Babies are an unlikely lot to enter into the advertising business. You would expect a slick group like Manhattan Transfer to promote a hi-fi brand or Danish pianist Victor Borge to help sell Danish Beer, but a punk band pushing cider? And not ordinary Cider at that, but the top tipple in Sussex 'Merrydown' - Made at Horam.

The band's weakness for the best vintage was revealed in a national music paper and the band told me that for a tour of the north, last week they took a couple of crates of the stuff with them to keep up their energy.

"We smuggle bottles into tour gigs in our drum cases" admitted Ogs and fans have also been spotted swigging Merrydown.

The news that Merrydown is a new punk rock craze surprised the company managing director Richard Purdey.

"We are delighted they enjoy it," he said, "As long as they don't bring the product into disrepute, jolly good luck to the band - I hope it helps to make them a good sound."

Peter and the Test Tube Babies, whose home in Brighton is christened the Anarchy Ranch have had fan mail pouring in since their first single raced into the independent charts.

"We like to cheer people up with our music - we have a sense of humour and our songs are about everyday things that happen in life like getting banned from the pubs."'

To promote their album 'Plastic Surgery Disasters', we'd been invited as special guests on the Dead Kennedys' UK tour.

As soon as he'd left school, Trapper had started out on his first relationship, lost his virginity, got married and was expecting his first child. Busy morning.

His new wife Karen had given him the standard musician's ultimatum: *"It's me or the band"*, so Trapper told us he wouldn't be able to do the tour. Bruce Maxwell Smith, a friend of Ogs, was hired to play bass. Trapper did, however, show up uninvited to our Southampton and Brighton shows and grabbed his bass back and started playing. His new bride must have shut up shop as he kept trying to hit on Theresa, the wife of the Dead Kennedys' lead singer Jello Biafra, which became excruciatingly embarrassing for the rest of us.

It was at one of those DK support slots that future Test Tubes drummer 'Caveman' Dave O'Brien recounted seeing the band for the first time.

"The Dead Kennedys were going to be playing in Brighton! This was big news, the Dead Kennedys were our favourite band in the world, this event could not be missed so we sent off for our tickets.

The hallowed tickets arrived in the post and, printed thereupon was mention of a support band called Peter and the Test Tube Babies, we were dimly aware of them as a local band who'd had a few records out, but we knew very little about them. On the big night, we dressed in our finest punk rock raggedy clothes and caught the train to Brighton with our friend Steve, all our little hearts racing with excitement, I was proudly wearing my 'Nazi Punks Fuck Off' armband that had come with the Dead Kennedys single of the same name, we also intended to be there in time to catch the local support band.

The Test Tubes took to the stage, and we were deeply impressed, they were musically tight and powerful, conveying a good deal of arrogant punk rock swagger whilst at the same time they were hilarious and self-deprecating, through the atmosphere of saliva and phlegm with which the band were being drenched, we knew we were witnessing a very interesting live act. I knew none of the song titles but some of the riffs stuck in my head, this lot were alright. The next day, after school, I went to my local record shop and bought 'Pissed And Proud'."

In Brighton, Siobhan and Jackie, two punkettes from the local school, overheard their mums talking and tipped us off that the neighbours had signed a petition to have us evicted from the Anarchy Ranch.
The demolition of the building from the inside out was almost complete so it was time to move on. Fellow rancher Danny Bell and I moved in with our roadie Toot to Number 4 Bloomsbury Place, a four-storey house in a renowned area, close to the sea and just a short walk into town.

After Mrs Biafra's 'Noncey punk fuck off' episode, Trapper had another crack at wedded bliss for a year, then one morning he turned up at Bloomsbury Place in his mate's car, packed to the roof with all his belongings. He had left his wife again, this time for good. Uninvited once again, he was planning to move into our sitting room, much to the annoyance of Toot.

Luckily, he had a colour television set, which swung the deal.

Millions of Dead Cops, a punk rock band from Austin, Texas, were also on the bill with the Dead Kennedys and after some of the southern dates, singer Dave Dictor and a few other members of the band stayed with us at Bloomsbury Place in Brighton. While lounging around one afternoon getting stoned, the film 'Carry On Camping' came on and we were taken by surprise when Dave's girlfriend started yelling *"sexist"* and pointing angrily at the TV. As it turns out, she was way ahead of her time as that type of seaside postcard humour, characterised by homophobic jibes, fat gags, and relentless groping of female characters is no longer considered the ultimate in family entertainment.

Mwap mwap mawar! Cor, blimey guvnor.

CHAPTER 5 – BONKSVILLE, USA

During the early eighties, the Test Tubes seemed to be constantly on the road and after five years we had become pretty good musicians, blending a mixture of tight energetic punk rock with in-jokes and drunken sarcastic comedy.

On stage, Peter and Trapper would take verbal swings at each other, much to the amusement of the audience, but sometimes it would physically spill over into the dressing room after the show.

Trapper's method of getting the final word:

"You can take a free run up and hit me as hard as you can in the face. Then it's MY TURN."

We were also getting great live reviews and were about to start playing our first headline shows. We've always detested headlining, because it means you can't get completely shitfaced until the very end of the night. Well, you can, but it's not such a great idea, as anyone who has experienced one of those shows will testify. We used to love to rock up early, use all the headliner's equipment, steal the show, and then drink all their booze while they were on stage. Even today, we still try to negotiate our way down the bill and offer to swap with other bands who seem to think that going on later has some sort of prestigious value. At one particular Norwegian festival, we managed to swap our 10pm position on the running order with another band's 6:30pm slot. They pulled the plug on us after half an hour as that was the other act's allotted time. It turned out that the other band didn't have enough songs to fill an hour, so they had to end the show early. Ha!

In 1983, we began recording our first studio album at Pink Floyd's Britannia Row Studios. A three-storey building at 35 Britannia Row, Islington in London, Pink Floyd had recorded their 'Animals' album there, as well as parts of their album 'The Wall'. One boring afternoon I went for a wander around the building. I opened a door at the top of a metal staircase and was confronted by the still inflated giant pig from the LP cover of 'Animals'.

Peter recalled the recording session...

"Following 'Pissed And Proud', the live debut, it was now time to record our first 'proper' album. The year was 1983 and it was around this time that we somehow acquired a manager, Mr Nick McGerr. He persuaded us

to ditch No Future Records and set up our own label - Trapper Records. In theory, it sounded a good idea and it certainly seemed to work well… but nobody in the band ever saw any money from it.

Nick arranged a distribution deal with an advance, booked us into Britannia Row in London, and roped in Barry Sage (who had just finished some work with the Rolling Stones), to produce the album.

Rather than commute every day from Brighton, we all stayed with Nick's mate Marek in Brixton for the duration of the recording. God only knows how he put up with us!

Extensive gigging around Europe had improved us significantly and the fact that Del and I had written some great songs meant that we were very keen to do well in the studio. I also think we might have all been in awe of Barry Sage, and the fact that we were recording in Pink Floyd's studio. I am proud of this album. For a bunch of snotty-nosed kids, I think we did exceptionally well. Maybe one day we'll make some money from it!"

Peter was right, that studio must have been costing us a fortune with its over helpful receptionists and full-size snooker table, but we were young and naive so didn't bother to ask how much. I was still skint and was having to hitchhike back down to Brighton to sign on at the dole office, leaving the Brit Row engineers twiddling their thumbs instead of their knobs. My fortnightly dole cheque totalled £62.50 yet the studio must have been charging five times that, per day.

A lot of punk bands around that time were releasing records with what I used to describe as, the 'bee in a jar' guitar sound. As this was going to be our first studio album, I made a decision to try to do something different. I had managed to save up enough of my dole money to purchase a couple of guitar effects pedals, a Boss Delay and a Boss Chorus pedal. I still use those pedals to this day.

Lee Terry reviewed the album…

"Peter and the Test Tube Babies' studio debut is the wonderfully titled 'The Mating Sounds Of South American Frogs'. The lyrical approach has not matured in any way, the overall theme of glorious losers' anthems exemplified by titles such as 'The Jinx', 'Blown Out Again' and 'Never Made It' but musically their skills have expanded, with guitarist Del, in particular, displaying a much more dextrous style and a distinctive sound, especially on 'Let's Burn' and 'Blown Out Again', and a more ambitious sound is in evidence all over, with a crystal clear production and touches like the female backing vocals throughout. The Wham! pastiche 'Pissed Punks (Go For It)' raises a grin and the stream of righteous ire in 'Wimpeez' (originally 'Wimpys Are Shit', but presumably the title was

edited by more legally-minded heads, even if the lyrics weren't) is a joy to hear."

Sue Wade fondly remembered her own involvement in the recording...

"Nick McGerr was quite a character with his John Lennon glasses and cool, classic Citroën DS car which had this crazy kind of hovercraft suspension. I think he was a decent guy, but he was attempting to manage the unmanageable and that was never going to end well.

During the sessions at Britannia Row Studios for 'The Mating Sounds Of South American Frogs' album, I was asked to do something fun (at last!) - backing vocals on 'September', that classic ode to the psilocybin season. I sang alongside Suzie O'List, a professional session singer with a string of recording credits, and I could feel an attack of Imposter Syndrome coming on. But Suzie was lovely, generously calming my nerves and it all went well.

The next day, Nick McGerr decided we should host a preview of the album recordings for a select gathering of press and associates at the handily located Islington studios. Nick gave me a few tenners and I found the local supermarket. One laden trolley load of booze and food (crisps), plus a round of calls to leave messages for the usual suspects at Sounds, Melody Maker and NME and the sophisticated PR junket was all set.

Maybe it was optimistic to think anyone would actually show up, but those were the days when a late afternoon invitation resulted in a full house by 6pm. The words Britannia Row, Peter and the Test Tube Babies and free drinks (not necessarily in that order) worked their magic and people started to arrive. Among others, Carol Clerk from Melody Maker came along, and the party soon got started...

Everyone there seemed genuinely astounded by the power of 'Frogs', which sounded amazing cranked up through the Brit Row speakers. As usual, it was back to reality pretty fast. Back home to Brighton with Ogs, living on fresh sea air and not much else, until the next adventure..."

'The Mating Sounds Of South American Frogs' was mixed and finished at the more reasonably priced Southern Studios, a recording room in a garage behind some terraced houses in Wood Green, North London, used by Essex punk band Crass and their record label Crass Records. Three singles were released from 'Frogs': 'Blown Out Again', Wimpeez' and 'The Jinx', a story about the calamities that would befall us on a night out with Trapper.

Peter reveals here how we arrived at that album title…

"Whilst recording the album, we were of course constantly trying to come up with a title for it, as we had none. I remember one afternoon Trapper and I were bored in the studio, so we started looking through the sound effects albums. We could not believe that there was a whole album of frog noises entitled 'The Mating Sounds Of North American Frogs'. So of course, we nicked some frog noises from it... and then ripped off the title. With the title agreed, we set to work on the sleeve. Just down the road from Southern Studios was Wood Green Library. Trapper and I were in there one day and found a book with some great photos of frogs in it. So, we tore out a page with two frogs shagging and that became the front cover."

So, the frogs you can hear at the beginning and end of that record are North, not South American frogs, but you knew that of course... and what of the frogs making love on the front cover?
We later found out that they were in fact, toads!

After a busy year on the road, recording, releasing and promoting 'Frogs', our manager Nick decided to finish us off, physically and mentally, by sending us to the United States for our first-ever tour there.
On arriving, we discovered that the majority of the tour had already been cancelled, so we ended up playing just a handful of shows in California and Arizona.

Sue was given the thankless task of babysitting us Stateside...

"Nick was unable to go to LA for the Californian dates, so he asked me if I would stand in for him. He gave me a pep talk about following up licensing opportunities for the new studio album (...wait, what? Another job role?) and he also handed me an official-looking letter that I was to wave at immigration, if necessary. It must have worked because they let us into the country, although none of us looked exactly wholesome. I think we were booked in at The Tropicana Motel, but a friendly girl, Carrie, who worked for the promoter took me under her wing and I ended up, with Ogs, hanging out at her place in West Hollywood. She was mates with the legendary Texan band The Butthole Surfers who came round one day to play their first release - an eponymous EP. The next morning, I entered the kitchen to see an upturned pan on the floor with an enormous, meaty, long tail protruding from underneath. A note written by one of the Surfers simply said, 'This is one fucking big rat'.
For some reason, I travelled to the San Diego gig with Carrie in her car. We got lost somewhere on the city outskirts and she stopped to ask directions from a random hitch-hiker at the roadside. He offered to

show us where the venue was and hopped in the back seat. Things went downhill as he started rambling about his favourite drugs, then proceeded to say 'Ladies, this is a stick-up'. As he was sitting behind us, I couldn't see if he actually had a gun or not, but a well-lit McDonald's forecourt turned out to be our saviour as we swerved into it and dived out of the car doors. He seemed to lose heart then and ambled off to terrorise some other lucky people. Glamorous this was not!"

Our first ever show on American soil was at Oakland Annie's in the East Bay region of the San Francisco Bay Area. It was there that we had our first taste of American weed, which, at the time, was so much stronger than the hash available in the UK. We were unaware that toke and pass was customary, so we hogged the joints and got so stoned we could barely play. During the show I had no idea where we were in the songs… or even which song we were supposed to be playing! Maybe an unheeded warning of things to come?

The next show on that first trip was at the 'On Broadway', an old avant-garde theatre and nightclub in San Francisco. We were all starting to suffer the effects of jet lag and the previous night's excess, so we went upstairs during the support acts to have a snooze in the circle seats. After the last of the support bands said goodnight, I ran down to tune up and get ready. We started the set but there was no sign of Peter. He was still asleep in the comfy seats upstairs, but after a couple of songs, he woke up, saw us on stage and started stumbling down the aisle, carrying his brothel creeper shoes and climbing over people in an attempt to get up and sing.

The promoter in Southern California was Gary Tovar, who named his concert business Goldenvoice after a strain of marijuana which users claimed made them feel as though they were being spoken to by angels. He now acts as the Goldenvoice consultant, which operates the Coachella Valley Music Festival, the most profitable music festival in the US. Even though we'd sold out the Olympic Auditorium which held 4,000 people, at the end of the tour we received the gargantuan sum of $12 each. Peter, Trapper, and I decided to stay in Los Angeles and experience the American dream - or as it turned out, nightmare. Ogs, Sue and our roadie Toot were dropped back at LAX where our famous Frogs backdrop was deposited in the airport bin as Toot and Ogs couldn't be arsed to carry it.

Unsurprisingly, that $12 didn't get us too far, so now cent-less (and senseless!), we were adopted by a young girl named Pam who took Trapper and me under her wing. Our room was at her parents' large house in Santa Monica, where, every evening, we had to join the whole family for dinner. We became known as the weird young English punk guys, residing in the back. Pam really looked after us and every day after school, she and her friend drove us around and showed us the sights of LA, even taking us to Disneyland.

We didn't want to do that though, we were still in our early twenties, we were in California, and we wanted to get drunk, take drugs, meet women and hang out backstage at concerts.

A hippie friend of promoter Gary Tovar had filmed the show at the Olympic and wanted to meet up and show us the footage. She picked us up in a large convertible sports car at Pam's house and drove us up into the Santa Monica hills to her house on Mulholland Drive.

When we arrived, the place was in complete darkness, as apparently electric light weakens your auric energy field! She showed us into her private cinema and dished out some lines of cocaine on a glass coffee table. This was more like it. After a few glasses of fizz and a few more lines, it was time for the grand premiere, as she started to show the movie. It was complete crap, filmed through some sort of weird red and green filter. The band hardly featured at all, just a few unrecognisable distant shots beyond the backs of people's heads. At one point the whole thing was upside down with the camera zooming in and out, spinning around and swinging from side to side, making us feel physically sick. We started to realise that she was completely bonkers.

She then announced that she had a play running downtown and asked us if we would like to go and check out the show. At this point in the evening, we'd have done anything to get away from the sickening video nasty, so we jumped in her car and headed downtown to the theatre. When we arrived, the performance was over and the theatre was empty, so we just sat on the edge of the stage and got even more hammered.

The stage scenery for the play consisted of two apartments with cross-sectioned bedrooms facing the audience with the two lead characters living out their lives in neighbouring apartments. She continued droning on about saving the planet or some other incomprehensible bollocks and then burst into tears, so I got into one of the beds on the stage and crashed out. When I woke up she was gone, and Trapper was passed out on the other bed in the neighbouring cross-sectioned apartment. We didn't know where the fuck we were or what time it was, so we wandered around the theatre, eventually finding a fire exit and pushed open the doors, only to be blinded by the bright Californian sunshine. We were in some dodgy area of downtown LA and had no money for a cab, so we just started walking, even though we had no idea which direction we were headed.

Trapper remembers our horrendous Hollywood walk of shame...

"It was a time before phones or Uber, we had no cash and massive hangovers so Del and I had to walk in the boiling hot sun still wearing our leather jackets from the night before, past gangs sitting on cars, jeering and taunting us with their bandanas on. We must have looked like a couple of junior, teabag terminators."

We somehow managed to avoid being dragged into an alley at knifepoint and walked on for what seemed like miles, eventually finding our way to Grauman's Chinese Theatre on Hollywood's historic Walk of Fame. We begged a quarter and called Pam, who came and picked us up with a face like thunder, refusing to talk to us all the way home because we'd been naughty and stayed out all night.

One guy named Etch had mentioned we could stay at his apartment and offered to drive us around and take us to some 'happening' gigs. That sounded great, as we'd had enough of being mothered so we said yes. When Trapper told Pam we were moving on, she ran out of the house screaming, putting her arm through a glass window on the way out!

Etch worked for the AT&T phone company so we had the run of his flat during the day, but he soon got pissed off with the state of the apartment and we got told off because we left crumbs on the breadboard that apparently 'might attract animals'. We also blocked the toilet which also might have attracted even larger animals. One morning after Etch had left for work, Trapper started snoring so I thought I'd go and lay on Etch's bed. Later, when I woke up, I stretched and slipped my hand under the pillows, I felt something cold and pulled out a silver Magnum 45 revolver. Yikes!

Etch got us a job putting up Christmas decorations at his mother's house for $20 each. We thought it would be a cinch, putting a couple of baubles on a tree but Americans go large at Christmas, and it involved electricity, ladders and getting on the roof while doing our best punk rock Laurel and Hardy impressions.

Trapper recalled another of our work endeavours...

"We also got paid to wash Etch's Mum's white Mercedes convertible, so of course, afterwards we took it for a spin. I had no glasses for some reason and couldn't see anything, so without ever having driven in America and with no UK licence either, we drove off and hit an eight-lane freeway which freaked us out because we couldn't work out which lane we were

supposed to be in or how to get off it. I think we ended up on Venice Beach!"

Peter stayed on for a few months in California as the British music press back home reported that he had run away and married a model. Had he? Here's his story…

"Following the cancellation of most of the dates of our first-ever USA tour, we were left in LA in mid-December 1983 with return flight tickets that were still valid for another four or five months. It seemed rude not to take advantage, so Del, Trapper and I decided to stay on and have an adventure. I'm not sure how or why we split up, but whilst Trapper and Del went off to stay with this girl Pam, somewhere in Santa Monica, I ended up staying with an English guy, Harvey, who lived just a few blocks back from Sunset Boulevard. Harvey worked at a great shop called The Hollywood Book and Poster, close by on Hollywood Boulevard, and quickly got me a job there as well. Also working there was the most gorgeous girl I had ever seen, Christine Ameroux, and pretty soon we're going out with each other. I think we got together on New Year's Eve. Living where we were meant we were right in the thick of the action and we were out watching bands practically every night and often some weekend lunchtimes as well. Tex and The Horseheads quickly became one of my favourite bands. I remember once we were at a lunchtime gig of The Red Hot Chili Peppers who must have only just started. Later that evening Christine, Harvey and I went out to a party at someone's house and, lo and behold, there they were again playing in the front room!

Christine was very good friends with The Cramps and knew all of the coolest people so we were always on the guest list or at brilliant parties. I became known as 'that crazy English guy' since I rolled joints with three or five papers (normal to me), which was unheard of at the time over there. They were all rolling these ridiculous one skinners. One day in March though, Christine got a call, and it was from one of the band or our manager Nick. They had finally tracked me down and needed me back in the UK for an upcoming tour. The adventure was over."

The novelty of our first trip to America was starting to wear thin. After driving miles to punk rock shows, we were told on arrival that it wasn't cool to enter, so we had to stand around in the parking lot and drink Budweiser with the skateboarders. Awesome dude!

I ventured into a show once, it was empty apart from three bare-chested, heavily tattooed skinheads kicking the shit out of each other on the dance floor, not my idea of a happening punk scene.

We missed England, we missed Bloomsbury Place, and we missed our magic mushrooms. We said our final goodbyes to Bonksville, USA and flew back to Brighton, where we arrived just in time for New Year's Eve. Hooray!

Happy New Year!

CHAPTER 6 – PEELING CARROTS

The 'Meet The Wife UK Tour' (named by Nick 'Terrible Tour Names' McGerr) was about to kick off, so Peter flew in from the States and we drove up to Victoria Station to pick him up. We couldn't see him amongst the crowd, so we circled the station a few times before we spotted him leaning against a wall. It's no wonder we hadn't recognised him, he had undergone a complete image change, now wearing brown leather trousers, a tasselled poncho, and a neckerchief. All that was missing was Woody's Hat!

Peter confessed…

"I even had fuckin' cowboy boots as well. I came back totally Americanised. What an idiot."

American Idiot?

Years ahead of Green Day too!

His nickname for the rest of the tour became 'Clint Balsawood'!

Joining us again on this tour was Guy 'Double or Quits' Gillam, a loud Geordie who was selling our merchandise amongst other things. Guy remembered the first time he got sucked into the murky underground world of the Test Tube Babies…

"I first got involved with them when Brian Mckeich's Popworld promotions sent me off on tour with them to sell their merch on the 1983 'Jinx' tour. Del and I clicked straight away and remain friends to this day, with him later becoming the best man at my wedding, even delaying his own honeymoon by a week, as he had got married the Saturday before.
On that first tour, we drank like fish, took lots of hard drugs together and on a rainy windswept night in Leeds, fought in the street over a woman. I remember running down a dual carriageway trying to jump onto the car that Del, their roadie 'Toot' and the girl in question were driving away in. I was raging, and I'm not sure how I managed to track them down, but I ended up on the fifth floor of a block of flats in Bradford, hammering on someone's front door. The wrong door of course, but the commotion made another door open and guess who was standing there? Yes, Del, ha ha! We laugh about it now though.
We were all completely out of it that night, Trapper got into a fight with a one-legged barman whilst Ogs was arrested by the Bradford police;

however, they let him go right away because he was so completely off his face they didn't want to deal with him."

Later we arrived in Glasgow. On a previous visit we played at the infamous 'Venue' where the van was broken into before the show and all the 'Pissed And Proud' T-shirts were stolen, only to be sold later that night on the street corners around the club.

Several years later, Scottish chart-toppers Texas were playing at the Brighton Centre and I was there helping out with the catering. While I was peeling some carrots, guitarist Ally McErlaine noticed me and came over to say hello. He told me he was at that show and had been thrown out by the bouncers for being underage but still managed to climb back in through the toilet window.

This time we were staying at the Dorchester Hotel on Sauchiehall Street. In contrast to the iconic, swanky Dorchester Hotel in London, this version was more wanky than swanky. Guy and I wandered back after the gig and discovered an old upright piano in the foyer so we started bashing out some tunes, much to the amusement and annoyance of the other guests.

Jimmy the top hat wearing doorman strolled over:

"Dae ye boys want some girls fur a pound?"

A few embarrassed looks were exchanged before we decided to head up to our room. Several cans later, the phrase *"girls for a pound"* was still rattling around in our heads, and we started discussing what Jimmy might have meant. After laughing over a few possibilities, our intrigue got the better of us, so we phoned downstairs to reception.

"Jimmy, what about these girls for a pound?"
Jimmy replied, *"Come doon 'n' gimme th' pund then."*

At around 2am, we jumped in the lift and headed down to the lobby. At the reception desk, we each gave Jimmy a pound. What next? Maybe the girls would pop out from under the front desk or Jimmy would retrieve them from behind the office filing cabinet?

Jimmy took our money and said:

"Hauld yer horses 'ere" and a few minutes later a cab driver pulled up, nodded at Jimmy, looked us up and down and in the thickest of Glaswegian accents said, *"Richt let's gang."*

I had been fully expecting, and secretly hoping, to be instantly returning to the room empty-handed, so I hadn't bothered to put on any shoes or socks. Now I was starting to worry where this was all heading. Guy kept insisting...

"Come on, let's see what happens. It'll be a laugh."

Barefoot and a little less intrigued, I followed along. After a few minutes the cabbie pulled up to a burger van, rolled down the window, and shouted:

"Seen Cheryl th' nicht?"
"Na nae th' nicht" came the reply.

The meter kept running and the search started dragging. Finally, two girls were picked up. I use the term 'girls' loosely here. The moment they entered the cab, we noticed they were in their 50s, one of them had one solitary tooth, and the other was about 20 stone. Staring out into the rain-filled night sky, I started to wonder how this would end and began to consider possible ways I could escape and return to the safety of the hotel.

"It's a tenner back at the hotel or a fiver doon an alley."

Due to our gentlemanly nature, we, of course, agreed to take them back to our hotel. As we sat in the back of that claustrophobic black cab, one of them stared at us inquisitively.

"Sae, whit dae a coupla young lads lik' yi'll want wi' a coupla auld trollops lik' us?"

After we arrived at the hotel, Jimmy greeted us with a knowing grin as he let us in. I was starting to tremble with fear as we crowded into the hotel lift. How far was Guy going to take this? Suddenly he slammed his hand against the lift buttons, the lift door slid open and he was gone, leaving me on my own with Glasgow's finest.

"Where's he gaen?"

Could all of this have been pre-planned from the start as revenge for me stealing his date in Bradford?
The three of us arrived on the next floor so I started slowly walking along the corridor with the two working girls following close behind.

How was I to escape? In a moment of realisation I recalled that Ogs and Trapper were sleeping on the same floor, so in a last desperate attempt to save myself, I tried their door handle... Success! It opened. I led the girls/elderly women into the darkened room and once they were a safe distance inside, I made a dash for the door, slapping on the lights on the way out.

"It's a fooken set up."

These were the last words I heard as I pulled the door shut, ran to my room, double-locked it and slumped face down on the bed. My heart was pounding out of my chest, as a huge sense of relief washed over me.

There was no pound of flesh for us; Jimmy's pound was merely a commission for introducing us to the delights of the Glaswegian red-light district.

That scary night was a lesson learned... if something seems too good to be true, it probably is. Especially when it's *"girls for a pound."*

Nick McGerr was enthusiastic about how things were going, telling people we were going to be *"bigger than the Who by Christmas"*. In 1984, to promote the next single 'Blown Out Again', Nick brought in a publicist and booked an extensive UK tour. The new publicist came up with the ground-breaking idea of renaming the band - from 'Peter and the Test Tube Babies' to 'The Test Tubes'. Where do we begin with that one? Is it more commercial? Was the name change going to propel us up the charts? Does the Pope shit in the woods?

I guess that's just what managers do... interfere with the original idea. Anyway, I violently disagreed with him, and to exacerbate the situation further, it was time for a bit of self-harm...

It was a leap year and back in Brighton, I hit the headlines for all the wrong reasons. I don't remember much about the incident, but I do remember waking up at the Sussex County Hospital being unable to walk and with a broken wrist. After a boozy night out at Subterfuge Nightclub underneath the Apollo Hotel in Brighton, I had been walking along the seafront with a young lady on the way home when I attempted a less than impressive balancing act on the railings overlooking the promenade. I slipped and fell 20 feet on to the concrete below. Ouch! Nick rushed down to Brighton to try to help me get fit for the tour and even drove me up to London's Harley Street to visit a private specialist. He also booked me an appointment with an acupuncturist, to try to help speed up the healing process in my wrist bone. Alas, the tour started without me. Marcus Mystery played most of the lead guitar parts until later on in the tour, when I was fit enough to twiddle along in the background.

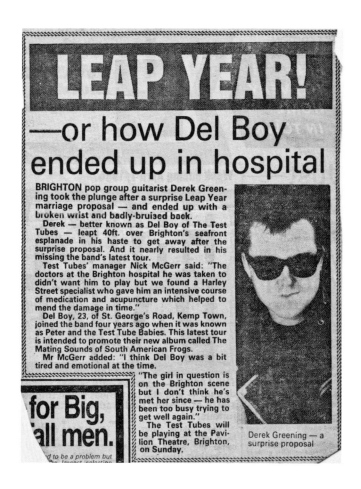

LEAP YEAR!
—or how Del Boy ended up in hospital

BRIGHTON pop group guitarist Derek Greening took the plunge after a surprise Leap Year marriage proposal — and ended up with a broken wrist and badly-bruised back.

Derek — better known as Del Boy of The Test Tubes — leapt 40ft. over Brighton's seafront esplanade in his haste to get away after the surprise proposal. And it nearly resulted in his missing the band's latest tour.

Test Tubes' manager Nick McGerr said: "The doctors at the Brighton hospital he was taken to didn't want him to play but we found a Harley Street specialist who gave him an intensive course of medication and acupuncture which helped to mend the damage in time."

Del Boy, 23, of St. George's Road, Kemp Town, joined the band four years ago when it was known as Peter and the Test Tube Babies. This latest tour is intended to promote their new album called The Mating Sounds of South American Frogs.

Mr McGerr added: "I think Del Boy was a bit tired and emotional at the time.

"The girl in question is on the Brighton scene but I don't think he's met her since — he has been too busy trying to get well again."

The Test Tubes will be playing at the Pavilion Theatre, Brighton, on Sunday.

for Big, all men.

d to be a problem but

Derek Greening — a surprise proposal

With positive reviews for the first couple of singles and albums, we were hurried back into Pink Floyd's studio to record the turgid 'Zombie Creeping Flesh'. I hated the song and the lyrics, which consisted of a half-finished riff and a description of some zombie movies that Peter liked at the time. Ogs decided he needed to hire in kettle drums, timpanis and bell trees for the drop-down middle eight, a far cry from the drunken trip to Herne Bay to record 'Banned From The Pubs'.

The flight cases containing Ogs' hired percussion began rolling in as Peter played snooker in the studio recreation room. Peter looked across rolled his eyes and screamed:

"WHAT THE FUCK HAS THAT GOT TO DO WITH PUNK?"

There was a massive buzz around the band after the UK tour, especially as Radio One's Kid Jensen had been playing 'The Jinx' on his daytime radio show. 'Zombie Creeping Flesh' was about to be released and we'd sold out the 2,000-capacity Brixton Ace in London. No pressure then. Manager Nick 'first 10 zombies get in free' McGerr had hired the best lighting and sound engineers in town, but forgot about us, the band, so with no food or drink available, we all wound up at the Prince Albert on Cold Harbour Lane and got completely arseholed.

It was time to go on stage, so Nick sent someone to look for us. After the stop/start intro music, Peter attempted to stand on the beer-saturated monitor, slipping, and falling into the audience before he could shout an incorrect lyric. Excellent start.

Before the show, Toot was so wasted he had tuned the bass guitar an octave too high, so you could now shoot arrows with it. All the crowd could hear was a blackboard-scraping high-pitched bass jangle.

The band competed to see who could out-shit each other and as the show reached its 'peak', or to be more precise, 'trough', Peter and Trapper decided to take all their clothes off and do the rest of the gig naked. This was punk Jim, but not as we know it!

To hide the embarrassment, Toot attempted to operate the dry ice machine at the side of the stage, but couldn't figure out how to turn it off, so now all the crowd could see was a cloud of smoke and a couple of knobs flapping about.

From punk rock heroes to box office zeroes, in a single evening. If only samplers had existed back then, the sound engineer could have simply triggered the Benny Hill Show theme tune.

CHAPTER 7 – THAT'S THE WAY TO DO IT

Camp entertainer Mike 'Sargeant' Stone was Britain's longest-serving Punch and Judy puppeteer and a typical Brighton eccentric. On one UK headline tour, we took him and his X-rated puppet show with us. The Newtown Neurotics, an English punk rock band formed in Harlow, Essex, were also on the bill, and we all travelled together on the same bus and became good friends.

At that time, teeny pop band Kajagoogoo were at number one on the UK Charts and they'd previously used this same tour bus. 'Kajagoogoo on Tour' was still emblazoned along the side with their hit single's title 'Too Shy' being written on the destination plate. The driver apologised and offered to get it all removed as soon as possible but we ordered him to leave it. This led to a large number of young screaming girls running alongside our bus as we pulled into cities around the UK. Of course, once they had clocked our ugly mugs as we waved back at them, their eager, excited smiles turned to looks of puzzlement and disappointment as their frantic running slowed to a frustrated trudge.

Mr Punch would appear on stage each night smoking a huge spliff and as the puppet policeman arrived to arrest him, Mike would have to erect an umbrella inside his booth as half-full beer glasses were hurled in the direction of the stage. Toward the end of his performance, he would introduce us...

"Ladies and gentlemen, it gives me great pleasure to introduce tonight's headlining act. Peter - and - the - Test - Tube - Babies. There's nothing like a good band and they're nothing like a good band."

In an interview with The Sun newspaper in October 1990, former Brighton footballer Justin Fashanu announced he was gay. The fact that he was the only man (until very recently) to have come out as openly gay during his playing career, tells you how brave he was at that time. At the Upper North Street dole office, Peter was in the queue reading the paper when, from the adjacent line, Mike Stone noticed the headline: £1m Football Star: I AM GAY.

Sergeant Stone rushed across and grabbed the newspaper.

"Hold on a minute, I used to shag him."

In April 2005, Brighton lost a very colourful character when Mike 'Sergeant' Stone departed to the great puppet show in the sky.

As 'Frogs' was now sitting pretty at the top of the German alternative charts, it was time to inflict some good old Test Tube shamboholic touring shenanigans on continental Europe...

Previously, we'd made a few minor trips across the channel, but this was to be our first full European tour. Mixing our front of house sound, as well as tour managing, was Mark 'Big Food' Botting, a big rugby-playing bloke who always got the job done and was just what was needed to keep a bunch of drug-addled drunken wasters like us in line. Guy Gillam was now taking care of the equipment, so Danny Bell had been brought in to embezzle on the merchandise stall.

On those early European tours, we always played in Hamburg, usually at the Markthalle located at Klosterwall in Hammerbrook. This is one of our favourite venues with the best technicians and stage crew, Louis and Chris, and of course the lovely promoter Evelyn Mommsen. One year, for some reason, we were booked at the Fabrik, in the Altona district and joining us on the bill were London goth rockers Flesh for Lulu.

A full-scale riot was taking place on the street in front of the building, the kind only seen in war zones. Punks and skinheads were fighting with the German police, who had started firing tear gas canisters to disperse the crowd. I chatted to Flesh for Lulu backstage as they were putting on their makeup. They were worried about their safety and asked if they would be okay out there? I assured them it would be fine, maybe a little less blusher.

The lead singer for Flesh for Lulu, Nick Marsh, watched our performance from the side of the stage. I remember making eye contact as he raised an eyebrow and gave me a knowing nod. Later that evening, Nick, Rocco Barker, and I, along with their sound engineer Harvey Birrell all ended up drunk on the Reeperbahn, the street in Hamburg's St. Pauli red light district. A good time was had by all and friendships were struck.

We had arrived at the hotel quite late that night. It was like the German version of Fawlty Towers and the overweight, chain-smoking, moustachioed owner told us in a thick Turkish accent that we couldn't check in yet and that there was to be:

"No shitting on the bed!"
"What?"
"There is no shitting on the bed, here."
"We're not going to shit on the bed."

Then we realised he was trying to tell us that the beds did not yet have sheets.

Trapper reminded me of another story while trying to check in:

"Yes, I remember that hotel in Hamburg. It was late and there was nowhere open to get anything to eat, so while the owner was fumbling about looking for keys, a couple of us snuck into the kitchen (I think it was Peter and me) and smuggled this massive leg of ham up to the room and tried to eat it. We didn't have a knife so it ended up being covered in teeth marks. After realising it was impossible to eat and worried that the owner was going to discover it missing, we decided to get rid of it. We tried hiding it in the room without any luck and then someone suggested chucking it out the window. We were on the top floor about four floors up and when we opened the window, we saw the big fat owner standing on the front steps smoking a cigarette. Dan came up with the idea to throw it on the roof. Bearing in mind this is a fucking great big bit of pig leg, he leans out and with all his might, chucks it up over what we thought was the ledge of the roof. Unfortunately, it bounced back, came back down past our window and hit the hotel owner on the bonce, so, not knowing what to do, we reverted to what we always did in these situations, quickly turned the lights off and pretended to be asleep."

Back across in France, after a big boozy night in Montpellier, we greedily bought eight grams of cocaine, one each. We couldn't finish it all, so I uncunningly hid what was left of mine in the front zip pocket of my leather jacket.

The next morning we set off in a drunken haze and as we were heading down a country lane, the 'Douane', a mobile French customs unit, suddenly flagged us down. We were all sleeping in the back when an old French plod began poking me and telling me to get out of the bus.

As I was being bundled out, I didn't have time to locate my jacket but soon enough, they found it for me, went through the pockets and found the coke. Danny Bell tried to hide his in his mouth, but as the paper dissolved his face turned a worrying shade of purple. The police must have thought they'd won the national gendarme promotion lottery as we were promptly arrested and taken to the nearest police station, where they telephoned for a forensic team. Since none were available, we were locked up in separate cells until the lab boys arrived.

They then searched the bus, removed all the merchandise and started counting it. In those days you were supposed to declare any saleable goods at the border. It was now looking more and more like we were going to miss that night's show and tour manager Mark Botting was fuming. Eventually, the lab guys arrived, and I got taken into the office where they were testing the drugs. Through the window, I could see the local gendarmes going through our bus, trying on our merchandise and laughing. Before the tour, Guy Gillam had come up with the idea of designing some 'Pissed And Proud' baseball caps so I laughed out loud when a couple of armed police officers entered the room wearing them.

After testing the coke with various pH papers, the guys from the science team looked up at me and declared…

"Oui, bon, it is good cocaine."

Great. I didn't get ripped off then, so I gave them the thumbs up. They also found the merchandise accounts.

"For the cocaine, you must pay us 800 francs and for selling the T-shirts without permission, the French customs tax will be 850 francs."

Ouch!

So, the fine for the illegally imported merchandise was heavier than the class A drugs. After we'd paid the fines and were released, we stopped at the tree near the arrest spot on the way out of town. Earlier, Guy managed to shake his cocaine wrap down the leg of his pants and kick it behind a tree, so we were delighted to find it and celebrated our escape with a big fat line on the way to the gig. We eventually made the show by the skin of our teeth, played a blinder and sold over 1,700 francs worth of illegal merchandise.

Customs 0 Test Tube Babies 1

We also encountered trouble with the merchandise on another occasion, at the Swiss/French border. Switzerland isn't in the EU, so once again, you need to declare any commercial goods. They found the T-shirts, records, hats and CDs before adding up the total value of all those saleable items. Then they presented us with another huge fine which Peter paid on his credit card. At the next payphone, we cancelled the payment by contacting his credit card company and reporting that his jacket containing his wallet and cards had been stolen at the show the night before.

Customs 0 Test Tube Babies 2

After reaching the South of France, the promoter told us there was a restaurant and buffet available behind the stage, where we could sit in the sun and help ourselves to whatever we liked and he would be along later to pick up the tab. Whilst we were enjoying our French food selection, Trapper came back from the buffet with a snail. Declaring that he'd never tried snails before, he put on some salt and vinegar and downed it. When the promoter arrived, Trapper told him that the snails were 'good'. The promoter looked confused and told him that snails were not on the menu.

Raised eyebrows all around. Wild snail. Mmmmm!

Nature 1 Trapper 0

Dave Harrop, our driver, and I decided to stay on in Paris for a while and then hitch down to Barcelona for some after-tour beach action. A friend dropped us on the outskirts of Paris and we started hitching. This is easy we thought, as we got a ride almost immediately and got dropped in the middle of nowhere about 200 kilometres south of Paris.

We found another spot on the hard shoulder and stuck out our thumbs again. After enduring five hours of disappointment, it was getting dark and cold. Finally, we gave up and began walking across some fields in search of the nearest village to find some sort of refuge for the night. We arrived at a half abandoned-looking railway station, but we couldn't see any information signs for the next train. By now it had started raining, so we were glad there was a waiting room available where we could sit and eat what was left of our provisions (half a baguette and some red wine). Soon after, we heard a train approaching and, after squinting our eyes in its direction, we both cheered as we spotted 'Lyon' written across the front. The city of Lyon is at least halfway to Spain, we thought. We could catch it and restart our mission to Barcelona from there. The train was empty as we climbed aboard and there was no ticket inspector. After about four hours, it was beginning to get light as we approached our final destination.
'Gare de Lyon' was back in the centre of Paris!

At the end of the Test Tubes' Scandinavian tour, we drove to Gothenburg to take the ferry back to the UK with our Swedish representative, Petra, who later went on to manage both The Cardigans and Europe (the band, not the continent).

Petra, or 'Peanut' as we had now dubbed him because of his short-cropped hair, was holding our tickets for the Tor Gothenburg ferry home, telling us that the boat was leaving at 5pm. As we arrived, we saw that there were no cars lining up at the terminal and even more worrying, no boat.

To our dismay, we discovered that the ferry had already set sail at

15:00, not 5pm and due to some weird Swedish holiday, there were no more crossings that weekend. The information office was closed so Peanut made some phone calls while we all took turns to stare cluelessly at the map. After several stupid suggestions, a decision was made to drive back up the coast of Sweden and catch a night ferry to Frederikshavn in Denmark, and then head home via Esbjerg the next day - at least we'd be heading west.

On arrival, we bought the tickets, drove up the ramp, parked the bus and made our way upstairs to commence the search for alcohol. Much to our delight, the bar was like a floating Wetherspoon pub with a large dance floor in the centre. We soon came to realise that this was the weekend party boat travelling from Sweden to Denmark and back again to take advantage of the cheap Danish booze. During that time, the Swedish government held an alcohol monopoly called Systembolaget, where beer was divided into three classes and you could only buy Class III, starköl (strong beer over 3.5%), and spirits at a Systembolaget store. I remember attempting to buy some vodka in one, I had to queue for ages and then once I'd had my ID confirmed by a guy in a white scientist's coat, he went off to get the keys to a glass cabinet before sealing it in a brown paper bag and eventually taking my money and handing it over.

The cheap booze was flowing as the party boat sailed across the Skagerrak Strait towards Denmark. Everyone on board was getting more and more shitfaced, and we certainly needed no invitation to drink away the worries of the day. In the middle of all the chaos, we hadn't realised that the boat had docked in Denmark and while looking out the window, I could see our tour manager Mark Botting running along the quayside trying to get our attention by waving his arms about and going disembarking mad. Mark's histrionics had proved too late; the boat had set sail back to Sweden with us still on board.

Peter, driver Dave, and I continued to drink and dance the night away and as there were no more crossings back to Denmark, Mark, Trapper, and Ogs checked into a hotel to wait for us. In the hotel bar, an investigation was launched and, after a few drinks, tempers frayed as they blamed each other for the latest mishap. As a result, rugby-playing Mark wrestled Trapper to the ground and punched him hard in the face.

Motion carried.

I woke up the next morning in a strange bed, in a strange house, in a strange country to the sound of Swedish voices arguing loudly in the hallway. A pretty blonde girl entered the room and translated that her father wanted me to leave immediately, but she had already told him...

"I can't throw him out, where is he supposed to go? He is English and has lost his friends."

The buffoonery had reached boiling point, with half the band in one country, and the other half in another. Trapper and Ogs decided to continue on with their journey back to the UK, while Mark, like the soldier who blows himself up with the bridge to save his comrades, stayed behind to meet us off the next ferry from Sweden.

The new day was about to deliver up a fresh set of unpleasant surprises, as we met Mark off the boat and drove to Esbjerg, only to discover there were no more crossings to England for another three days.

To relieve the boredom, we bought a football and took penalties against each other in the local park. There was certainly no need to practise any more spectacular own goals!

CHAPTER 8 – THE CRINGE CLUB

At Bloomsbury Place in Brighton, Dan, Toot, Trapper and myself had a macabre stroke of luck. Our landlord, Morris, was sitting at a casino table at Brighton's Duke of York when someone walked in and murdered him by slitting his throat. As a result, he was no longer able to come and collect the rent, so we rigged the electricity and gas meters so that each time you put a 50p piece in, it immediately came straight back out again. Living rent-free, signing on and receiving housing benefits meant those were the glory days of living in Brighton. The dole office was on strike so you didn't even have to go and sign on.

A typical day back then would consist of waking up in the afternoon, cashing your giro, going to the pub, going to someone's house for a mushroom brew or a hot knife session, getting stoned again in the evening, and then going out to a concert or party. We'd do it again the next day and the day after that and the day after that…

There was no doorbell or telephone at the house, so if there were any upcoming tours, I'd have to be woken up by the driver throwing stones up at my bedroom window…

Hurry! Passport into my back pocket, a couple of cans into a carrier bag and onto the tour bus. Nowadays, preparing to embark on a lengthy tour is a far more complicated affair. Passport, check, keys, check, wallet, check, reading glasses, check, driving glasses, check, phone, check, laptop, check, chargers, check, headphones, check, international mains adapters, check, credit cards, check, blood pressure tablets, check, chafing cream, check!

One night at the house, while out of our minds on magic mushrooms, we decided to build a bonfire in the tiny back garden. We sat and watched in amazement as it spread to our neighbours' fence until the tiny window to the garden was smashed in, through which, an axe-wielding fireman's head and helmet appeared as three fire trucks blocked the street outside.

On top of that, we grew cannabis plants on the roof and were again tipped off by a punk neighbour, who heard her landlord on the phone to the police. We managed to relocate everything before the raid, but the police still found our five-person hash pipe made from a 2-litre plastic lemonade bottle with five tubes sticking out through holes drilled into the top.

"…What do we have here then?"
"That's a helicopter from the future, mate", we replied.
(An early drone prototype, perhaps?)

All of us had citizen band radios (also known as CB radios), which allowed short-distance, person-to-person communication. Users would meet on the communal channel and then take their conversation to a separate channel agreed upon by both parties. My handle was 'Captain Haddock', Dan's was 'Terrapin Man' (because he kept terrapins), Toot's was 'Joe Bonesnapper' and Walnut's became 'Gnasher' (broadcasting from Peacehaven). Walnut even managed to get a real-life girlfriend after going for an 'eyeball' (meet up) with 'Little Mo'.

I thought I'd try my luck and started chatting to a girl with the handle 'Desperate Lady'. Sounded promising.

"Why did you choose the handle, Desperate Lady?"
"You'd be desperate too if your old man was in Wolverhampton nick."

Click.

We took pleasure in winding up local CB enthusiasts by going on random channels and shouting…

"Clear the emergency channel…"
"This is not the emergency channel; this is channel seventeen. The emergency channel is channel nine."
"Clear the emergency channel…"
"I just told you, this is not the emergency channel, the emergency channel is channel nine."
"Clear the emergency channel…"
"Are you stupid or something…?"
"Clear the emergency channel…"

Dan used to interrupt private conversations by saying in a high squeaky voice:

"Is that right, maaate?"
"Hey, breaker on the side, this is a private conversation please use an alternative channel. Over."
"Is that right, maaate?"
"Breaker on the side please leave this channel now. Over."
"Is that right, maaate?"
"Who is this? I repeat, this is a private conversation please use an alternative channel. Over."
"Is that right, maaate?"
"Are you taking the piss? I'm gonna triangulate your signal and come over there and kick the fucking shit out of you… Over."

Twat!

I tended to have this effect on women
New Year's Eve at the Alhambra, Brighton 1979.

Test Tubes at EMI
Manchester Square Studios, London 1979.

The Resource Centre above The Vault
The building was destroyed by an arson attack later that night, Brighton 1980.

The Anarchy Ranch
With the gloriously named 'Skweech' on bass, Brighton 1982.

Pissed and Proud
L-R Trapper, Del, Ogs, Peter. Brighton Nudist Beach 1982.
(Photo: Tony Mottram)

Where's Woody's Hat?
L-R: Del, Clint Balsawood, Trapper & Ogs. London 1983.
(Photo: Luc Carson)

The Cringe Club

"Is that right, maaate?... Is that what you're gonna do, is it?"

The evenings just flew by.

Of more historical significance, one morning just before 3am we heard a large explosion as the IRA attempted to assassinate Margaret Thatcher at the Grand Hotel. We watched the fire from the roof. Dan wanted to go down there and shake his fist at the building and shout 'See what you get, Thatcher' like Rik from The Young Ones.

A couple of French punks, Doume Septier and Marco, appeared unexpectedly at Bloomsbury Place one afternoon. On hearing our records they had made the pilgrimage from Paris to Brighton to try to meet us but, after visiting the fan club in Regency Square, Sue Wade had given them our address to get rid of them. Doume couldn't speak English, but his friend Marco had an English parent and was fluent. They offered to take us out and buy us drinks and as we didn't have much money we gladly accepted and took them clubbing. When we arrived home in the early hours there was nowhere for them to sleep so we said they could stay on the roof in their sleeping bags amongst the cannabis plants. After a few days, they left, and Doume left us his address in Paris, in case we ever wanted to visit.

One afternoon during a rare tidy up, we came across Doume's address so Dan, Trapper and myself decided to go over and take him up on his kind offer. When we arrived in Paris, we were expecting to be sleeping on the floor of a filthy punk squat but were surprised to discover that they all had nice apartments. Doume and his friends treated us like kings, taking us out for dinner and drinks every night and making us all feel mightily guilty for making them sleep on the roof back home at Bloomsbury Place. Years later, Peter took their Gallic generosity a step too far by marrying, and having a child with, one of their friends and getting Doume's brother's girlfriend pregnant.

Doume (or 'Duvet' as we had now nicknamed him) later started his own punk band, Trotskids, and when they visited London to record their debut album, I was on hand to help out with the production.

Doume recalled our first encounter...

"I remember when we first arrived in England, I felt like an idiot because I didn't understand English or what anyone was talking about, but I soon became a small brick in the legendary saga of the Test Tube Babies when they allowed me to design a picture of the band as half human frogs for the inner sleeve of their next record. I still haven't been paid for that, Ha Ha!

Anyway, the years have passed, and we are still good friends and still see each other from time to time, sharing a pint and a good laugh, which is the most important thing for me."

I had first visited France in the mid-seventies on a day trip from Newhaven to Dieppe with Peter and Trapper, skipping school. It only cost a fiver each, so our friend and international diplomat, Simon Gaul, travelled with us and announced on the ferry that when we arrived in France, he was going to hit the first French bloke he saw. He did not disappoint and as we docked in Dieppe, he ran down the gangplank and did indeed punch the first Frenchman he clapped eyes on. We were arrested, taken to jail, and spent the rest of our trip in the cells. A wonderful holiday.

The endless summers at Bloomsbury Place came and went, and I was starting to become restless. It was high time for a change, so I decided to step off the drink and drugs merry-go-round and made the decision to move up to London to 'get on with my life'. One incident made up my mind…

I'd invited a friend from Leeds to come down for the weekend, Bev from the band Civilised Society? She arrived with her friend and during their stay, some money went missing. Clive and Ben, who lived downstairs, accused her and her friend of stealing it. Their logic being…

"It must be them. We don't know them, and we wouldn't steal from each other."

I was infuriated by the accusation as I knew the girls would never do anything like that. I was even more pissed off after Bev and her friend had left and the downstairs tenants discovered the 'stolen' cash under the mattress… Stoned idiots.

In the 1980s, King's Cross in London was a seedy hotbed of crime, drugs, and prostitution. Our manager, Nick 'Five Storey' McGerr had decided to rent an office in Wharfedale Road just around the corner from the main station. It was a large five-storey building dusty and covered in cobwebs, with a small pub next door, The Queen Victoria. I decided to go and live in the office rent-free, transforming one of the downstairs rooms into an apartment (well, a mattress on the floor with an outside toilet).

I instantly fell in love with my new life in the capital, bunking the Tube, blagging our way into West End nightclubs, and gate-crashing boat parties on the Thames.

Drummer Ogs had broken up with his girlfriend Sue Wade, and moved in with Marcus Myers and Carmen Denton just off Ladbroke Grove. Marcus, despite not being in the band, had begun helping us with recording and touring. He didn't want his real name to be used for fear of hindering his rise to stardom, so he was listed on records as Marcus Mystery. At the time, even Marcus didn't seem to know which band he was in. He had formed Midnight and the Lemon Boys with Ogs, briefly replaced Jaz Coleman in Killing Joke, and then formed a band with KJ bassist, Youth, named Brilliant.

Guy Gillam, Ogs, and myself set up the new Test Tubes fan club in the room next to Nick the manager's office and called it the Cringe Club. We used to stay up all night taking speed, drinking cheap brandy, and making Cringe Club membership cards. We wrote to all the fans personally, made fanzines and put together a cassette of rare live audio clips, unreleased demos and recordings from the office answer machine and called it 'Journey To The Centre Of Johnny Clarke's Head', named after the infamous autistic local Brighton promoter and table tennis wizard Johnny Clarke. It was only intended to be a freebie to Cringe Club members but eventually became a bit of a cult classic. One day, a familiar face appeared at the window of the Cringe Club office, it was Steve Brown from Jungle Records. We invited him to the Queen Vic next door for a drink, where he told us he'd been getting phone calls from customers asking where they could purchase 'Johnny Clarke's Head'. A deal was struck to distribute the fan club tape through Jungle and he handed over a cheque - drinks all round!

Previously, Trapper had the label number 'Trapper 1'. Peter had 'Chin 1', so it was time for 'OD 1'. 'Ogs and Del Records'.

Trapper had built a soundproof studio beneath the Cringe Club, and The Fits, a punk band from Blackpool now living in London, signed with Trapper Records and started practising down there. I lived across the hall from the studio so, as I couldn't sleep or hear the TV when they were rehearsing, I would just plug in and play along with them. Later, I was invited to play second guitar on a couple of The Fits' UK tours.

Nick was becoming more and more disgruntled and who could blame him? We were now using his office to licence our own recordings, sell our own merch, rehearse and I was living there rent-free. Each morning when the post arrived, Nick would have a pile of bills and we would have huge piles of cheques - Cheers!

CHAPTER 9 – DUNCOKE SPIRIT

Suspicions were aroused at Cringe Club HQ, when some strange characters started turning up with instruments and making their way downstairs to rehearse in the studio that Trapper had worked hard to build. Nick the manager used to lock his office before he went back home to Somerset for the weekend, so one night, we decided to heat the putty around his office window, take out the glass and squeeze through the small empty frame for a nose around. Even without studying the accounts too carefully, it appeared that there was a lot of money coming in for Test Tubes' releases but a lot more going out to support other acts, some of which we'd never even heard of. I always liked Nick, his heart was in the right place and I don't believe he ever intentionally intended to rip us off. He certainly believed in us, but there seemed to be a lot of money changing hands, while we were always skint and our equipment remained shit. We resolved to make some changes and decided to sack Nick.

Amongst those weird characters arriving to rehearse, were a band named Joe Public, featuring American singer Cindy Jackson and the late ex-Angelic Upstarts and Long Tall Shorty guitarist Tony Feedback. Cindy was some sort of plastic surgery celebrity, frequently appearing on TV to talk about her operations and held the Guinness world record for the most cosmetic procedures. Guy and I took a break from Cringe Club activities to play bass and drums for them at rehearsals. If I was hungry Cindy would take us out for an expensive curry afterwards. A scuffle with Cindy backstage at Dingwalls eventually led to Guy getting fired, so I was promoted to bass. Ogs got a whiff of the free curry and took over on drums.

Garry Bushell wrote a glowing review in Sounds:

"Joe Public are the latest in a long line of talentless tossers turned on by the possibility of rock 'n' roll as an unprincipled swindle. But what the heck? They may not be peddling a particularly original sin, but they're a good grin and live their gigs have to be experienced to be believed. These Skid Row Joes are ringmastered by a terminally dodgy sex goddess, named Cindy Jackson, whose meagre vocal attributes fade into insignificance next to her alluring habit of blowing johnnies up to John Bindon size proportions on stage to "Find a man to fill this darn thing". Modesty forbids... Her partner in grime, Tony Feedback, is used to sharing a stage with a non-singer having strummed the old six strings for the Angelic Upstarts after making a minor name for himself in non-league Mod band 'Long Tall Shorty'. The dubious duo are backed up by a rhythm section

akin to the one that powers yon Peter Test Tube. No, it ain't a rat you smell, but lovable Del-boy and Ogs. Their set of massacred covers and 'orrible originals - sort of sixties pop played at demolition derby - falls apart more often than a flasher's mac on Clapham Common!"

A few months later, Joe Public toured with Edinburgh punk rock legends The Exploited. When we were on their bus, singer Wattie would drive while snorting speed with one hand and reading the address of that night's venue from the back of a fag packet with the other. In Blackpool Dingwalls, a young drunk member of the audience suffered first-degree burns after he fell asleep at the front of the stage and was set on fire. Upon finding out the victim was the son of the local police superintendent, the police sealed off the whole building and we were all held back for questioning.

Later on that ill-fated tour, we were booked to play at the Pavilion Theatre in Brighton. The U.K. Subs were also on the bill, so a large firm of us, Guy Gillam, Kev Hammer, and Upstarts' roadie, Chuck, drove down from London in ex-Banshees' roadie and U.K. Subs guitarist Captain Scarlet's van. As soon as we arrived in Brighton, we steamed into the first off licence, took whatever we liked, and walked out without paying. I recognised Alistair behind the counter as the senior draughtsman from my very first job. I was too embarrassed to stay and chat, so I just nodded and legged it out with the others. That night became infamous around Sussex and is now referred to as the 'Famous Brighton Riot'.

As soon as we finished our set, all hell broke loose with fighting breaking out, before spilling over onto the stage. We were trapped in the tiny dressing room so Kev Hammer pulled out his trademark hammer so if anyone with any violent intent came through that dressing room door, they would have almost certainly wished they hadn't.

Local writer for 'Brighton and Hove News' Nick Linazasoro was in attendance that night to experience it:

"On 15th February 1985, I witnessed a full-blown riot at The Exploited show at the Pavilion Theatre in Brighton, there were herberts there and you could smell trouble. After Joe Public played, the U.K. Subs abandoned the show during 'Warhead' after playing just five songs. People were being attacked and chairs were being thrown, the U.K. Subs singer Charlie Harper was trying to calm people down, but he eventually gave up and left the stage as the police came running up the stairs and stopped the show."

We were now ready to break the bad news to Nick, but before we could do so, we had to remove all our equipment from the rehearsal room at the office in Wharefdale Road. We saw in his desk diary that he was due to attend one of his other band's showcase gigs, so we took note of the date and time and hired Captain Scarlet and his van to move everything out of the building. As we were loading out, the police pulled up, and for reasons unknown, Scarlet ran away. He was either over the limit, banned from driving, or didn't have a licence to begin with.

Having now sacked ourselves from our own record company, I had inadvertently rendered myself homeless, so I started sofa-surfing around London, switching between Guy Gillam's in Willesden Green and Marcus and Carmen's in Ladbroke Grove. Guy shared a flat with fellow Swagmeister Michael from Edinburgh who we nicknamed 'Scotch Egg'... Of course.

Carmen, Marcus and Ogs shared a flat on the top floor of a large Victorian three-story house, on the corner of St Marks Place and Oxford Gardens. Carmen recaptures those fun times…

"At 95 Oxford Gardens, we lived on the top floor, the landlord was a bit of a git, nothing ever got repaired. We never met him, but Glenn Gregory from the band Heaven 17 lived in the basement and notoriously superglued all his furniture to the ceiling when he moved out (…or so it was reported in London's Time Out magazine). It must have once been a beautiful house, with a glorious sweeping staircase that contained three bedrooms of varying sizes, mine being the largest. Ogs got the smaller one, but I don't think he minded or even noticed. It was last decorated in the 1950s and we still had the original fridge and boiler to prove it. It was always freezing cold with an Arctic wind blowing through the hallway, no matter what the season. In the winter the insides of the windows would frost over with sheets of ice. We had many visitors staying, mainly friends from Barcelona, such as Alberto (Pirata) who was searching for bands to play in his home town (Brilliant and the Test Tube Babies both played there). His beautiful girlfriend Maribel and Moises Sorolla, the drummer of the Rockabilly band Los Rebeldes, as well as various Barcelona DJs such as Joan Grau, came over to buy records from Rough Trade that were unavailable in Spain. Ogs had moved in when Sue Wade, his then-girlfriend, found new love with Bruce Maxwell Smith. Ogs was always very drunk, but sweet, he did the washing up when I left it in his bed. Along with Ogs, came the rest of the Test Tubes, often fast asleep on the sofa or floor, with the cover of the Test Tubes' 'Rotting In The Fart Sack' being photographed in the living room. They were all old friends from Brighton bands, Marcus had moved in with me while still in Brilliant but

left as they were about to sign their big record deal. I think he dodged a bullet as they went on to be produced by Stock, Aitken and Waterman. Mind you, Jimmy Cauty, best known as one-half of the duo The KLF, co-founder of The Orb and as the man who burnt £1 million did well out of it, as did Youth who went on to become a top music producer going on to work with Paul McCartney.

We used to go out of a night, after listening to 'Subterraneans' by Flesh for Lulu, whilst glugging down Merrydown cider, our drink of choice. The Earl of Lonsdale on Portobello Road was where we would all meet, or the Batcave in Soho on a Wednesday night (Brilliant and Flesh played there often) and I think I was a goth in a sort of Spanish flamenco style, but weren't we all, for about five minutes?"

While I was crashing on the sofa there, Nick Sayer and Wendy James from Transvision Vamp were also staying, so Wendy and I would meet up every afternoon at five o'clock in the front room to play Blockbusters: a TV general knowledge quiz show where you had to complete a path of hexagons across a lightboard. Merriment ensued...
I'll go for a P please Bob. I'll take an E, etc... Chortle!

I received some good news when a room in a house became available in Brixton with an old friend, Annie Godfrey. This new abode at 57 Hubert Grove was a two-storey terraced house, situated underneath 'Death Bridge', so named because you could hear the screams of people being mugged crossing from Clapham North into Brixton. My upstairs living room and kitchen were shared with Andy Allen, who played bass in Steve Jones and Paul Cook's post-Sex Pistols band, The Professionals. The two of us got along fine, although he was sometimes a bit of a fusspot. I certainly wasn't allowed to use his favourite plate.

Andy was also a bit of a man about town, with his white Rasta dreadlocks, leather jacket and cap, he featured in photoshoots for trendy magazines like ID and Blitz. Many of his celebrity London friends would turn up at the flat and he would drag me along to showbiz parties where I felt uncomfortable, like a (strange) fish out of water.

From time to time, the smell of burning plastic and chemicals would creep up the stairs from our landlady's apartment. Peter came to visit me just a few days after I had moved in. We were alone in the house when we became alarmed by a loud hammering at the door. As I peered through the spyhole, I saw eight Old Bill with a battering ram about to break down the front door. In an effort to prevent it from being smashed, I stepped back and quickly pulled the door open as the police came tumbling into the narrow hallway, falling over each other with the momentum of the flailing battering ram.

"HANDS ON YOUR HEAD AND UP AGAINST THE WALL. NOW!"

Andy designed jewellery to sell in Kensington Market and had left a pile of crystals on a mirror, which he planned on using as eyes for some snake earrings.

"Gotcha…"
"No. You have not."

We were inevitably questioned while the premises were searched and subsequently told they would go easy on us if we confessed. (To what?) I later discovered that everything illegal had been moved somewhere else due to a tip-off. Eventually, the police apologised and left us a complaint form on their way out.

Welcome to Brixton town.

Coincidentally, a few members of Flesh for Lulu lived in the same street, at number 99. I knew singer Nick and guitarist Rocco from that infamous night hanging out on the Reeperbahn in Hamburg.
Rocco, formerly of narcotic glamour post-punk band, Wasted Youth, was the 'rock star' while Nick, with his pitch-perfect velvet voice was the naturally competent musician. I was instantly drawn to Nick's talent but unfortunately, like those old forgotten leather trousers tucked away at the back of your wardrobe, they came as a pair.
We would meet up in the Prince Albert pub on Coldharbour Lane, Brixton, a hangout for punks and goths. My new flatmate Andy had got me into their latest album 'Big Fun City', an upbeat record packed with original well-written songs and some great guitar riffs. We became like-minded regular drinking buddies and one night Nick told me the band were searching for a new guitar and keyboard player as he felt restricted playing the guitar and needed more freedom to move about on stage.
I drunkenly boasted that I could do both, even though I only knew a few piano chords. I'd talked myself into helping Flesh out so went home to start practising. Never thinking that I would still be in the band eight years later.

Following our split with manager Nick, Peter and the Test Tube Babies now had nowhere to rehearse, no van and nowhere to store our equipment. We needed a fast cash injection and Red Rhino Records, run by Tony Kostrzewa and his wife Gerri, had recently offered us £6,000 to make a new record. We didn't have any new material to speak of so they asked if we had any old recordings stashed away. We did have some demos that we had recorded at Chestnut and Seaford Studios back in the seventies, but the tapes had been so badly stored they were unplayable.

We desperately needed that six-grand but how could we acquire it? I came up with the idea to re-record those old demos. There weren't quite enough unreleased titles, but I had also been drumming for my brother's band 'Walnut and the Wankers', so we ended up asking him if we could use some of his songs to pad out the Red Rhino album commission.

We booked into Alaska Studios in Waterloo in the morning and started rehearsing and writing. There was also a recording studio in the building, so after lunch, we dragged the gear over there and played the songs live straight to 24-track. Trapper had the flu and went home so I played the bass and guitar on it, Walnut also played some guitar, and the backing vocals were shouted by Ogs, Walnut and Guy. Most tracks were recorded in one take with all the mistakes left in… intentionally.

During the recording, we all got totally wrecked and the engineer started mixing at around 2am. We had already arranged for the acetate to be cut at Porky Prime Cut, which opened at 8am, so with the sun coming up, we left the studio with the masters. At that time, George 'Porky' Peckham was known as the most accomplished at mastering vinyl records, with his master discs famously known as 'Porky Prime Cuts'. They often bear a cryptic or humorous comment etched onto the run-out grooves. As he hadn't played on the record our cryptic message read…

'Can you hear Trapper?'

As we were leaving, Noddy Holder and Jim Lea from Slade were waiting outside for Porky to work his magic on their latest offering. Peter and I then went straight over to Mayking Records in West London to hand over the acetate and design the sleeve. We'd brought all our old Kodak colour photos and press cuttings for the front and back cover. I wrote out the label for the record by hand and came up with the new record company name - 'Hairy Pie Records'. Peter then got the train up to York to meet Red Rhino and picked up the cheque for £6,000. We had pulled a few favours but the whole thing had cost us around £1,500. We used the balance to buy a tour bus and we called the album 'The Loud Blaring Punk Rock Album'.

The tagline read:

All the songs on this album were recorded in 1979 and constitute two days of heavy drinking in the studio. They were never meant to

be anything else but demos. This is not the band's follow up to 'The Mating Sounds Of South American Frogs'.

A loud, blaring, bare-faced, Boris Johnson-style lie!

We did it though, an 18-track album written, rewritten, rehearsed, recorded, produced and with the artwork designed and the cheque banked all within 24 hours. Wham-bam-thank-you-ma'am.

Now that's what I call, Duncoke Spirit!

CHAPTER 10 – THE HAND OF GOD

In 1985, the success of 'Johnny Clarke's Head' led Jungle Records' Steve Brown to ask the Test Tubes whether we would be up for recording an album of new songs, so we returned to the studio to start our second official studio album. I stayed with Marcus and Ogs during the recording, and every night after everyone had gone to bed, Marcus and I would sit at the piano and come up with silly ideas for songs.

I wrote the lyrics to 'Every Time I See Her', 'Ghost In My Bedsit', and 'All About Love', a pastiche of a power rock ballad, the lyrics of which later appeared in a Swedish school textbook, teaching Scandinavian students to read and write English. Every year, BBC Radio's Steve Lamacq plays the song during his Valentine's Day radio show.

The album was recorded and mixed at the Greenhouse in Old Street, London, with Noel 'Asteroids' Thompson engineering (his nickname alluding to an Asteroids gaming machine situated in the studio lounge, where he spent most of his time outside of the control room). London was buzzing at that time with bands such as Big Audio Dynamite (featuring Mick Jones of The Clash), Westworld and Transvision Vamp (whom Ogs lived with at the time) using electronics and sequencers influenced by 1970s glam rock bands such as Suicide and the New York Dolls. The British new wave band Sigue Sigue Sputnik were at number 3 in the UK singles chart. Ogs used this as an excuse to get out of setting his kit up and wrote some of his drums on a LinnDrum digital drum machine. We used the results on 'Every Second Counts' and 'Key To The City', which became the first single from the album.

I had called Trapper asking him to come up to play his bass parts and, the evening before, Noel and I managed to get a decent bass sound. The next day I had to attend a seminar on the Enterprise Allowance Scheme, a programme created by Margaret Thatcher's Conservative Party, which guaranteed an income of £40 per week to unemployed people who started their own business. This avoided the need to sign on while away on tour and also helped the Tories maintain low unemployment figures. I somehow managed to blag on to it twice, even though you were only permitted to take part once. Since I didn't have a business plan, I called mine Parallel Universe. Ogs created a vehicle-less haulage company named 'Truck Off!'

Trapper was left alone in the studio to work his magic.

"Don't worry," Trapper said.

"By the time you get back, everything will be finished."

I returned to the studio late that evening to find Trapper had already fucked off back to Brighton. Listening back, it was disappointing at best. On some parts, I could barely work out which key it was supposed to be in. I got straight on the phone to Trapper's girlfriend at the time, Rebecca, who was reluctant to get him out of the bath.

"Get him on the phone NOW. It sounds like he played it in the fucking bath. Underwater."

Once she realised I was serious, she passed the phone across. After that, I worked on guitars and keyboards for a few more days before Peter came up to do the vocals. Marcus Mystery added a few parts and Chris Gent played some saxophone before Noel and I finished the mixing. We wanted a one-word title like 'Quadrophenia'. A few phobias were suggested. Papaphobia – fear of the Pope. Lipophobia – fear of becoming fat (oh the irony!). Arachibutyrophobia – fear of peanut butter sticking to the roof of one's mouth. Andy Allen, however, was the one who hit the nail on the head with 'Soberphobia'.

Lee Terry reviewed it as follows:

"Soberphobia is a bit jarring after two solid albums worth of two-chord foolishness. It's a huge step up in quality; the musicianship is massively improved, the lyrics are cleverer, the palette of sounds is much wider. Del's guitar has taken on a semi-Gothic, jangly timbre (he was also playing with Goth-glam pioneers Flesh for Lulu by this time). 'All About Love' is a brilliant deconstruction of the power-ballad genre; 'Spirit Of Keith Moon' makes a reappearance in a more polished form, as do 'Boozanza' and the celebratory 'Key To The City'; 'Louise Wouldn't Like It', 'Allergic To Life' and 'Every Time I See Her' are good solid punk/rock tracks with unusually thoughtful words for such an unapologetically daft band, and 'Ghost In My Bedsit' is disarmingly poignant."

Since the early eighties, as summer approaches, I prepared myself for the annual pilgrimage to Somerset to lose my mind in a muddy field for a week. Glastonbury Festival in Pilton is the UK's largest festival, attended by around 200,000 people, although gatecrashers, of whom I was one, before I started working there in an official capacity, sometimes caused the numbers to swell. Well before the days of spotty teenagers with pink sunglasses and green glow bands, the festival was a much grungier affair with the travellers' field bursting into life after midnight.

One year, 1986 (although all my Glastonburys now seem to have blurred into one giant psychedelic flashback), we had brought both of the huge Test Tubes' fireproof stage backdrops and constructed a giant marquee between two buses. Inside we had a small portable black and white television hooked up to a car battery so we could watch the World Cup, which was being held in Mexico that summer. It was there in our makeshift teepee that we witnessed the most controversial moment in English football history, that infamous 'hand of God' goal by Diego Maradona for Argentina against England in the quarter-finals. Where was VAR when you needed it?

Another year, I arrived late to the festival and after clearing accreditation I made my way to the backstage area to find somewhere to pitch my tent. Having driven around in circles in the dark for over an hour, I eventually came across a large area of grass with no other tents on it. Perfect I thought, as I quickly unloaded everything, set up my tent and wriggled into my sleeping bag. Around 7am, the whole tent started vibrating with loud engine noises, and a strong smell of diesel filled the air. After crawling outside on all fours to see what was going on, I discovered a large hot air balloon hovering a few feet above my tent. As I looked around, I saw Guy Gillam in his giant multi-coloured shorts laughing his head off outside his tent. In the dark, I had stupidly pitched up on the Glastonbury CND Balloon landing pad.

I don't know if LSD was a lot stronger back then, or maybe I have built up a resistance over the years, but one year at the festival I dropped two tabs of White Lightning and Jesus it was potent. Never mind Maradona and the hand of God… I could now see the face of God!

As it started to take hold, my flatmate Andy Allen showed up unexpectedly and dragged me across the field and backstage to meet The Cure… the last place I wanted to be. It was a hot day and I was standing in their stuffy dressing room tripping off my bollocks and desperately wanting to leave. Fortunately for me, Andy got stuck in a deep muso conversation with someone, so I managed to duck out without him noticing.

For those of you who are unaware, sometimes when you take a lot of LSD your bowels need to evacuate rather sharpish. Due to my heightened senses, the infamous smell of the Glasto toilets seemed a thousand times more putrid, so I gave them a wide berth. As the call of nature grew louder, I headed out of the festival and found a small, wooded area with a babbling brook. I had discovered mother nature's restroom fully equipped with some large soft leaves as a possible toilet tissue substitute. As I squatted by a tree, I finished my business, grabbed some leaves/bog roll and stood up to wipe my arse. It was at that moment that everything came into focus, and I had a sobering realisation. I had forgotten the golden rule of defecation - pull your trousers down first. Fortunately, the babbling brook was not an hallucination and I was wearing wipe-downable leather trousers. The babbling brook soon became shit creek as I cleaned myself off, returned to reality and headed back to the hustle and bustle of the festival.

So kids, remember this important piece of advice…

Next time you take too much acid make sure you are wearing washable trousers… in case you shit yourself!

Guy Gillam was a constant companion during the Glastonbury years and here he looks back at those insane times…

"By 1991 I'd started my own merchandise company, 'TCB' (Taking Care of Business) and in 1993 I was offered the official Glastonbury merchandise concession. I would put a crew together, and we would set off early to get set up on the Monday morning, seldom making it on-site before midnight due to the multiple stop-offs (pubs) on route. The crew were a mad collection of people all hanging out in the TCB area. We had security guards, musicians, professional footballers, drug dealers, and all sorts of weirdos with most of them staying up all night and going to work selling the official merchandise, still out of their heads at 8am the next morning.

On hand to help with the heavy lifting and even heavier partying was all-round brillllliiannnt geezer and man-mountain, the late, great Callum Henderson. I'd known Callum since I was a kid back in the early seventies and we formed a punk band together called 'The Condemned', playing our first gigs in Berwick-upon-Tweed in 1980. There were some shows we didn't even get to play; I remember one in particular when we were chased out of town before we'd even had a chance to soundcheck.

Callum was one of the best party-loving, hard-working blokes to have around. Always looking for excitement, full of optimism and living life to the full. He was listed in the Guinness Book of World Records as being the youngest person to climb the north face of The Eiger, he helped underpin the Rock of Gibraltar and even painted the nine-mile-long Firth of Forth bridge in Scotland. Callum would phone you up at four in the morning to tell you how much he loved you. He once said to me - 'If I was anywhere in the world and I had one phone call for someone to find me I would call you Guy, as I know you would sort it'. I wish Callum was still here, for so many reasons but also because he can tell a much better tale than I can."

Guy, having snatched up the opportunity to run the official Glastonbury merchandise, meant we could head down to Shepton Mallet at the beginning of the week to get the party started early. In order to gain access to the much sought-after soft toilet paper, we would pitch our tents in the backstage area of TCB. Guy's section also backed onto the V.I.P. area of the site, so after a quick snip with Callum's bolt cutters, we had our own secret entrance to the free booze and would get stoned, take acid and go and take the piss out of the 'celebrities'. The three of us stuck out like a trio of red-faced sore thumbs – sweaty, scruffy, muddy-booted geezers amid a sea of trendy North Face jackets and brand-new Hunter wellies… and with Callum around, no one would dare to try to kick us out. Wonderful days.

The Soberphobia European tour was under way, and Marcus Mystery had joined us to perform the second guitar parts from the new album live. As we entered the Spanish coastal town of San Sebastián, we heard the news that three Spanish Policia Nacional officers had been shot dead in a café by an ETA gunman. The area was covered in graffiti, echoing Northern Ireland during the troubles. We left the hotel after checking in and went out for a late drink. As we were walking back, two men appeared behind some bushes, smelling of alcohol and waving pistols around. They flashed their badges and said they were plain-clothes cops. They calmed down as soon as we produced our passports and said we should be more careful since we could easily have been shot. Gulp! Later that evening, when our set began, the audience looked wild-eyed and crazy, and there was an electric atmosphere in the hall. One of the crowd immediately jumped up on stage, grabbed Peter's microphone stand, and bent it over his own head. Another guy was dancing in front of me holding a switchblade knife in one hand and swigging surgical spirit from a plastic bottle in the other. As soon as he got bored dancing, he climbed on stage and slashed my guitar strings with his knife. Without the guitar, we were unable to continue, which was a great excuse to get the fuck off the stage. A full-scale riot erupted. Ralph and

Scottish Al from our road crew at the time made it back to the small dressing room, but there was no other way out, so Al smashed a bottle of Jack Daniel's on the table and said…

"First uninvited person through that door gets this in the face."

Marcus however, recalled a pleasant turnaround to the evening:

"That San Sebastián gig where there was a riot, yes, I remember it well. I was recently talking with a friend who lives in Spain, Tom Beker, who had lived in the Basque Country for a while, and had heard about the riot, as it had become a bit of a legend in musical circles in the North. I remember the place was trashed, although, for some reason, they hadn't smashed our equipment up... but they did slash the tyres on the tour bus.

I especially liked it when two hours after we'd abandoned the stage, the Spanish promoter came into the dressing room with a bottle of Cava and six glasses, congratulating us for playing five songs, as English rockabilly band, King Kurt, the week before, had only managed three."

Meanwhile, in the foyer, Marcus' half Spanish girlfriend, Carmen, was attempting to run the merchandise stall, amidst the chaos…

"I remember that it was full of heavy skinhead types drinking pure surgical spirits. Total mayhem and madness, dancing wildly and baying like wolves. I was working on the merchandise stand with a security guard by my side. After the third shithead had jumped on my stall and nicked a T-shirt, I decided that enough was enough, so I asked to be escorted through the crowd of nutters, to the backstage area. 'They're all off their heads, it's scary out there' I warned the band. Shortly after that, a riot broke out, and I ran out on to the stage screaming down the microphone in Spanish for calm. Marcus dragged me off the stage into the tiny, enclosed dressing room where we all sat it out, whilst the smashing, screaming and banging could be heard all around us. At one point we thought the door would cave in. We later found out that all the van's tyres had been slashed and the whole place had been smashed to smithereens with bottles strewn everywhere. The Cava, when it eventually arrived, was much needed. That show has now become a legendary gig in Spanish music scene circles."

Later on that tour, in Germany, we arrived back at the hotel after the show to discover that it had an indoor swimming pool. Woohoo! Anyone up for a drunken midnight swim?

Even though it was all locked up we still managed to break in but couldn't figure out how to turn the lights on. Determined to be first in, I climbed up to the top board in the dark and dived in. That's when I painfully discovered that the pool was being serviced and had been drained. I crashed into the concrete on the bottom and broke my arm. I went to bed and in the morning, we drove to Nuremberg. I was in terrible agony and every time we went over a bump in the road, the excruciating pain would shoot up my arm. When we arrived, I got taken to the hospital where the fracture was confirmed. Upon returning to the backstage area, Ogs tried to force my guitar onto me, cutting a couple of holes in my plaster cast to see if I could still play. Ugh!

Marcus had to step up and take over the lead guitar duties. In such a short time, he managed to learn all the songs, and I flew home. Later, I heard that Ogs had decided he wanted to include a new, untried song in the set, 'Spirit Of Keith Moon'. Marcus told him he'd never heard that track before.

Ogs' response was…

"Just play anything!" …and boom, another tour saying was born!

The day arrived when Ogs decided that he was now a professional drummer and was no longer going to drink before the show. Due to the fact that he now didn't drink, he logically supposed the rest of us shouldn't either. To ensure this would take place, he confiscated the whole backstage rider. This was also to make sure there was enough booze for him to get totally paralytic after the show. One night, two of the tequila bottles smashed together in his bag and soaked all of his belongings. The next afternoon, he was attempting to dry all his sweaty stage clothes and piss-stained jogging pants on the radiators in the backstage area. The stench of tequila, piss, and body sweat filled the dressing room to such an extent that after a few minutes you would have to run to the fire exit to catch your breath as your by-now streaming eyes began to sting and burn.

Had the time come to join a band that allowed you to drink your own rider?

CHAPTER 11 – MUSTN'T GRUMBLE

'For the sun stopped shining and darkness fell across the whole land.'
Luke 23:45

After the punk rock explosion, everyone was on the lookout for the arrival of the next subculture. Notable punk and post-punk artists such as Siouxsie and the Banshees, Bauhaus, and The Cure contributed to the development of the new 'gothic' movement. Gothic rock stood out due to its darker sound, with the use of primarily minor or bass chords, reverb, dark arrangements, or dramatic and melancholic melodies, covering subjects such as sadness, nihilism, dark romanticism, tragedy, horror and death.

Mummy, I'm scared.

While living in London, I plucked up the courage to visit the dark side, frequenting clubs such as Alice in Wonderland at Gossips and the Batcave, every Wednesday at the Gargoyle Club in Soho. The Batcave was run by Specimen's singer Ollie Wisdom and guitarist Jon Klein. Originally, it specialised in new wave and glam rock but later turned to gothic rock. I attended, not because I loved the music, but because they were the best alternative clubs around at the time. I spiked my hair up and wore black but drew the (eye) liner at wearing makeup. These clubs often had guest bands such as Alien Sex Fiend, Specimen, Southern Death Cult and Flesh for Lulu.

In addition to Nick and Rocco, Flesh for Lulu's line-up now included Nick's fellow-founder member James Mitchell on drums and ex-Specimen bassist Kevin Mills, who had also taken on the role of band manager. The band had just signed with Wandsworth-based Beggars Banquet Records. Back in 1977 I had bought The Lurkers' 7" single 'Shadow' and their subsequent album 'Fulham Fallout' – Beggars' first independent release.

Flesh were about to start making their third album 'Long Live The New Flesh' with producer Mike Hedges, who had previously worked with U2 and The Cure, as well as The Associates and Siouxsie and the Banshees. They were recording at the oldest purpose-built recording studio in the world, Abbey Road Studios, best known for being the creative base for The Beatles. In fact, the original Hammond RT-3 organ used on Sgt. Pepper's was still sitting there in the corner of Studio 2. I was invited to play guitar on a few tracks (by Flesh for Lulu not The Beatles), where I contributed the intro riff to 'Sleeping Dogs' and played some parts on a few other tracks. The studio's small canteen was only open for a few hours each day, so every lunchtime we'd have to squeeze in, elbow to elbow, with The London Symphony Orchestra.

Flesh had the song 'I Go Crazy' featured in the Paramount Pictures movie 'Some Kind Of Wonderful', a 1987 romantic drama written by John Hughes and starring Eric Stoltz, Mary Stuart Masterson, and Lea Thompson. They also featured on the trailer, so to promote the film and the soundtrack album, we began a co-headline US tour with Leeds gothic rockers, The March Violets, who also appeared in the movie. Both bands shared a tour bus and I became friends with singer Cleo Murray, guitarist Tom Ashton and their keyboard player Aaron Davidson. One night while travelling between shows, I went to visit Rocco's bunk, but he wasn't in it. I heard giggling coming from Cleo's bunk and when I pulled back the curtain, they both slurred in unison…

"Ssshhh. It's a secret." The rest, as they say, is history.

Paramount were picking up the tab for the whole promotional tour and on arrival in Hollywood, both bands were invited to a private screening at Paramount Studios. We ate at the best restaurants, stayed in five-star hotels and got driven around in limousines. At the end of the tour, 'Some Kind Of Wonderful' premiered at the Chinese Theatre and we played at the star-studded after-party at the Hollywood Palace on Hollywood Boulevard. I was living an alternative reality as on previous US tours I would have been squashed in the back of a van with nine other hairy-arsed farting geezers living off 99 cent burritos.

On release, Flesh for Lulu's album had been licensed to Capitol Records in America and Polygram in Canada. Aerosmith's Joe Perry said that 'Long Live The New Flesh' was his favourite album of the year, so it looked like the planets were starting to align and I'd got involved at the right time. Capitol Records were not impressed with the UK version of the album cover so they ordered a brand-new photoshoot of the five of us. However, when the US version was released, some record company executive had decided to crop me out of the band picture. Maybe I was too ugly? Surely not! Fortunately, James was leaning up against me so at least my shoulder made it on to the front cover. Ha!

On our next American tour, we opened up for identical twin fronted British rock band Gene Loves Jezebel. The tour was in full swing when we reached the historic First Avenue Club in Minneapolis. After a smooth soundcheck, we walked across the street to check into the Loews Minneapolis Hotel where we arranged to meet back at the venue to get ready for the show. As stage time approached, Kev was yet to arrive backstage, so we dashed back across to the hotel, but there was no answer from his room. After the concierge let us in with the master key, there was still no sign of him, or his luggage, and the room had not been disturbed. The previous night, there had been a heated band debate as to whether or not our current US agent, New Yorker and blonde Betty Boop lookalike, Janet McQueeney, should become our full-time manager. Things hadn't gone the way Kev had hoped and subsequently, he'd been in a lousy mood throughout the day. We considered the possibility that he had simply had enough and flown home. We returned to the venue hoping he might still show, but he never did, so, reluctantly, we had to cancel the show.

And the answer to the great Kev no-show…?

The previous night, Kev discovered his room hadn't been cleaned, so asked to be moved, but they forgot to update the system. The next morning, he was sitting in the hotel lobby diner having breakfast, as if nothing had happened. We weren't even sure if he realised he'd missed the show.

Later on that tour we arrived backstage in Detroit where an open plan dressing room was made available for both bands to use. Near the kitchen area, an overweight guy, wearing an oversized comedy chef's hat was busy spit roasting a pig.

"You guys are going to love this. I've been basting this baby all day."

The chef continued to pour his homemade marinade sauce over the revolving/revolting pig, kissing his fingers and pointing to the sky. His mood soon changed when the tour manager walked in and told him that none of us ate meat. He angrily pulled off his chef's hat, hurled it across the room and stormed out shouting…

"Fuckin' limey teabags. I'm gonna go buy them some hamster food and a big fuckin' wheel to run around in."

'Long Live The New Flesh' reached number 88 on the US Billboard chart, so a happy Capitol Records gave us the green light to make the next Flesh record, 'Plastic Fantastic'.

On return from the US in March '88, I went for a beer in the West End with Ogs and Guy Gillam where they told me of a three-bedroom squat that had become available next door to where they lived in Bermondsey. Squatting (living in vacant buildings rent-free) was commonplace during the 80s, so I thanked them and moved on to Tyers Estate. Tyers was a run-down square of two-storey flats, inhabited by squatting Geordies who had made their way down from the north to London to look for work. I met up with one of the Geordie boys in the Horseshoe pub on the corner of Melia Street and gave him £50 to sort me out. He broke in, changed the locks, fixed the gas and electric, and returned to the pub with a set of keys. We lived across the river from the City of London, so after a late night out in the West End, you could drunkenly stumble home across London Bridge. Rory Lyons, the drummer from King Kurt, was squatting next door while Ogs and Guy Gillam lived next door but one. I became friends with most of the residents and even learned to speak Geordie. Despite a great year of partying, we all soon got evicted by the local council, except for Rory, who had secretly obtained a court order to remain in his apartment without telling the rest of us. God bless!

In need of new digs again, I started moving up in the world, well, geographically at least. Kev from Flesh for Lulu and a girl named Lucy Wisdom offered me a small room upstairs in a house in Parliament Hill Fields, an area near Hampstead Heath in northwest London. Dr Wisdom, Lucy's father, actually owned the house, he was also father to Miki, and Ollie, who was the singer of Specimen.

Initially, from the street, it appeared to be a suburban, one-up, one-down family home, but upon entering, futuristic sculptures adorned the interior, fluorescent paint enhanced the walls and a trapeze hung from the ceiling in the hallway. Some mornings, I would pull back the curtains to find circus performers rehearsing their acts in the back garden. Lucy was the secretary of the Mutoid Waste Company run by Joe Rush, a performance art group influenced by the movie Mad Max and the popular Judge Dredd comics. They also specialised in organising illegal London parties and became notorious for building giant creepy mechanical sculptures out of old machinery and used car parts. These also featured in the Flesh for Lulu promo video for the single 'Siamese Twist'. Lucy drove an original Volvo 244 nicknamed 'The Fish' as it had a giant fin and grey scales welded all over the body. We used to turn heads as we drove through the city. Moreover, she held a fake driving licence under the name 'Miss Anne Chovy'.

To avoid enforced after-breakfast juggling practice, I decided it was time to get back into doing some songwriting, so I set up my four-track studio in my tiny upstairs bedroom and started working on some songs. One morning there was a knock on the door.

"I hear tunage."

It was Nick, who had stayed the night on the sofa downstairs. He came in and sat on the bed, so I quickly rigged up a microphone and gave him the lyrics, he then grabbed a tambourine and was soon singing along.

"These tunes are great man… who are they for - Test Tubes or Flesh?"

"I just like writing songs, they're not for anyone in particular."

"Would you mind if we tried a couple at the next rehearsal?"

A decision had been made to record the next album 9,500 miles away in Australia with producer Mark Opitz, an Aussie who'd produced Australian bands like Cold Chisel and Jimmy Barnes. Part-owner of INXS' Rhinoceros Studios in Sydney, he naturally suggested we do it there. I can't think why Beggars Banquet and Capitol Records agreed, maybe they hoped a little bit of INXS' success would rub off on us, anyway, it suited me, I'd never been.

Since we were going to be there for at least six weeks, we decided to rent an apartment. The first place we stayed was infested with nightmarish scuttling cockroaches, so before we went out for the evening, we would hunt them down and squish them with our shoes to avoid them crawling over us while we were sleeping. We assumed we'd killed the egg-producing queen, a giant one we found in the hallway, as we took turns to run up and whack it as hard as we could until it was in tiny little pieces.

Insects 0 Humans 1

Unfortunately, Nick managed to blow the electrics in the apartment by plugging his UK voltage crimpers straight into the wall, so when we got home from a night out, we would have to conduct a cockroach hunt by torchlight. We stared in astonishment when we saw that the resilient egg-producing queen began moving again. We thought it must have reassembled itself, until we realised another huge cockroach was on top, eating the dead queen underneath - Equaliser.

With no power and an infestation problem, we had to evacuate quickly. Thankfully, Janet McQueeney, who was now our 'acting manager', located a large comfortable four-bedroom flat in an apartment block in Elizabeth Bay, a harbour-side suburb in eastern Sydney.

We were welcomed into our new temporary home by Ronny, the singer from Rocco's first band, Smak, who turned up with some disco biscuits (MDMA tablets) so that night we went out and hit a few bars. Outside one, Nick was sitting on the wing of a car chatting with some girls when a giant Aussie guy rushed out of the bar and smacked him hard in the face, crushing his cigarette in his mouth and sending sparks flying up into the night sky.

Every night after recording we would have to walk home along Darlinghurst Road through the red-light area of Kings Cross. Colloquially known as 'The Cross', you would have to navigate your way through hookers, drunken fights and people jacking up in doorways. We eventually started taking taxis. One night, after a long wait in a taxi queue, we were finally at the front when another huge Aussie guy ran across the road and shouted…

"HERE'S ONE MATE" as he pushed James over a wall and got in.

Kev also remembered running into trouble with the local police:

"I remember walking back to our apartment block one night on my own when I became aware of a car kerb-crawling next to me. I turned around; it was a police car containing two evil-looking cops. The one on my side wound down the window, and said, 'Hey fuckhead, where you going? Oi, you cunt, I'm talking to you!' He was just trying to get a reaction out of me so I ignored them and kept walking. Luckily, I was just outside our building so I did a swift left-hand turn into the lobby. They were about to get out of the car and give me a kicking, I'm sure of that. The Cross at night was a right dodgy place to walk through."

I also recall one evening sitting in the front seat of a cab when some big geezer took a dislike to my appearance and tried to smash me in the face through the windscreen. A lot of Sydney residents told us we should have made the record in Melbourne, as it was more conducive to the arts and that New South Wales was a dangerous place, full of violence and racism. It wasn't clear why we were regularly assaulted, maybe our leather jackets gave the impression that we were some sort of pommie biker gang!

Apart from the daily violent attacks, our stay in Sydney was also filled with many fun experiences, including a Christmas Day barbeque on the beach and an evening hanging out at an after-hours bar with Guns N' Roses, who later invited us to their show at the Sydney Entertainment Centre. However, dark clouds were looming over the Flesh for Lulu camp.

Rocco later explained why he was feeling disillusioned at the time.

"It all started back in London at Abbey Road; we were recording one of Kev's songs 'Way To Go'. A good song but the way we recorded it made it sound like Simply Red. I remember being in the studio and saying this sounds terrible. What are we doing? Kev said he wanted it to sound like

Motown and I was like, we're not Motown, we're a bunch of white geezers from London. Nick got carried away with it and it ended up like it ended up.

That's when it first hit me. When I was playing guitar on Nick's songs, never a problem. When I was playing guitar on my songs, never a problem. As soon as I played guitar on one of Kev's songs or one of James' songs, there was a big problem. Whatever I did was never right. Even Mike Hedges, the producer, looked at me and rolled his eyes. There was a Duane Eddy type part on it. I must have spent two days recording that. It was never right. It was always wrong or slightly off. It just went on and on… And on.

I just sort of dismissed everything as a blip and we went on tour, and everything was great. Then we went and did 'Plastic Fantastic'. During those rehearsals, James would be reading the newspaper and Kev would be staring at the carpet. They were both insecure and both control freaks. Kev felt like he had to control everything but Nick and I didn't give a shit. The final straw was when we were in Australia. Again, any of Nick's, or mine or even Del's songs, no problem.

That one song, 'Slowdown'… a terrible, terrible song. I remember at the time saying this ain't a great song. James got really fucking upset. I said, 'we gotta be upfront about it, haven't we?' I carried on with it and did the guitars on all the songs but what really, really got to me was when I came to do the last song. That was 'House Of Cards' which was one of Kev's. I went and got some really good coke and bribed the engineer Al Wright to stay up all night and record. I just kept dishing it out, so I kept him there until the next morning and we just worked on that one song. I remember thinking, those are the best guitars I've ever done in my life. Nick wasn't even in the studio. The next day when Kev came in, he listened to the first few bars of the song and said it was total shit. Get Nick to play it.

He didn't even listen to it all the way through. He shot himself in the foot there. He didn't even hear what I'd done. If he wanted to bash me over the head again, he could have at least waited until the end of the song. But he didn't, he waited like two bars and then 'stop, stop, stop. Rubbish, absolute rubbish. Get Nick in.' So I thought. That's it. That is it. I'm not in this band any more. If that's the way it is, I'm not in it. That was the moment I knew I was gonna go.
I was still in Australia, so I just did what I had to do on that record and just went out and enjoyed myself. To be honest I just walked out halfway through it.

I just thought, fuck it!"

Short Live the New Flesh?

CHAPTER 12 – BANANA SHOOT PUSSY

While I was absent touring and recording with Flesh for Lulu, Peter and Walnut started a side project called The Masked Raiders of Love, or, as my mate Paul H renamed them, 'The Market Traders in Gloves'. They were a sort of weird punk band gone wrong, dressed in leather clothes and leather masks. They proclaimed themselves 'metal' as the guitar solos were a couple of minutes longer than a normal punk track. Promoters advertised them as 'PETER of THE TEST TUBE BABIES' Masked Raiders'.

Marie, Peter's French girlfriend, decided to dip her toes into the world of promotion by organising a tour in France for the band. One night they arrived late in a small village to find the promoter standing at the entrance of the venue with the doors already open. Aside from a few barmaids, the cavernous venue was empty, and there was no sound system to be seen. The band decided to rectify this glaring omission by routing the vocal microphones through the bass amplifier and the bass into the extra channel of the guitar amplifier. As stage time approached, they sneaked a peek through the stage curtains and saw that the hall was still completely empty. Ex-childhood traumatised Anarchy Ranch visitor and now Masked Raiders' lead guitarist, Andy Aggro, then had a stroke of genius.

"Let's turn on the smoke machine and fill the whole venue with dry ice. Once everyone hears the music, they'll all come rushing in from the local bars and restaurants, and then when the smoke clears, the place will be packed and everyone will be dancing and going mental."

They pulled on their leather masks and hit the stage. As soon as the smoke subsided it became clear that there was still not one paying punter in the vacuous venue. The barmaids had pulled down the bar shutters and the promoter had fucked off home with the empty cash register!

The Masked Raiders later asked me to produce their first album. The recording studio was in a large country house near Eastbourne. As soon as I found out the place had a swimming pool, I packed my trunks and tennis racquet and headed down. Future Test Tube drummer Caveman Dave O'Brien wrote about my arrival in his journal:

"The Masked Raiders were writing more songs but we still had no singer, so it seemed inevitable to ask Peter. The line-up of the Raiders was me on drums, Andy Aggro on lead guitar, Walnut on rhythm and Mark 'Skweeech' Verrion on bass. This was now exactly the same line-up as

Walnut and the Wankers and so the bands became identical, the difference being that one was a punk band and the other heavy metal. A record contract was offered to the Wankers and we accepted the deal, which was £1,000 up front to record an album, but we didn't tell the company we were going to record a heavy metal album as the *Masked Raiders* using their money. ell... the band members were the same, so it didn't seem to matter. The studio was booked, a large country house near Eastbourne, copious quantities of drugs and alcohol were stockpiled and the services of a 'top producer' were engaged: one Del Strangefish. After a couple of days of struggling to find any sober time, I finally got the drum tracks laid down and felt that I could relax. I was sitting in the library with Skweeech, we had been flicking through M. C. Escher books and marvelling at his works. After drinking a large breakfast of Special Brew and taking a couple of tabs of acid we'd decided that I would draw what Skweeech was playing on an acoustic guitar. At this point we, two drooling vegetables, looked up from our pages of incoherent scribble to see Del arriving at the studio. The great god of rock 'n' roll arrived in a white Vauxhall Chevette from which he emerged clutching a briefcase. The album continued on its downhill trajectory. When the record company heard the finished masters, a full metal racket with lengthy guitar solos instead of the hoped-for chugging oi!, they pulled the plug on the finances, and we were unable to pay the studio or Del or the engineer. All very embarrassing, but we had the most enjoyable time. I left the Masked Raiders to concentrate on working hard and buying a house. Fucking disaster: I ended up being repossessed and living in a truck."

Later, in 1989, I was asked to produce the next Masked Raiders album entitled 'Dear Executioner', at Esselle Studios in Brighton. As I hadn't been paid for the last one, I wasn't interested at first, but the studio told me there were tennis courts across the street, so I packed my racquet and trunks again and headed south.

Listening through the glass of the control room, my favourite conversation of the session went like this:

Walnut to the drummer:

"Dan, mate. You keep speeding up and slowing down."

Dan the drummer, in reply:

"No, I don't. It's you lot, you're out of tune."

Later in the session, I asked guitarist Andy Aggro, through the mixing desk talkback, if he could try an arpeggio guitar part to accentuate the stabs in the chorus. The reply came back...

"You swallowed a dictionary or somethin' mate?"

The new record company accidentally paid me twice for this one! Swings and roundabouts (a far better title).

The recording of Flesh for Lulu's album 'Plastic Fantastic' in Australia was over, and with it, our adventure down under. Kevin had arranged for the record company to buy the most expensive flights with Qantas Airlines so we could break the journey on the way home and spend a few months in Thailand. Since I had been living off free cheese toasties in the studio rather than going out to eat, I had managed to save up enough per diems to bring into effect my 'stay as long as you can in Southeast Asia' plan. Who in their right mind would want to return to a doormat covered in red bills in the cold, dark doldrums of the UK in January? Brrrrrrrr!

After a few days in the intense heat of Bangkok, we decided to head to the closest island, Koh Samet in the Gulf of Thailand, described as 'heaven on earth' in Kev's second-hand Lonely Planet guide.

"At Diamond Beach Hotel (Sai Kaew Beach) a luxurious experience awaits you!"

Another enticing quote from the out-of-date travellers' bible, convinced us to give it a go. On arrival, we waded in from the boat with our rucksacks on our heads to the palm tree-lined stretch of beach. We immediately spotted a sign for Diamond Huts, and thinking that this must be 'it', we quickly paid and checked in.

On closer inspection we discovered that it wasn't 'it' when, after opening the backdoor of my hut, I discovered a shingle-heavy, oil-stained beach with a dead dog on it.

A luxurious experience indeed.

After dining out on that first night I started to feel unwell and developed the worst food poisoning of my life. As a result, I spent my entire stay laying in a sweat-sodden bed in my miserable 'Diamond' hut. To ease the pain, I would try and force myself to sleep, only to wake up totally dehydrated, then gulp down a litre of water before sprinting to the bathroom again. I had to get my shit together because we had arranged to meet Janet, Nick and Rocco for New Year's Eve in Bangkok.
In keeping with the 'stay as long as you can budget' guideline, we

decided to buy the cheapest bus tickets back to Bangkok. The seats on that rust bucket of a bus were made of wood and every time we went over a bump in the road, I thought I was going to shit myself again. I lost over a stone and a half on that trip, at least I was now ripped for our journey south.

As soon as we arrived back in Bangkok, we went to our old hotel on the Khao San Road, but the guy at the reception desk was stressed and less than helpful…

"No room, no room ready, room being cleaned, come back in one hour, we have room for you then."

I was still feeling sick and desperately needed to get out of the intense heat and go to the toilet again, so I told him that we didn't care if the room wasn't clean, we needed it now. Eventually, we managed to talk our way in and make use of the bathroom. Next thing we knew, the Thai police were kicking down the door with guns drawn. The guy at the desk must have thought we were opium addicts and needed to use the room to fix up. Luckily Kev had smoked the last of the Thai sticks before we'd left the island… and exhale!

Imagine the scene as a sea of tourists are reduced to a state of stunned amazement as two leather-clad Brixton cowboys strode down the Khao San Road wearing mirror shades, leather trousers and cowboy boots in 110F dry heat. It was Nick and Rocco.

They were only due to stay for a couple of days as they had to get, in their own words, 'back to our birds'. That evening Kevin and Janet went on a tour of some temples and palaces, but, as it was New Year's Eve, Nick, Rocco and myself decided to wander around Patpong, the infamous red-light entertainment district in Bangkok's Bang Rak neighbourhood. Rather predictably, by the time midnight arrived we were steaming and plucked up the courage to visit a ping-pong show, a type of sex show in which women use their pelvic muscles to either hold, eject, or blow objects from their vaginal cavity. We made our way upstairs into the crowded smoky room and, as the clock struck 12, we witnessed a line of Thai girls touching their toes on the bar playing the Robert Burns classic 'Auld Lang Syne' with whistles in their vaginas. Each one of the ladies played a different note from the song. We knew it was time to leave when we saw another girl performer fill her vagina with beer, expel it into a glass and invite an audience member to drink it. Classy.

Eventually, we made our way back downstairs and walked off into the night where a small boy, no more than eight or nine years old, started running along beside us and tugging at Rocco's sleeve.

*"Hey, Mister. You wanna see banana shoot pussy?
Banana shoot pussy, you wanna come see banana shoot pussy?"*

Nick declared that there was absolutely no way… but Rocco drunkenly insisted.

"Yes, let's go and see bananas shoot pussy. It'll be a laugh, a one-off experience, come on…" was Rocco's 'reasoning' as we allowed ourselves to be ushered along down an alley.

We entered a dark bar through two large creaking wooden doors and a topless girl showed us to a small table in the corner. She then invited some more topless girls to join us, attempting to sit on our laps and order expensive drinks. I refused, fearing the damage it may inflict on my 'stay as long as you can budget'.

The show began and after having to endure some of the most unsexiest dancing known to humanity, it was time for the main attraction. On the dirty floor next to our table, a naked girl appeared with a banana and did the backwards crab. She then placed the banana inside her vagina with her feet, peeled it with her toes, and then with a sudden pelvic thrust, shot it into the air, caught it in her mouth, chewed it, and then swallowed it to a round of applause.

Whoever said vaudeville was dead?

"Right, we've seen banana shoot pussy, now let's get the fuck out of here."

We left some change on the table and scurried towards the two large wooden doors through which we had entered. What a surprise, they were locked. Two huge Thai wrestler types emerged from behind a curtain and stood in the doorway, one with arms folded while the other pointed menacingly at the cash register. Although I don't recall getting back to the hotel that night, I do remember waking up with no money.

Rocco and Nick went back to London while Janet flew home to New York. Kev and I took the 12-hour sleeper train south to Surat Thani to meet up with some friends, Miki Wisdom, the brother of Lucy, and his girlfriend, Charli. On the train, I was awoken at around 5:30 in the morning by a hand coming through the curtain and placing a plate containing two fried eggs on the pillow next to my head.

Eggstraordinary!

Surat Thani is the gateway to much of Thailand's beauty, especially its Gulf Coast islands, so from there, we made our way across to Koh Phangan, Ko Samui, Koh Tao and then on to Krabbe. Late one evening we decided to cross the sea to the party islands of Koh Phi Phi, but on arrival we discovered that there was some sort of festival going on with every hut on the adjoining islands fully booked. As we'd missed the last ferry back to the mainland, we decided to rough it and walk up into the jungle. Pushing back branches and squeezing through prickly bushes, we came across a small run-down fisherman's hut full of nets, baskets and dusty old buoys. This'll do, we thought as we rolled out our sleeping bags on the sand and arranged a few candles to make the place look a little cosier.

Miki rolled a spliff and placed the remainder of our stash in the middle of the makeshift table and we started a game of cards. We were pretty stoned when a helicopter flew overhead, breaking the silence. All of a sudden, the whole hut filled with light, the door burst open, and the Thai police entered, this time with machine guns. The smell of cannabis hung in the air as we were made to stand against the wall with our hands on our heads while they emptied our rucksacks.

A split-second earlier Miki, who was a member of a travelling circus, had heard the sound of a twig cracking underfoot and, with sleight of hand, quickly whipped the cling-film bag of Thai sticks off the table and into his underpants. I noticed that two of their party were dressed in civilian clothes and after the search was complete, the officer in charge marched across to where they were standing and slapped them both hard across the face.

The police trooped off back into the jungle leaving us alone with the two, now nervous-looking civilians. They turned out to be local fishermen who had spotted our flickering candles from the bay and assumed we were some sort of drug-smuggling cartel, instead, the police had discovered a few stoned idiots playing gin rummy.

As we stood there in the silence of the clearing, trying to come to terms with what had just happened, one of the two fishermen tried to exchange pleasantries and laugh it all off. Giving us a knowing wink, he asked if we had anything to smoke? Nice try. We ignored them and they eventually wandered off as well.

No huge reward for them but more than a lucky escape for us.

CHAPTER 13 – ICH BIN EIN FRANKFURTER

Tick. Tick. Tick.

In March 1989, I arrived back from my travels to a ticking time bomb.

I was still living with Kev at Dr Wisdom's North London house where the constant pressure of having to play for and manage Flesh for Lulu was getting the better of him. I began to notice how much of his personal time he was dedicating to the group, constantly on the phone, sometimes into the early hours of the morning, and I could also see how he was becoming increasingly frustrated with Nick and Rocco's disruptive rock star behaviour. His ultimate plan was to hand over the management to Janet so he could concentrate on his songwriting. His efforts eventually paid off when he landed a major US tour opening for English post-punk band Public Image Ltd, formed by ex-Sex Pistols singer John Lydon.

As he was about to start making the initial arrangements, he received a phone call from Nick…

"Rocco and me don't wanna work with you or James anymore."

Tock… the ticking stopped…?

"OK, but after the tour, yeah? Let's go out on a high," Kev replied.

After a lengthy conversation, Kev realised Nick's mind was made up and he and Rocco didn't want to go on tour with him or James any more.

Rocco and his partner Cleo Murray had discussed the situation after returning from Australia, and the two of them had decided it was time to move on – so Rocco told Nick he was leaving.

Initially, Nick was shocked but, after a while, he called back and declared…

"I'm leaving as well."

Rocco and Nick then called a meeting in a pub in the West End, at 11 the next morning.

"I was in at half past ten," said Rocco.
"I was drinking whisky before they got there. I was dreading it."

Drummer James explained his perspective on the split in a later interview:

"In my opinion, we were all up our own arseholes and lost the plot. We didn't have strong outside management because Kev was doing it all, and that was wrong. Being the manager was a disaster for Kev and we all took him for granted. We were lazy and should've written together. I should've nurtured my baby, but I was also guilty of letting it fall apart. The strength that propelled Flesh for Lulu at the start was the bond between Nick and myself and I feel bad that I let that slip. We should've been locked in a room together to write, and no offence to Del, we should've stayed a four-piece. I lost sight of what made us good. Nick was the only really good musician and the rest of us were limited. I do feel bad for giving Rocco a hard time about practising the guitar when I was no Topper Headon myself! Nick and I originally got a deal from following our noses and writing together all the time, so we messed up when it became about how well we could play our instruments, that was never what it was all about. I guess in the end if we'd had good management, if we'd knuckled down and written songs together, if there hadn't been so much booze and drugs, who knows what we could've come up with? Or not..."

Nick later stated:

"The reason Flesh really split up is because... to coin the oldest cliché of them all, there were musical differences, two separate trains of thought."

James' partnership with Nick had been taken over by Rocco, which must have been heart-breaking when it resulted in him being chucked out of the band he had originally formed.

To avoid any fallout from the blast, I thought it best to put myself in a position of neutrality. A basement flat just off Ladbroke Grove in Cambridge Gardens became available in the same building as old friends Carmen and Marcus, so I quickly grabbed it.

One interview after the break-up seemed to imply that I joined the group with an agenda. Nothing could be further from the truth. I worked hard at learning my parts, reluctantly agreed to dress like an idiot in video and TV appearances and even helped out with the songwriting. Even though I accepted opportunities, I never asked for anything. Another interview stated that I received £40,000 for my songs on 'Plastic Fantastic'. This is also complete nonsense. Oh, if only. All I got was Andy Heath of Momentum Music chasing me around London trying to add me to Flesh's existing publishing deal, of which the advance had already been spent. Why would anyone in their right mind sign that? Later, I did receive $15,000 (£11,500) for submitting my song 'Next Time (I'll Dream Of You)' to the soundtrack of the movie 'Flashback', an adventure comedy starring Dennis Hopper and Kiefer Sutherland, but I put that back into the band to keep Nick and Rocco's wages paid. I sometimes wondered whether my arrival had upset the balance in the band but, on reflection, it probably would have fallen apart anyway, maybe I even prolonged it?

After some legal wrangling of which I knew little, Nick and Rocco decided to continue as Flesh for Lulu and asked me if I would be willing to carry on playing with them, filling in on bass guitar. They also needed a drummer and a Swedish guy named Hans Perrson had come highly recommended by a friend of Nick's, so we set off to The Intrepid Fox in Wardour Street to meet him. After a few pints, we got along well and partied until the early hours at Soho's Raymond Revue Bar, a club hosted by ex-Specimen drummer and club promoter Jonathon Trevisick. A good time was had by all, which meant Hans was in without lifting a stick.

That summer, Nick and Rocco started getting bored of sitting around getting drunk in the beer garden of the Earl of Lonsdale on Portobello Road. They were desperate to get back 'out there' and start playing again. Consequently, the four of us began doing mystery guest support slots around London under the name The Infidels, playing Iggy Pop, David Bowie and Prince covers. I returned to filling the gaps in my diary by booking more Test Tube shows…

Germany and especially Berlin had always been Peter and the Test Tube Babies' most successful stomping ground. Many buildings there had become abandoned due to the decline in industry during the Cold War as a proliferation of bars, clubs and squats opened up all over the city. A lot of German punks moved to West Berlin before the reunification because, if you lived there, you weren't eligible for national service in the West German army.

On November 9th, 1989, we witnessed one of the most important European events since the end of the Second World War: the fall of the Berlin Wall, and I am not referring to the later pathetic Hasselhoff, Clinton and Pavarotti firework display. Nein…

A couple of months earlier, the Iron Curtain had begun to weaken when some of the Eastern Bloc countries began to relax their borders to East Germans. Many of them were able to sneak around the corner through Hungary and visit West Germany for the first time. Due to this development, the East German government had drawn up plans to soften travel restrictions. The person chosen to announce these new measures was Günter Schabowski, leader of the Socialist Unity Party in East Berlin. Having not been properly briefed, he responded in true Test Tubes style by saying that as far as he was concerned, it would take effect immediately. Ha!

That same night, the Test Tubes were due to perform at the Ecstasy Club in West Berlin. Lighting tech Paul Goth and Danny Bell were the long-suffering crew at the time and after we'd finished sound-checking, we decided to go and find a bar. When we emerged into the daylight from the darkness of the club, a large number of hysterical Germans ran past us, shouting and crying. Unaware of what was going on, our first instinct was to join the party, so we followed the crowd until we reached the wall. In both West and East Berlin, news of the relaxation of border controls had been making headlines.

In true western capitalist style, Trapper grabbed an old lady's umbrella and started to chip away at the wall to get some souvenirs to sell when he got home. Others also hacked away at it with anything they could find. I clearly remember standing there taking it all in as people pulled each other up to dance on the wall. Two nations were reuniting, and we were lucky enough to be there for that unique moment in history.

A year after the fall of the Berlin Wall, the Test Tubes represented the United Kingdom at the historical MTV East/West party at the SO36 music club in the Kreuzberg area of Berlin.

'The Mating Sounds Of South American Frogs' had been at the top of the German alternative chart for months and a German friend of mine once told me...

"You couldn't enter a bar without hearing Mating Sounds."

Germany certainly had become very liberal.

Every year since 1983 we have toured Germany in December, except for 2007 when Peter had some personal issues and 2020 and 2021 due to coronavirus. We always have a tour theme. ABBA, Hippies, Convicts, Dead Rock Stars, American election candidates, to name but a few. Personally, I have never been a fan of this pantomime version of the band. I always thought we should just let the music do the talking but Peter explained that he needed to dress up as some sort of theatrical crutch.

Our tour manager on these tours was Henry Klaere, a German friend and promoter, who had the same sarcastic sense of irony as the rest of us, so fitted the bill perfectly. Back then, he lived in Dreieich, a suburb of Frankfurt, and he told me he used to listen to 'Mating Sounds' every day. He became a Test Tubes fan after first seeing us at the Batschkapp in

1983. He also recalled meeting Peter at the Batschkapp for the first time:

"I was in the Elfer bar downstairs from the Batschkapp. Peter had a broken leg, and I had a broken arm, so we chatted about fractures. After Peter left, a fan came across to me and asked if I knew Peter and could I get him his autograph? I faked Peter's autograph on a beermat under the table and sold it to the guy for a beer."

This must have been the moment that planted the seed in Henry's head – there's money to be made from these gullible drunken Brits…

10 years later he became our tour and European manager.

But Henry doesn't stop there…

"In 1989, I worked for Hammer Promotion with Michael Löffler. Michael 'accidentally' forgot to pay his foreign artist tax and went bankrupt so I started my own touring company called HHK. I booked the Test Tubes for a festival and put, sound engineer at the time, Bernie Schick in charge. The festival got cancelled but Bernie had already paid them so they went home with the money. In 1993 they agreed to do a tour for me so I could make my money back. I had a deal going with a bus company and booked them a sleeper bus and we've used one ever since."

That was my first experience of life on a sleeper bus, or a nightliner as they are sometimes called. I liked it. No more dragging your suitcases up some dodgy hotel staircase at two in the morning to get up at 7am to pack for another tedious van trip to the next show.

Later, after becoming a tour manager myself, I learned to walk the diplomatic tightrope and make friends with everyone on the tour. This even included psycho drummers, but most importantly I made it a priority to befriend the bus driver. Chat with them in their cab until the early hours and invite them out to dinner even if it means having to discuss the latest European driving regulations or the importance of tyre gauges. A positive working relationship with the driver makes your life so much easier. They will reverse down small alleyways, attempt impossible 360s and even fiddle the tachograph. Take them for granted and load-in will become your worst nightmare, with your equipment trailer being resentfully detached streets away from the venue.

It's difficult to comprehend the mentality required to sit behind a steering wheel for hours on end, staring at endless white lines on a motorway while the band parties in the lounge behind you staring at endless white lines on a mirror. The majority of bus drivers start the tour eager to help and assist, but that doesn't last long. On arriving at the venue in the early hours, the driver will leave the cockpit to find that everyone has gone to bed leaving the lounge tables covered in half-drunk bottles of alcohol and half-eaten pizzas. Later in the day, while attempting to sleep, the hungover band start yelling and slamming doors before heading off to the luxury hotel to freshen up. The disgruntled driver, now filled with hate and resentment, begins to unwind his toy vacuum cleaner to begin the clean-up.

Bill, sound engineer for the English electronic music band the Dub Pistols, told me over dinner they once had a bus driver who turned out to be a serial killer. After dropping the band off at the hotel each night, he would then go out on a killing spree.

Occasionally the driver will put in an appearance backstage to comment on what the band are wearing or how the stage should be set up. Monitor engineer Dan Bartley, who worked with me on the British electronic band Sneaker Pimps' European tour, once summed it up nicely during a soundcheck by yelling at an interfering bus driver...

"SHUT UP AND DRIVE!"

On one European tour we had an ex-Dutch Marine behind the wheel who went by the name of Diestel, but we named him Diss. Every morning he would make us stand by our bunks and have our bedding ready for laundry. Despite our protests, he kept fiddling around with and tidying up our stuff. He even washed Walnut's wank sock, even though Walnut had been hoping he could get it to stand up on its own by the end of the tour. On a few of the dates, a female journalist was travelling with us covering the tour. Taking a shine to the bass player, she became increasingly upset and would burst into tears whenever he shunned her advances. One night on the bus, she was upstairs in the sleeping area wandering up and down the aisle trying to figure out which bunk he was in. The following morning, he was downstairs, proudly telling us how her hand had appeared under his curtains, grabbed his penis and wanked him off. His face turned as white as a ghost when I explained she wasn't on the bus last night but I'd seen Diss, the ex-Dutch Marine, with his arm through someone's curtains!

On our first tour with Henry, to help cover the cost of the bus, our tour merchandiser sold off any extra tour posters on the stall. After the final show, Henry went to claim his poster money, but the merchandiser informed him that Trapper had already collected the money at the end of each night. Henry challenged Trapper on this.

"Trapper, what happened to the poster money?"

"We used that to buy coke."

"That wasn't the deal."

"Too late. It's gone now!"

The German Christmas tours would always finish at the Batschkapp in Frankfurt on the 23rd of December, and the next morning we would get dropped off at Frankfurt Airport at around 5am for a 7am flight back to the UK just in time for Christmas. It would be freezing, getting light and the end-of-tour party would still be in full swing. The band and crew would be in a terrible state, inebriated and befuddled.

British Airways had once announced on Teletext that they were not taking any drunken passengers over the festive period, ticket or no ticket. Henry taught me an important German phrase to use just in case the airline refused to let us on board.

"Ich gehöre nicht zu ihnen - ich bin ein Frankfurter."

(I'm not with them. I'm from Frankfurt.)

CHAPTER 14 – BLUE SHARK ATTACK

Peter Cook (my neighbour, not the late comedian), hammered in a fierce shot from the edge of the box, the goalkeeper spilt it straight into my path and BANG! I tapped the ball into an empty net from four inches out. A goal my granny could have scored, and she's been dead for 30 years. That was my only goal at under-16 level and as we trotted down the tunnel at half-time 1-0 up, I received a huge pat on the back from the coach. It all went downhill after that, as in the second half we were kicking uphill and went on to lose 1-11. Team selection was easy back then, anyone good up front, hoofers in central defence, the two worst players left and right back and fatty in goal. Losing 11-1 was a close contest compared with the lowest lowlight of my playing career...

Peacehaven 1 Bevendean Badgers 33 (Thirty-Three).

At least we scored one.

In a true 'Roy of the Rovers' inspired turnaround, we caused a major cup upset two weeks later when we went to the Badgers' set and turned them over 4-3.

As a football 'fan' my motivational mantra was…

'Never let a football match ruin a good Saturday afternoon out at the football.'

I would spend many an afternoon with my hand over one eye watching two balls, two referees, four linesmen and 44 players. Hic!
Yes, football, 99% despair, 1% glory. Mind control for the masses. A once free-flowing exciting game played with pride and passion that would brighten up our grey lives on a Saturday afternoon before we were lowered into the pit to have our life expectancies shortened on Monday morning.

Once upon a time, neighbouring towns would compete on the village green for a prize ham. Now, most football stadiums are just glorified shopping centres owned by petrochemical-producing nations, where 'fans' are assigned 'customer numbers'. I never went to football to support a brand; I went to support my local team.
I still get goosebumps when I think back to those early days when I first started attending Brighton and Hove Albion games. The whole matchday experience would cost just one pound. I would walk two

miles to call for my old school chum, Tim Dawes, at Broomfield Avenue in Telscombe, then walk another mile across the Telscombe Tye to catch the Green Southdown Number 5 bus from Saltdean to Sackville Road in Hove, just around the corner from the famous Goldstone Ground. We'd pop into the newsagents and go halves on ten No.10 cigarettes, then stick them down the front of our underpants because if a copper searched you and found them, you'd be redirected to the adults' turnstile to pay the full matchday admission. There was an electric buzz of excitement in the air as we made our way through the cold clunky metal turnstile and on to the North Stand to inhale the smell of fresh-cut grass and cigarette smoke. Having paid our 65p admission and bought a programme, we still had enough money to share a bag of chips on the bus home - a perfect day out, win, lose or draw. Usually, lose.

Tim recollected those early treasured football memories…

"They were fuckin' crackin' days. We were only around 14 or 15 years old and if there was any crowd trouble we would run behind the bigger lads in the North Stand. Whenever there was a shot or an attack, we would get carried down the stand as the fans bundled forward in anticipation of a goal. You would have to dodge the railings and stanchions and we would always end up with fag burns on the backs of our necks, I remember my Mum going mental when I got one in the back of my brand-new Parka. There would always be a large space at the front of the crowd which we would surge into if we were about to score. Sometimes a couple of newbies would be attending their first match, would see that space, and shout 'here's a free spot'. Then, as soon as Tony Towner would set off down the wing on one of his trademark runs, the crowd would surge forward again and the newbies would end up face down in their coffees.

Shortly after Del's brother passed, we went to Crystal Palace away. We were looking for a punch up to let off some steam but couldn't find one for love or money. We ended up nicking a Palace scarf from a 9-year-old boy, but he started crying, so we felt sorry for him and gave it back."

Pwopper Nawty.

My first ever home game was a friendly against Chelsea in 1972, in which we lost 2-3 and my first away game was a 0-1 win over Aldershot in 1974. That year I saw player-manager Bobby Charlton steer Preston North End to a 0-4 victory at the Goldstone Ground. Hard to imagine Sir Bobby rampaging through the mud wearing tights, woolly gloves and a snood.

A couple of years later I went to all three games in our epic FA Cup battle with bitter rivals Crystal Palace. For those of you who don't already know, this is my understanding of how that rivalry began…

Ex-Spurs team-mates Terry Venables and Alan Mullery were the Palace and Brighton managers respectively. Mullery was critical of his opponent, complaining about Palace's negative tactics. Stamford Bridge hosted the second replay, as the tension was ramped up by the fixture being postponed twice due to bad weather. When the game eventually got under way it was pissing down and the Palace fans were in the uncovered end getting soaked while we were warm and dry in Chelsea's famous Shed. We were dominating the game and then, in the 78th minute, we were awarded a penalty, which was 'scored' by Brian Horton, only to be disallowed by referee Ron Challis who judged that some players had encroached into the penalty area before the ball had been kicked. Horton retook it but this time it was saved. We were knocked out of the cup, eventually losing 0-1. After the final whistle, Mullery approached Challis to 'discuss' his decision and had to be escorted off the pitch by police while flicking 'V-signs' and telling the Palace fans to do one. The Brighton manager then burst into the Palace dressing room and threw a five-pound note on the ground, telling Venables:

"Your team's not worth that."

Mullery was fined £100 by the FA for bringing the game into disrepute.

Until that run of matches we had been embarrassingly nicknamed 'The Dolphins', but somewhere around that time, depending on who you talk to, the Palace fans were chanting their nickname, *"Eagles, Eagles",* to which a group of Brighton fans responded with a chant of *"Seagulls, Seagulls"* and thus a new club nickname was born.

On April 26th, 1997, the curtain finally came down on the famous Goldstone Ground after 95 years. Before our final match at home to Doncaster Rovers we had been propping up the Football League tables but were now only three points behind Hereford United. Our new chairman, Dick Knight, sat in the directors' box for the first time after the removal of money-grabbers Bill Archer, Greg Stanley, and David Bellotti. Stuart Storer scored the last ever goal at the famous ground as we won 1-0 to lift Brighton from the bottom of Division Three. After the game, the fans flooded on to the pitch to claim pieces of turf and anything else in the stadium that could be carried away. A week later, someone in the Green Dragon pub in Brighton tried to sell us the machine that painted the white lines on the pitch.

The following Saturday the Test Tubes were playing at the

Carnavalorock Festival in Saint-Brieuc, France, so for that final away game to 'new-bottom club' Hereford, I had my ear pressed firmly against my small transistor radio. We needed either a draw or a win to avoid being shamefully relegated out of the Football League but, typically, full back Kerry Mayo scored an early own goal to leave us trailing 1-0. Suddenly, through the radio interference, the news came in that Brighton had pulled back to 1-1, secured a point, and survived after earlier in the season being 12 points adrift at the bottom of the league. Woop! Woop!

I was overjoyed and to celebrate our 'Great Escape' I stage-dived head-first into a field of stinging nettles. The rest of that evening, every time my skin flared up and I felt that itchy stinging sensation, I smiled like an idiot.

Brighton's football ground was sold off and flattened to make way for a trading estate containing a Toys"R"Us and a T.K. Maxx among other corporate stores. A friend of mine regularly goes to visit the Burger King drive-thru there and when they ask him:

"Good morning sir. What can we do for you today?"

He shouts:

"PUT THE STADIUM BACK UP!"

… then speeds off without ordering anything!

Albion fans have always had a great sense of irony and humour, that's what got us through the troubled times. We have always been a target for homophobic abuse from rival fans due to the liberal attitude of the city and the club's embracing of the LGBT community.

When rival fans would chant....

"We can see you holding hands…"

Brighton fans' comeback would be to sing…

"You're too ugly to be gay" and soon, after going 1-0 up…

"We're gay, but we're beating you!" to the tune of Village People's 'Go West'.

After having to play our 'home' games in Gillingham for a couple of years, the team had just returned to Brighton at the Withdean Stadium, an athletics track where the away fans would have to watch the game through a discus cage. The Albion didn't have a pot to piss in, and we had recently finished 91st in the entire Football League (of 92 clubs)! Knight turned to the supporters, asking them to help fund buying players who might lift the club from being the second-worst professional team in England.

A star-sozzled line-up was announced for a Brighton and Hove Albion benefit concert at the Paradox nightclub (a decidedly better name than its previous one – The Pink Coconut!) in Brighton's notoriously rough West Street. This event was to raise money for chairman Dick Knight's new 'Buy a Player' Fund, with Albion fans encouraged to chip in whatever they could to allow Dick to reinforce our struggling Fourth Division squad.

Bad Manners, The Levellers, Peter and the Test Tube Babies, The Fish Brothers and Too Many Crooks, among others, were all to appear with Attila the Stockbroker as compere.

Hollywood actor Ralph Brown, best-known for playing Danny the Dealer in Withnail & I and some bloke in Star Wars, was also there to play sax with Attila as they'd released a charity single for the Albion. He seemed to spend most of the night glaring at our shenanigans through the open dressing room door.

Brighton centre forward David Cameron (no not the ex-prime minister) was presenting prizes to the winners of various raffles. The drugs and booze kept flowing freely backstage with lines of cocaine mixed with Viagra on the table. Cameron said he could no longer remain in the dressing room in case he inhaled marijuana smoke and there was a random drug test at the training ground. His wife ended up buying some so he could have a smoke after training. The next game he was hauled off after 20 minutes, with Brighton's assistant manager Alan Cork stating:

"Cameron was useless, full stop. If he wants to be a professional footballer he has got to liven up. On that performance, it will be a long time before he plays for us again."

We were scheduled to play at 9pm, with the Levellers closing the show at 1am. As we drank in the pub next door and prepared to head back, word came through that the Levellers were taking our 9pm slot, condemning us to the graveyard shift. The half an ecstasy tablet I had just taken in preparation for the show had just started to kick in, so my girlfriend Rachael suggested I take the other half to 'level me out'. By the time our 1am slot arrived, I was extremely drained and floaty.

Second or third song (could've been any song really), I forgot which year it was and started riffing out like Jimi Hendrix back in 1971 (he died in 1970). After a while, the bass player gave up, put his bass down and walked off, followed shortly by the drummer. While still trying to solo, I was escorted away from the stage by security.

Always leave 'em wanting less, that's what I always say.

As the presentations were being made at the end of the night, I was physically thrown out through the back doors by the bouncers who forgot to reclaim my V.P.I. pass (Very Pissed Idiot). Wasting no time to get back into the swing of things I quickly climbed over the black bin liners, jumped out of the skip, and ran around to the front of the venue, flashing my accreditation to the girl in the box office. As Attila started thanking everyone (except me) for a wonderful evening, I sprinted on stage and attempted to pull his pants down while wrestling him over the monitors to forcefully simulate anal sex on him.

Since that night, whenever I bump into John (Atilla) at the football, he bemoans that moment like a broken record or one of his monotonous rants.

With the money raised, we helped the club buy Rod Thomas, a fast, entertaining winger who would have you off your seat whenever he got the ball. At 14, while in Watford's youth set-up, he had been hailed as 'the next Pelé', however by 23, he was playing for Carlisle in the Fourth Division. Unfortunately, it all went tits up as usual. Thomas got injured and failed to see eye to eye with new manager Micky Adams who favoured solid professionals rather than the speed and trickery of Thomas, so like my benefit performance, his Brighton career fizzled out into insignificance.

A few years later, our new Uruguayan manager Gus Poyet got us promoted to the Championship and we proudly relocated from the 5,000-capacity Withdean Athletics Park to our new 30,000-seat home ground at the Amex Stadium in Falmer. I bought a season ticket for the first six seasons and, apart from having to remortgage my house for a bag of Mini Cheddars and endure the enormous queues for overpriced, warm, flat pints, I enjoyed watching Poyet's free-flowing, possession-based style of football. Amazingly, 25,000 'lifelong' fans appeared from nowhere, some who had once called us crap and rubbish back when the club was really in need of their support. You know who you are!

Ironically, our first competitive match at the new stadium was against Doncaster Rovers, our last opponents at the old Goldstone Ground.

Unfortunately, I was stage managing 300 miles away at the Rebellion Festival in Blackpool, but I wasn't going to let this piece of history pass me by. Myself and fellow season ticket holder Steve Potts, nicknamed 'Muscle Mary' for his pumped-up, hernia-ripped, tattooed gym body, left Blackpool at 5am. Stocked up on cider, we drove five hours to Brighton arriving at the new ground well before the 3pm kick off.

During the game, Brighton were typically behind 0-1 until Will Buckley, our first ever million-pound signing, entered as a second-half substitute. It took just eight minutes for the debutant to equalise, rifling home from the edge of the box. As the game entered the sixth minute of injury time, Brighton winger Craig Noone's quick feet slipped Buckley in one-on-one with the Rovers goalkeeper. The North Stand held its breath and the stadium erupted as Buckley coolly lifted the ball over the stranded keeper to make it 2-1. One word: Bloodyawesome!

Steve went home to Worthing, so I celebrated alone on the train back up to Blackpool. I had left Paul H in charge of my stage and told him that if anyone asked where I was, to tell them that I'd be back in five minutes. 16 hours later I arrived at the festival completely hammered as headliner and Crystal Palace supporter Captain Sensible was about to take the stage. I planted a Seagulls flag on the end of his guitar which was instantly removed, thrown to the floor and stamped upon during the first song.

A few seasons later, after a 2-1 home win over Wigan Athletic and a celebratory pitch invasion, we had secured our place in the top flight after a painful 34-year struggle. The journey to the promised land was finally over but as The Clash once sang:

"You got the future shining like a piece of gold…
I swear as we get closer, it looks more like a lump of coal…"

You can love your goldfish, but you don't have to love the water it swims in. The English Premier League is a cold unwelcoming place where money is king and all but the so-called 'big six or seven' foreign billionaire-owned clubs struggle to do much more than tread water in an annual battle to avoid relegation, season after season.

After the introduction of the dreadful VAR (Video Assistant Referee), I began to lose enthusiasm for the beautiful game. Instead of free-flowing football, robust challenges and the crowd spontaneously celebrating goals, we now had to stand around or go and get a cup of tea while a couple of idiots fiddled around with some technology to see whether the centre forward's pubes were in line with the last defender.

Along with the over-commercialisation of football came the emergence of the modern-day fan, wearing the £65 pink, third away shirt with someone else's name on the back. What's wrong with a rosette and a rattle? At one recent game, I ended up 'seated' (don't get me started) between two kids commentating loudly in high pitched voices, and Mr and Mrs Heart Attack chewing away at boxes of stinky fish and chips. Children now hold up signs asking Manchester United or Chelsea players for their shirts. If you support Brighton, why on earth would you want a player's shirt from another club? The kids might not know any better, but the parents bloody well should. What next? Groundsman, can I have your white-line painter?

There are now facial recognition cameras to make sure you don't sit in the wrong seat or, God forbid, stand up, along with designated singing areas, and laser-guided 'Class A' drug sensors on every toilet seat... OK, maybe not the last one. 'Bottletopgate' also occurred when staff removed the tops of bottles when you bought soft drinks or water. Eventually, the club was outfoxed by the fans who smuggled in their own replacement bottle tops.

Call it inverted snobbery if you want, but I miss the excitement of being kettled out of away grounds by a cavalry of police horses, fag burns on the back of your neck, and standing in the rain getting hammered 0-1 at home by nine-man Walsall. I mean, who wouldn't?

My seat at the new stadium (or standing area, much to the annoyance of the stewards) was at the very back of the North Stand among fellow punk rockers Steve Potts, Chemical Coskin, Jake Potts, Neil from Constant State of Terror, Jim Rogerson from Age of Chaos and some failed skateboarders. For a bit of fan fun, we clubbed together and made a large blue banner with skull and crossbones, reading 'BHAFC PUNK ROCK'. We also made a few hoodies and T-Shirts which became highly sought after, so I made a Facebook page. I then received a cease-and-desist letter from the club's legal team advising me that the acronym BHAFC is a trademark registered to Brighton & Hove Albion F.C. and cannot be used without the club's permission and that they were unable to allow us to continue to use their trademark on any clothing. I was given seven days to take down my Facebook page or face legal action for trade infringement. As I was unsure how to respond to being stamped on by the authoritarian corporate football machine, I called my partner in crime, wheat-intolerant Steve Potts, but was told:

"Nothing to do with me mate, take my name off it. I've got too much to lose."

It was a massive slap in the face from the club, after all the years of support and all the fundraisers I'd gone to the trouble of being thrown out of!

CHAPTER 15 –
BLUE SHARK ATTACK 2: THE REVENGE

Back in the equally unrewarding world of rock 'n roll, Flesh for Lulu were on a mission to find a new bass player for the upcoming 1989 Public Image Ltd US tour. Nick wanted me back on guitar and keyboards, so he and Rocco spent a couple of days auditioning potential bassists at Samurai Studios in London Bridge. Nick's flatmate Eva delivered the bad news to each hopeful on the way out as none had succeeded on either ability or style. Unfortunately for me, I had both (chortle), but I didn't want to play bass; I'd already destroyed the top end frequency in my eardrums with the guitar, so I had no wish for the bottom end to abandon me as well. Pardon?

We finally settled on a guy named Mike Steed from Southend, a tall good-looking lad with a broad smile and a knowing wink. He was also a great player and a bit of a 'Jack the Lad', a worrying contrast to the rest of us mild-mannered gents. (Err, cough!)

In October 1989, on the opening night of the PiL North American tour, we arrived in our empty dressing room to the sound of loud farting noises coming from the bathroom. After a shout of *"ARRSENALLLL"*, Johnny Rotten emerged fastening his pants.

"Alright lads. Sorry about that, I didn't want to stink out my own dressing room."

Charming!

Before the tour, Nick and Rocco told me they were thinking of hiring ex-Test Tubes drummer Ogs as our backline technician. My protestations were ignored, so I resigned myself to a month of gigs with a fat bloke standing behind me on stage constantly taking the piss. Those 'hilarious' jibes culminated at the tour's big sell-out show at Culver City's Universal Amphitheatre in Los Angeles. Before I went on stage for the so-called 'big gig', Nick hassled me to go the extra mile and wear a three-piece white suit, so to keep him happy I reluctantly agreed. As I made my way down the stairs to the side of the stage, Ogs couldn't believe his eyes and while almost choking on his beer, shouted:

"Greenback, you complete wanker!"

Just the confidence one needs when preparing to perform in front of 6,000 people.

We became friends with Lydon, well, he seemed to want to hang around with us whether we liked it or not. It soon became evident there was a mild case of schizophrenia at work, but then again, why wouldn't there be after having to play that role for so many years? As long as he was on his own or in safe company, he was funny, friendly and sensitive, but if a stranger approached, the leering belching Johnny Rotten would rear his ugly head and his 'Fuck You' defence mechanism would be engaged. At one show he'd be up for drinks and chats, but at the next, no one would be allowed in his backstage area. The latter usually coincided with a hangover.

One night he attempted to steal the tour bus. The bus driver, recognising the sound of his engine, rushed to his hotel window only to see Lydon's contorted face trying to figure out how to get it into gear. After scrambling for his pants, the driver rushed downstairs to prevent an almost certain disaster.

Rocco meanwhile hit it off with the legendary late PiL guitarist John McGeoch, remembering their friendship on that tour:

"A lovely guy. Scottish, always pissed. I used to call him 'The Chardonnay Kid', he'd call my room most mornings. 'Hey! Ah'm in tha Jacuzzi, man! Wi' a bottle o' Chardonnaaaay!' I mean, literally 9am, it's McGeoch, ringing you."

We were at the Minneapolis First Avenue Night Club, where we'd lost Kev on the previous tour. Lydon walked in and sat down at a table and announced…

"Not this shithole again. That's it. I'm getting pissed." As he pulled back the ring on his first can of Red Stripe.

One night somebody in the audience spat on him.

"That's it. I don't want your American AIDS…" and he walked off stage.

Every night he'd end the show with:

"Right, that's your lot, if you wanna hear any more you know the procedure…" before he walked off stage to stand behind the curtain with his arms folded.

One of the lighting guys on the tour was a muscular American surfer dude with curly blond hair and a wide selection of Hawaiian shirts.

While up in the rigging focusing the stage lights he used to do pull-ups without a harness. We were struck by the cultural differences between our West Coast colonial cousins and us Brits when Dave Peters, our deadpan Brummie bespectacled tour manager, wore his duffle coat to breakfast. The bare-chested surfer dude bounded into the catering room with a beaming smile and shouted to glum-looking Dave:

"HEY MAAAN WHAT'S HAPPENING?"

Dave Peters: *"Not a lot."*

Surfer dude: *"ALLRIIIIIGHT!"*

A beautiful sunny morning greeted us at one of the first-ever US boutique hotels, The Phoenix in San Francisco. We were sitting in the courtyard by the mosaic-tiled pool with Lydon and a few other members of PiL, drinking Blue Shark Attacks. A Blue Shark Attack is a cocktail made with rum, pineapple juice, blue curacao, with a large blue rubber shark stuffed inside. A large number of blue rubber sharks had been collected and were now piled up on our table. Our marketing lady from Capitol Records arrived to take us to do some radio interviews. Despite the lack of space in the car, Lydon insisted on coming. He ran beside the car, shouting, 'Don't leave me!' and dived in through the rear window, lying on his back across our legs, gobbing backwards out of the car window. Most of our interviews that afternoon featured Lydon swearing and shouting *"booooring"* in the background. After our 'boring' interviews, the record company rep took us to see The Waterboys' matinee show at the Berkeley Theater. Despite Lydon's desire to return to the hotel, we managed to persuade him to tag along. We enjoyed the show and when I asked John what he thought, he shrugged his shoulders and in an automated response shouted *"boring"* again, but I could tell he really enjoyed it.

We then returned to the hotel and continued our Blue Shark Attack session by the poolside. A young blonde girl in a bikini appeared and started doing her yoga routine. This proved far from boring as she walked up the ladder on her hands and did a handstand dive from the top board, for which she received a loud round of applause.

After the show at The Warfield, the previous day's drinking party reconvened back in my hotel room. There was a knock at the door, and it was the blonde yoga girl from earlier in the day.

"Mind if I join the party?"

She sat around drinking for a while before turning up the radio and disappearing off into the toilet. The bathroom door then swung open and she danced out, doing a striptease routine wearing all the towels and the hotel dressing gown. We watched in disbelief as she then continued her yoga in the centre of the room, completely naked!

After finishing her routine, Hans got his camera out and snapped some major blackmail material, including one rather embarrassing shot of Hans and me positioned side by side with her legs wide apart.

Lydon then came up with an eyebrow-raising request.

"Let's see a little poo stick its head out."

That was the signal to call it a night, we all went back to our rooms, and she went back to her poolside yoga. We had no idea that later that night John McGeoch would stumble back into the hotel after a night on the tiles and whisk her away to his room. The next day she was sitting on the tour bus and announced herself as his new girlfriend. We couldn't resist, so that afternoon we went in search of a darkroom to get the previous night's photos developed. We got some large naked yoga girl blow-ups made and at the next show, during the changeover, we secretly stuck them up on McGeoch's amp and in various other positions around the stage.

Lydon then bounced on stage for the first song, looked around at the pictures of the blonde yoga pool lady taped to John's amp, and cracked up with laughter; proceeding to bugger up the first couple of lines of the opening song 'Warrior'.

The tour was a real success and PiL were great, when not hungover. At the last show, Trigger, PiL's production manager, came to say goodbye and told me he used to play in an 80s punk band named Erazerhead, and had remembered Ogs and me from back in the day when he had supported the Test Tubes at the 100 Club.

After returning to the UK, Mike Steed was sacked and will be worst remembered for sleeping with 50 women on the 36-date Public Image Ltd US tour. How is that scientifically possible, I hear you ask?

'Steedy' and I got along well, and we had a lot of fun sharing a room. One sunny morning in New Jersey, we looked out of our hotel room window and saw a strip club in full swing across the street (or a 'titty bar' as Americans called them). After Mike had dragged me across for a lunchtime drink, a stripper came dancing along the bar, grabbed his bottle of Heineken and put it where the sun probably does shine quite often. Mike complained to the manager that his beer was now undrinkable and we were given a free bar tab for the rest of our session as long as we kept the tips coming. Somehow, he ended up inviting the 'lady' in question back across the road to the hotel for a different sort of afternoon session, so I went and watched TV on the tour bus.

After that evening's soundcheck, the local record company representative hopped on the tour bus to say hello. Steed shouted out *"do-able"*, much to the embarrassment of the rest of us, yet he still managed to have sex with her on the tour bus before the show. That was a sackable offence right there, but we were in the middle of a US tour and there was no time or money to fly in a replacement, which granted him a stay of (s)execution. Later that night the record company girl was discarded and Steedy managed to pick up another girl at the after-show party and take her back to the hotel. Three in one day, I was exhausted just finding out about it.

On another occasion, we were checking into a Dallas hotel when a long-haired, suede-tasselled, leather-trousered, mirror-shaded Bon Jovi lookalike group came sauntering down the carpeted marble stairs with a couple of giggly blondes in sparkly hot pants and cowboy hats. Maybe it was Bon Jovi; they all look the same to me. The girls continued to hang around in the lobby after the metal band had left. After collecting his key, Steedy turned around and shouted...

"OI! YOU TWO, BACK UPSTAIRS!"

They giggled and followed him up.

Mike had his bass guitar customised to include a mirror scratch plate on the front so while playing he could deflect the stage lights from his guitar into the audience and on to the face of his next victim. After another show, I entered the tour bus alone and made my way down the narrow corridor to the back lounge. On pulling back the curtain, I discovered Steed on the job on the back seat. Whilst still in the act, he looked me in the eyes, punched the air and shouted *"ENGLAND!"*

Mike Steed was a PR accident waiting to happen and the camel's back finally gave way when we returned to the UK to do a live TV show at Wembley studios. We were hanging around on set between rehearsals when the presenter, Paula Yates, complained that she was feeling unwell and asked if anyone could get her a thermometer. Mike Steed yelled out:

"STICK IT UP YOUR ARSE!"

The production team and performers all looked over at us to try and figure out which one of us had said it. We had all been tarred with the same blusher brush so Rocco went nuts. We could no longer let him represent the band in that way. As a result, Mike was gone, and I was demoted back to four strings for our upcoming tour of Scandinavia.

Skål.

CHAPTER 16 – BERSERKERS

1990 was an eventful, hopeful, exhilarating, exhausting, scary and strange kind of year. Nick, Rocco, and I spent January putting together an acoustic set to promote Flesh for Lulu's new album, 'Plastic Fantastic' on radio and TV. A track written by myself, 'Time And Space', had been selected as the next single by Capitol Records. Flesh toured Scandinavia. Another song of mine, 'Slide', was used in the John Candy movie 'Uncle Buck', my American girlfriend got deported and the Test Tubes recorded 'The Shit Factory', an album of Stock Aitken Waterman songs.

Err, wait… what?

Nick, Rocco, Hans and I travelled to Germany to perform on a TV show called 'Flash'. SPV Records had licensed 'Plastic Fantastic' in Germany and their rep, the appropriately named Thomas Beer, was there to meet us at Cologne Airport. As we dragged our guitars through baggage claim, I introduced myself to Thomas and he could not believe it was me, as he was a massive Test Tubes fan. Later on during that trip, over a few beers, he told me that SPV were setting up a small alternative label named Rebel Records and asked if we would be interested in doing something. As I had been so busy recording and promoting with Flesh for Lulu, I had not written many songs, so I had to come up with a proposal on the spot. I had been mulling over a couple of ideas for covers albums, either recreating Bob Marley's 'Exodus' in a punk rock style or a collection of Stock Aitken Waterman covers. I pitched the ideas to Thomas, expecting him to turn around and tell me to fuck off. Unexpectedly, he enthusiastically embraced the SAW concept.

Back in London, I had met and was dating an American, half Irish, half Cherokee Indian girl named Arcturus. Yes, her mother was a hippie. Arcturus was working at a US-style diner in Chiswick named Tootsies. US citizens can only stay in the UK for six months on a holiday visa and cannot work here without a permit, however, Arcturus had been living and working in the UK for over a year. The restaurant had begun asking for her National Insurance number and she was unsure what action to take next. Annoyingly, I had been constantly reminding her that she needed to go back to the States and get it sorted out. Eventually, she caved in, booked a flight and headed out to Heathrow. At UK immigration, they noticed her expired visa and took her to an interview room to inform her she would no longer be able to re-enter the country.

The next day she telephoned me from Los Angeles in tears…

"…they interrogated me and kicked me out. I've lost everything. My job, my flat and my friends. What am I going to do? I can't return now. I've got nothing here in LA."

In choosing my next sentence, I had to be very careful. My two choices were:

a) See you around… or
b) Will you marry me?

Of course, being a true gentleman, I proposed and on the 2nd of March 1990 we tied the noose at the Los Angeles County Courthouse.

The night before the wedding, my stag night had taken place at the Cat and Fiddle, a noisy hangout for failed British musicians on Sunset Boulevard. I met up with ex-Anarchy Ranch hand and Walnut and the Wankers/Masked Raiders' bassist, Mark 'Skweeech' Verrion. Skweeech had recently been on a trip to America with his girlfriend but they had fallen out and she'd stormed back home to England. He was now stranded in the US as his visa had expired and his car had been broken into, with all his belongings being stolen, along with his passport. To this day, over 30 years later, he has still not yet made it back to the UK!

In an attempt to earn some money to buy food, Skweeech had started washing car windscreens at a traffic intersection but had been chased away and threatened by the black gang that owned that corner.
I didn't know many people in Los Angeles, so I asked him to be my best man. I was marrying an 'illegal' immigrant so why not have another as the best man? He turned out to be the 'worst man' as on the day he couldn't find anywhere to park and missed the ceremony.

Arcturus' Mum Karen drank champagne from her stiletto shoe on the courthouse steps and we had the reception back at her best friend, Hayley Rose's house just off Hollywood Boulevard, which she shared with her friends Tara and Rizelma. Coincidentally, the house was overshadowed by the Capitol Records Tower which was only a block away, so I popped in for a meeting and presented them with some of Flesh's new material.

One day, when Arcturus and Hayley were out shopping, I was home alone lying on the sofa watching some enthralling American daytime TV (probably 'I Love Lucy' or 'Bewitched'). Slowly, a huge ceramic plant pot started to make its way across the living room floor. My first thought was that it was some sort of paranormal activity, but I had been unaware of the magnitude of the situation as I had just witnessed my first earthquake. When Hayley returned home later, I was shocked when she announced it had reached 5.7 on the Richter scale, causing 30 injuries and $12.7 million worth of damage.

A ground-breaking experience!

On our return to the UK, Arcturus moved into my three-bedroom flat in Cambridge Gardens. We were happy enough for a while as we hadn't really known each other for that long but, as in a lot of cases, once you get over the initial butterflies of meeting, you then have to get down to the nitty-gritty of trying to live with each other's flaws.

Soon enough, the archaic 'hard-working waitress versus musician between albums' battle soon commenced.

One night, I was watching 'Match of the Day' on the portable TV when she arrived home in a bad mood after a particularly long shift.

"How long is this going to be on for? This is always on. Why can't we watch something good?"

She had a point, but I explained that everyone needs 'mindless activities' from time to time to recharge their brain and relieve stress. However, my flimsy justifications fell on deaf ears. As the bad vibes escalated, I picked up the TV, went into the spare room and never came out again.

Arcturus remembered our first meeting…

"I met Del in LA at a dinner party after the premiere of the movie 'Some Kind Of Wonderful', then two years later, I had gone to see Flesh for Lulu play in the West End of London where I met Carmen and after the show, she introduced us. I was immature and jealous back then and Del was older than me and I was in a foreign country, aged 17 with no friends or family. We never argued and it was a shame that we gave up so easily. I moved into a bedsit while Del toured the states for six months and I used to call him on tour from the record store that I worked at in West Hampstead. I got in sooo much trouble for that, in fact, I think that's why I got fired!

We broke up because I was insecure. I remember we were having a Bonfire Night party in our garden in Cambridge Gardens, loads of people were invited and after lots of mulled wine, I started thinking that he was into Cleo, Rocco's lady, but as I say, we should have tried a little harder to stay together... I kept his last name though... ha ha ha!"

Around that time, the Test Tubes were asked to open for Die Toten Hosen, a platinum-selling German punk rock band, on their European tour. We stayed at five-star hotels, singer Campino invited us to share their tour bus and all the shows were sold-out sports halls and arenas. Also on the bill was Honest John Plain from Seventies punk band The Boys. John couldn't look any more rock 'n' roll if he tried and is rarely seen without his mirror shades, cowboy boots and bandana. Each night he would appear for the encore to perform a couple of Boys classics and then we would bumble on for the last song of the night to perform 'Leader Of The Gang'. After the show, the entire tour entourage would pour back to the hotel and designate Honest John's as the party room. John would soon crash out and everyone would help themselves to his minibar and stick the porn on until around 5am.

Passing the hotel check-out the following morning we would witness Honest John craning his neck toward the receptionist so he was out of earshot from the rest of the guests in the queue, insisting...

"I never watched any porn, and I didn't have anything from the minibar."

The following night, Honest John invited everyone back to his room again. Of course, John crashes out, the minibar gets emptied and on goes the porn. The next morning he's back at the front of the queue arguing with the receptionist again.

"I never watched any porn, and I didn't have anything from the minibar."

This continued after every show and later on the bus, as the tour manager was dishing out everyone's PD's (daily allowance), John was informed... Sorry, there's nothing for you mate, I've had to cover all your room charges with the band credit card.

"But I never watched any porn, and I didn't..." etc...

He never learnt but he did have the honour of earning his very own Test Tube nickname...

'Minibar John!'

On return to the UK, the new Flesh for Lulu line-up had been booked to play some European dates and without Kev and James reining us in, the driverless carriage now became a no-holds-barred, self-destructive drink and drug-taking machine, much like being on the road with the Test Tubes.

We once played in the middle of the desert, near Valencia in Spain, and after we'd finished sound-checking in the afternoon we were driven back into the town for dinner, close to the hotel. After endless refills of red wine carafes, I asked the promoter what time we were expected on stage... *"Four thirty a.m."* came the reply. WTF! I was teetering on the brink of being unable to play, foolishly assuming that we'd be on stage around 9pm like in normal countries. It was time for an attempt at sensibility, so I went for a lie-down.

In the early hours of the morning, in the total darkness of my room, the silence was shattered by the deafening extended ring of an old-fashioned telephone... *"Hello?"*

"You need to come downstairs now Del, you're on stage in half an hour."

A few questions urgently needed answering...

Firstly, where am I? Secondly, what time is it? And thirdly, who am I?

I was already hungover, and we hadn't even played yet. I fumbled around in the dark, quickly got my clothes together, and we were then driven back out to the club in the desert. On arrival at the show, the whole audience was wild-eyed, dribbling and drugged out of their heads. I began to feel like a sacrificial virgin from an old Hammer Horror movie being nervously led towards the stage, sober and hungover with the contorted faces of evil devil worshippers laughing, shouting and shaking their fists. When I woke up the next afternoon I tried to figure out if it had all been a dream, like the entire ninth season of Dallas?

Having recently taken British rock band Then Jerico on tour in Spain, Trapper was brought in to take a crack at being Flesh for Lulu's new tour manager.

Following frontman Mark Shaw's departure from the band, Marcus Mystery had now become Then Jericho's new lead singer. He later told me a story about when they arrived at one venue in Spain to find a life-size poster of former singer Mark Shaw with his hands on his hips on full display outside the box office. During the show that night, two young girls made their way to the front of the stage, where one pointed up at Marcus and shouted...

"...THAT'S NOT HIM!"

Mike Steed was now history, so I was back on the bass for Flesh's tour of Sweden with wild kid Danny Bell joining us to take care of the merchandise and Trapper arranging everything. The dream team (cough!).

One afternoon we stopped at the side of the road for a piss in the forest, where Dan discovered a Fly Agaric mushroom growing on a tree stump. Those are the bright red ones with the white spots, the type that the Vikings ate during their raids on England to produce their berserker rages. When we arrived at the show, Dan started to cook the mushroom in the venue's kitchen area. The chef peered through the glass oven door and became instantly alarmed...

"If you eat that, you will die."

Despite this sage culinary advice, Dan finished baking it and crumbled the remains into a large paper wrap. The ferry home from Gothenburg takes about 26 hours and I can't remember at what stage of the crossing we thought it would be a great idea, but we decided to have a snort of Dan's Fly Agaric baked mushroom powder. Where to start? We went completely insane, drinking the bar dry, generally being a nuisance around the boat and hanging off the side trying to touch the water.

At one point, I passed the children's disco and saw Dan surrounded by toddlers dancing to 'Mahna Mahna' by the Muppets in his fur coat. The next morning, with all remaining dignity stripped away, we travelled back from Harwich through the City of London at rush hour. Everyone was in business suits on their way to work but we were still in Viking berserker mode and hadn't slept. Dan suggested...

"Let's get out and do some suits..."

Rocco liked the idea, but Trapper strongly advised against it.

Amid all this chaos and to keep myself busy between failures, I decided to put together another band. Err, why? Had I learned nothing? Mr Lyall (vocals) from Worthing's This Colour, Mick and Aaron from new wave band Modern English (bass and keyboards) and Ogs, ex-Test Tubes (drums). Transvision Vamp's manager Simon Watson put us in the studio to record some demos and we played a couple of shows. Singer Lyall came up to London for a brainstorming session so we could come up with a name for the new group. After two days of partying, we decided upon the name…

'There didn't seem to be anything strange about him until he took his hat off'

I'd lifted this from a 1963 comic book cover called 'Tales of Suspense - Prophet of Doom'. Lyall returned to Brighton and told his partner at that time, 'Journey to the centre of Johnny Clarke's sister' Dinah about the new name for our band…

"I feel sick," she cried.

We settled on Reactor (a device for containing and controlling a chemical reaction). I still preferred TDSTBASAHUHTHHO…

Could have been massive…

I'll get my coat.

CHAPTER 17 – WHILE MY GUITAR GENTLY SLURS

Guitars are boring planks of wood with magnets in them.

I always found music shops and the smug 'know-it-all' failed musicians who work in them tiresome and annoying. Visiting one was like going to the dentist; they would bore the hell out of you with theory, and then you'd leave with a headache. I never practise the guitar, but I enjoy writing songs and making up my own chords and scales. I will always pick up a guitar and play it just in case an idea strikes me.

As a musician my motivational mantra is:

'I'd rather play three chords in front of hundreds of people than hundreds of chords in front of three people'. (Guitar) case closed.

I have only owned one guitar; a 1974 Gibson Les Paul Gold Top which I bought for £250 from a smelly old hippie in Lewes… for the guitar bores among you: the Gibson Les Paul Deluxe replaced the Les Paul Standard 1969, with a new design to prevent headstock breaks (didn't work for me). I never carry a spare as I never hit the guitar hard enough to break a string and on the rare occasion that I do, I've developed a method of being able to change it while I'm still playing. It has been stolen once and lost countless times by various airlines. Four times the neck has been broken… Tip: never wave to the crowd at gigs with low ceilings while still holding your guitar.

On one European tour, after losing my luggage, British Airways sent my lost guitar to my hotel every afternoon after I'd already checked out. It followed us through Austria and Switzerland until it finally arrived just before we were about to go on stage at the Batschkapp in Frankfurt. I undid the catches on the case and lifted the lid, but unfortunately, my lost electric guitar had now morphed into an acoustic.

At a Flesh for Lulu show at the Cambridge Corn Exchange in England, we returned to the venue after dinner to find my guitar stand empty. Frenchie and Joe, our stage crew at the time, searched the venue for the guitar, but it was nowhere to be found. Expanding their search to the car park, they spotted it under a blanket, laying across the back seat of a car. The rear window was smashed and the guitar retrieved. It transpired that the perpetrator had lifted it, stashed it and then returned to the venue to watch the show. After the vehicle registration had been checked and the owner identified, he tried to make a break for it during the show as I happily watched from the stage as a Keystone Cops-style chase along the bar and across the dance floor ensued.

More recently Rancid, the million-selling punk rock band from the US, invited the Test Tubes to open a few shows during their 2012 UK tour. Guitarist Lars Frederiksen and I first met in Morecambe at a Rebellion Festival after-show party when he was playing with Charlie Harper in some kind of punk rock celebrity mash-up band. I was a little short with him when he approached me at the bar, thinking he was some sort of tattooed-up hassle merchant. My Les Paul was all he wanted to talk about. How old it was? Its value? Where did you get it? All that interesting sort of stuff. He'd watched our show and told me it was the best guitar sound he'd heard all weekend. He also explained how he'd flown to Sotheby's in London to take part in an auction for Pete Townshend's Telecaster guitar and after paying a lot of money for it, shipped it home only to discover that it sounded shit. At least I think that's what he was telling me? Once the penny had dropped as to who he was, I offered to swap my guitar for one of his houses in Beverly Hills. He thought I was joking, but I was serious and stood there awaiting a counter-offer.

As we pulled into the car park around the back of Portsmouth Pyramids live arena, Lars was standing by the loading doors and wandered over for another chat. I thought this may be a good opportunity to try to sell my guitar again. Early promise soon fizzled out as Paul H, who had been drinking all day, wandered across to queer my pitch by constantly interrupting and rambling loudly into his face.

Later that night, Lars squashed into our tiny dressing room where fellow Brighton North Stander, barrel-chested, tight-vested Steve Potts was sitting in the middle of the room taking up all the space with his giant pumped-up steroid arms. Lars told us that he had gone to our show in San Francisco when he was a little kid back in the 1980s. The memory of Peter getting him on stage and putting him on his shoulders had stayed with him to this day. As he left, he turned to the band and invited us to...

"Help yourself to any merch you guys want."

At the end of the night during loadout, it was raining, so I thought I'd go and get myself a Rancid hat. The girl behind the merchandise stall snapped at me angrily...

"You can't have anything else; you've already taken too much stuff!"

Of course, I hadn't taken anything, but as I boarded our bus, I noticed everyone was suitably clobbered up with Rancid merch. Huge Burden and Little Burden (Steve and Little Mark) had hats, hoodies, tote bags,

T-shirts, the lot. The grabbing hands grabbed all they can... all for themselves after all. It's a com-pet-i-tive world… and no guitar sale either, thanks H.

In the UK in the Eighties, you couldn't go anywhere without having to endure a song by the pop record producing trio Stock Aitken Waterman.

A truly awful period for music, particularly if you were over 12. SAW had written and produced some of the worst soulless music for the likes of Kylie, Jason, Mel & Kim, Sonia, Big Fun and the Reynolds Girls... the list goes on, even Cliff Richard released a SAW-produced song, what a truly horrific combination. They were successful from the mid-1980s through to the early-1990s, so I'd come up with an idea to wind up the punk police and do a SAW covers album.

At the first rehearsal, Ogs gave it his stamp of approval by stating:

"We're not going through with it, are we?"

I'd become friends with sound engineer and all-round nice geezer Ralph Jezzard while he was engineering for Flesh for Lulu. Now a producer, he'd just finished successful albums for alternative rock bands EMF and Jesus Jones, so we were lucky to get him to come down to Brighton to work on our new record. We recorded it at Esselle Studios during the Italia '90 football World Cup finals. Rehearsing next door were Beats International, a British electronic band formed by Norman Cook after his departure from The Housemartins, featuring actor and singer Lindy Layton and former Test Tube auditionee Luke 'Stomp' Creswell. Kevin Stagg, the studio owner, entered the control room midway through our recording and told us Norman needed the studio to do an urgent remix for GO! Discs. We agreed to vacate the place for the day on the condition that Norman did a remix of one of our tracks. This has never materialised so...

Fatboy Slim still owes Peter and the Test Tube Babies a remix.

The opening track on the album was a cover of ex-Rolling Stones child bride Mandy Smith's 'I Just Can't Wait'. I made it a point never to hear the song before we rehearsed it. I stole the chords straight out of a songbook and played them as fast as I could while Peter shouted the lyrics over it. I have no idea what the original sounds like, or even what it's about, hopefully not something dodgy, like underage sex.

A few of the tracks sounded a bit too much like the originals for my liking, which wasn't the point. The point was to mess them up like the Mandy Smith track. On pop duo Mel & Kim's classic 'Fun Love And Money', Trapper insisted on doing exactly the same bassline as their version, using his £2,500 Wal bass guitar which we nicknamed the 'Farty Rattler'.

Trapper recounted the noteworthy story of 'Farty'...

"I managed to blag a new Wal bass guitar from our then manager Nick McGerr so we drove up to, I think it was, High Wycombe. Mr Wal founder Ian Waller, who was a bass player himself, had hand-built it. He took me to the player's booth where I just strummed it discordantly. He just got up and walked out in disgust although he can't have been that upset as he sold it to us for £2,500. It was really shit for the music we were doing, and I think I eventually sold it to legless Paul H for £400."

Marcus Mystery helped out on the record again as did Rocco and Nick from Flesh and Trapper was guilty of bringing down Louise, Gabby, Sarah and Christine, the barmaids from the Green Dragon to do a terrible Bananarama impression on 'Love In The First Degree'.
Ralph and I finished the mixing at Gooseberry Studios in London.
The only single was a double A-side featuring Sinitta's gay anthem 'Toy Boy' (how did I coerce Peter into singing that?) and the Christmassy Nat King Cole classic 'When I Fall In Love', unoriginally covered by Rick Astley. We played it in a 'Great Rock 'N' Roll Swindle' Pistols style.
Stock Aitken Waterman had a studio in Borough named 'The Hit Factory' so, of course, we had to call it 'The Shit Factory' and we shot the album cover near my flat in West London. At that time, I was living with Scottish wheeler-dealer John McFarland who was importing American limousines into the UK and lent us one for the day. Photographer Lee Strickland, Trapper and I drove around Notting Hill looking for old homeless people living in doorways. We eventually found some horrible stinking tramps and paid them with a couple of crates of Tennent's Super lager to appear in the photoshoot. The only condition they gave as they climbed aboard was...

"...nae shit-stabbing."

Michael, our accountant at that time, was also Stock, Aitken and Waterman's, and, during a meeting, slipped Pete Waterman a copy of 'The Shit Factory'. He gave it a listen and warned Michael that this time, he would refrain from taking any legal action but gave us a word of advice:

"...If you're going to change the lyrics to any of the songs you have to get the permission of the publisher."

Fair play to him, lesser people would have taken out an injunction.

The album gained mostly favourable reviews, although some thought that the joke may have been missed by many. One review wrote:

'They rip apart the plastic nature of SAW with the precision of a surgeon wielding a chainsaw, in particular 'Especially for You' is very funny and 'I'd Rather Jack' sounds a damn sight better than the original.'

A more recent reviewer wrote...

'A jolly good romp at the time, but with over two decades of ageing now looks like a bit of a mistake. Nowadays every US pop-punker is putting out ironic covers of cheesy pop songs but this was not the norm when this came out and as such is the only time you could call Peter and chums innovators. What rescues this album is the quality of these pop nuggets (not what I would've said at the time, but then have you listened to the charts these days?) So, with former chart behemoths like Mel & Kim, Sinitta, Jason and Kylie, Bananarama, Brother Beyond, Rick Astley and the classic "I'd Rather Jack" by the Reynolds Girls being given their own aggro pop-punk spin, it's a good laugh for people of a certain age but little more. The most distressing thing about this album is that it doesn't contain anything by Bros despite a teasing picture on the cover. Ho-hum!'

The following year, Rebel Records foolishly picked up the option for a second Test Tubes release so I began looking for a studio to record the appropriately titled 'Cringe'.
    As a result of the breathing space that the SAW covers album had given me, I had written a good deal of new material. In fact, I had around 30 songs, all ready to be moulded into classics by my eager and hard-working bandmates. Not so. No one wanted to rehearse or spend any time in the recording studio, so with everyone pulling in different directions, once again it was down to the sound engineer and myself to try and produce some magic.

Trapper was having women problems, Peter never shows up until it's 'shouting time', while Ogs had decided he wanted to be paid for rehearsing and recording. The problem now was if I paid Ogs, I had to pay everyone else the same, so the budget got severely chomped.
    I've always maintained that you get what you pay for when it comes to

the quality of the recording, and if everyone hadn't been so greedy that album would have sounded so much better.

Ogs came out with some of his best classic drummer quotes at that time.

"I ain't drumming fast for your benefit."

And…

"If you lot go to the pub. I'm going home."

Around this time, I'd met a happy friendly chap named Shaun Harvey who was managing and engineering at Boundary Row Studios in Borough, South London (strangely enough, just across the street from SAW's studio). He gave us a great deal, including a promise to finish the record even if we went over budget. We got 18 tracks recorded and I'd chosen what I thought to be the best 12 when Trapper put in an appearance at the studio, heavily laden with booze and other band entertainments. As we listened through the mixes, Trapper gave himself the job of official timekeeper.

"We've got a major problem!"

"What?"

"We've only got a total of just over twenty-one minutes. That's nowhere near long enough for a whole album."

In a drunken wired-up panic we quickly remixed the remaining six tracks and put them on the record. Upon release, we realised that coked-up Trap had been adding up the track times at a rate of 100 seconds per minute, which made the album seem incredibly short, which, of course, it wasn't. As a result of this constitutional incompetence, the record ended up containing a load of unwanted tracks. Another towering effort on the slippery slope to abject failure. To celebrate, I designed a 'cringeometer' and put a free one inside every vinyl record sleeve.

We still await our invitation to appear on the British TV documentary series 'Classic Albums'.

CHAPTER 18 – HEADLOCK HOLIDAY

My concept of a holiday has always been synonymous with going on tour. Visas, jabs, airport, computer out, belt off, belt on, immigration, passport control, go into a little room, go in another little room, queue up for the plane, get on the plane, get off the plane, baggage claim, hotel, drag your suitcase up the stairs, unpack, pack and then do it all again in reverse. I could never see the point of lying around on a beach covered in sand, developing skin cancer and doing fuck all for five hours.

I would be pacing up and down the beach wondering when back-stage catering was going to open and what time were 'doors'? Being on tour for most of my life meant I was in a constant state of wanting to go home.

My first holiday without my parents was to the Norfolk Broads with The Scumbags, a punk band from Newhaven led by singer Allan Sherman who was nicknamed Allan 'Flares', due to his reluctance to ditch his bell-bottomed trousers during the early punk days.

Allan went on to be known as Allan Scumbag, which must have been a real icebreaker when being introduced at dinner parties.

The five Scumbags were on one boat and the Test Tubes on another, circumnavigating our way up the river from pub to pub. Initially, everyone wanted to steer and pretend to be the captain, but as soon as the novelty wore off, nobody cared any more. In the end, there was a stand-off as everyone refused to go up and sit behind the wheel as we careered blindly up the river until eventually coming to an abrupt halt running aground on the river bank.

There was always a race with the Scumbags to get the nearest mooring spot to that night's pub so you didn't have to stagger too far home at closing time. We'd found a prime mooring space and had begun manoeuvring in when we spotted HMS Scumbag hurtling towards the same space at full throttle. We managed to glide in with ease, but it was too late for them to pull out of their trajectory. A loud bang was heard, and a large crack appeared on the hull from bow to stern. Both parties had paid a £500 deposit at the start of the holiday but there was no way we were going to be losing ours, so we quickly obtained a written eyewitness statement from a bystander. Over the next few days, we took it in turns to stand guard through the night as the Scumbags attempted several times to sneak aboard, steal our witness statement, and destroy the evidence. One night however, our makeshift sentries got so drunk they fell asleep, allowing the Scumbags to cut through our mooring ropes and set us adrift. This treacherous act of piracy saw us waking up to find ourselves drifting out towards the North Sea.

While on the subject of drifting, even though it had cost £450,000 to make, Flesh for Lulu's 'Plastic Fantastic' failed to chart. Not great considering the Test Tubes could have made 90 albums for that amount! Nevertheless, the first single, 'Decline And Fall', became a top 15 hit on Billboard's Modern Rock chart, and the promotional video was directed by Flesh's former manager Peter Webber, who went on to direct 'Girl with a Pearl Earring' starring Scarlett Johansson and Colin Firth, which received numerous accolades, including three Academy Award nominations, two Golden Globe nominations, and 10 BAFTA nominations. (That's 'Girl with a Pearl Earring', not 'Decline and Fall'!) The follow-up single, 'Time And Space', reached the top 10 on Billboard Modern Rock but failed to appear on any other US chart.

One reviewer wrote:

"Flesh for Lulu bring the noise in Plastic Fantastic to gain more fans in America, but ironically, it's only the album's two most poppy love songs that found airplay in the United States. Released in 1989, when spandex metal was dominating AOR stations, Plastic Fantastic turns up the amps. 'Decline and Fall' and 'House of Cards' are passable rockers; they're much slicker than anything in Flesh for Lulu's early discography, so purists should be forewarned. Hidden in the rather forgettable material on Plastic Fantastic is the romantic 'Time and Space' and the sultry 'Every Little Word'. 'Time and Space' has Nick Marsh crooning love-stricken lyrics as dreamy new wave keyboards shimmer in adoration. 'Time and Space' could've been as fondly remembered as new wave ballads like Depeche Mode's 'Somebody' and the Psychedelic Furs' 'The Ghost in You' if it was released earlier in the decade. It's hard to chastise Flesh for Lulu for attempting to increase their audience on Plastic Fantastic; nevertheless, it's almost painful to hear gems such as 'Time and Space' and 'Every Little Word' surrounded by faceless guitar rock. And it flopped too."
(AllMusic Review by Michael Sutton.)

The 'Plastic Fantastic' promotion campaign came to an end and, as a reward for all our hard work, Capitol Records dropped us. A new album was in the works, so we started pulling favours and demoing new songs around various studios in London. Duncan Bridgeman, a double Grammy-nominated filmmaker and musician, helped set us up and recorded all our new songs live to tape at Moody Studios in Acton. After delivering the results to our management, we continued to rehearse and awaited their release.

And waited…

And waited…

Then all of a sudden… Nothing happened.

The wait went on too long, the wages and money for rent and bills started to dry up and frustration and boredom began to set in. A drunken Nick phoned me up late one night and declared:

"If this album's not out by Christmas, I'm going into acting."

Due to Nick's insistence, all our money had been spent on making the new record, so we began squatting a four-storey Victorian house on Fellows Road in Chalk Farm. We soundproofed the room next to mine with old mattresses to use as a rehearsal studio. Nick and Rocco's girlfriends TC and Cleo also rehearsed there with their new all-girl rock band 'Lovecraft'. In the kitchen, we all had our own fridges with padlocks on, so no one could steal each other's peanut butter.

By this point, I had lost interest in pointless rehearsals with no endgame, but Nick and Rocco had nothing else to do, so they would hammer on my bedroom door and shout:

"COME ON. LET'S HAVE A JAM…"

OK. I'm going to say it… I fucking hate jamming with a passion, always have, always will, ever since I first started playing the guitar. I develop a sense of utter dread whenever someone mentions the possibility that it may be about to occur. I find the experience to be an insufferable waste of time and energy. Hans and I would have to play some sort of 12 bar or a series of notes that Nick dictated and then he and Rocco would take turns to 'peel out' some solos. *"Take it, Rocco…"* Yawnaggedon!

One day I was in bed watching tennis on my black-and-white portable TV when I was once again summoned for another life reaffirming 'jam'. Picking up my TV and bringing it into the stuffy rehearsal room with me, I set it up on top of my amp so I could play bass and keep up with the order of the day's play at Wimbledon.

After breaking out into a mild sweat, it would then be announced that we should celebrate by going to the pub around the corner to discuss future plans. Translation: Get shitfaced.

Rocco then came up with the genius idea of 'starting again' with a new name.

"Fuck waiting around," he declared.

"Let's change our name and build up a following as we did in the early Flesh days when we sold out the Marquee once a month."

I could barely contain my excitement, erm, think of anything worse. 'Starting again' is not in my vocabulary so Rocco's proposition really signified the end for me. After one drunken meeting too many we decided to go our separate ways and the album never got released. It was all very amicable, but we'd all had enough of waiting for something to happen.

Years later, in 2014, I received the devastating news that Nick had been diagnosed with mouth and throat cancer.

Nick described the discovery in an interview.

"I had a funny sort of blip in the corner of my mouth, like a grain of rice. The doctors said it was nothing but I knew something was wrong, gut instinct, you know? Cancer had begun to spread into the lymph nodes under my jaw, so a massive section of my neck was also dissected and removed. After surgery, I had a six-week, intensive course of radiotherapy five days a week accompanied by six courses of chemotherapy. The sixth dose was withheld as there was a strong chance I wouldn't survive it, due to weight loss and dehydration…"

Hideously, the cancer then moved from Nick's jaw and into his brain, yet I still couldn't believe my ears when I heard the devastating news that Nick had passed away on the 5th of June 2015.

I attended Nick's funeral, a lovely sunny summer's day in the beautiful mature woodland at Greenacres in Epping Forest. His friends, family and ex-bandmates saw him off in style. The dress code said 'Dress Fabulous'. Nick always looked cool-as-fuck, dressed in vintage suits, great shoes and with his hair always perfectly sculpted.

"You're not going on stage dressed like that are you?"
he once chastised me.

"You look like a fucking roadie."

The Flesh for Lulu 'Joyride' was over and the Test Tube Babies were between record deals after cringing out with our last release.
It was time for some freedom. Woo hoo!

In the early 1990s, I started getting into the London party scene.

To keep the party locations secret from the general public and authorities, they would only be announced via word of mouth or by last-minute flyers in independent record shops or places like Kensington Market. Former working-class districts such as Old Street, Hackney Road and Bermondsey became playgrounds for eager clubbers who threw parties in empty properties, warehouses or anywhere else that had enough room to set up a sound system. When I lived in Brixton, my flatmate Annie used to drive us up to the Old Street area after midnight to visit the latest warehouse parties. The police would then raid, close them down and confiscate all the equipment as we legged it down the fire escapes to an alternative location where the party would continue into the early hours. As the sun came up, we would join the queue at the 'Beigel Bake' shop for a morning salmon and cream cheese bagel as Brick Lane Market burst into life. Eventually, the warehouse scene became more and more untenable, partially as a result of the police finally catching up with swift-moving club activities. Promoters got more creative. London party organiser Nicky Holloway threw a series of fantastic parties at the London Zoo, Lord's Cricket Ground and the Natural History Museum. Weekends were all about staying up until the first guilt-ridden rays of sunlight came streaming through the cracks in the curtains on Monday morning.

I gave up on clubbing when promoters, now fearful of police reprisals, began to move back into licensed premises. With overpriced drinks, heavy security and snobby guest list hags, the scene became trendy. As the ladies were marched straight into the VIP areas, the 'boyfriends' Stevie, Ben and myself would have to troop off to the night bus stop after being refused entry for wearing jeans and Dr. Martens boots.

Over in West London, Marcus Mystery had got his act together, his new band Hard Rain had signed to London Records. He married Carmen at Chelsea Town Hall and asked me to be his best man, which I gratefully accepted. I co-ordinated the guest list and reception arrangements with the matron of honour, Rachael Chappell. Rachael worked for Marcus' management, DHM, who also represented the reggae band UB40 and soul singer Robert Palmer. Rachael described herself as a 'party animal gone wrong' and I had many great nights out partying with her and her West London gang of girlfriends - 'The Fluffies' (or 'The Wiries' as Walnut now calls them). We would gather for pre-club entertainments at Rachael's sister Debbie's and Tina D's flat in Colville Gardens, just off the Portobello Road, then take taxis to clubs and parties.

Marcus and Carmen booked their honeymoon at Christmas in Goa, India, so Trapper and I, of course, tagged along. Rachael and the Fluffies would follow later...

CHAPTER 19 – DANCING WITH SQUIRRELS

Compared with the Norfolk Broads, the Indian state of Goa was a whole different kettle of sardines. With its palm-lined beaches, white sand and blue waters, it was a paradise on earth for those of us who wanted to escape the oppressive winter of humdrum London.

Originally a Portuguese province, Goa became known for its psychedelic trance and rave scene. It also became a popular destination for rich-parented dreadlocked Trustafarians pretending to be poor, while middle-class people like us waitresses, musicians and office workers pretended to be rich by dining out on lobster and buying cheap made-to-measure silk suits.

On arrival, Trapper and I rented an Enfield motorcycle and went off to look for some accommodation, finding a lovely three-bedroom house on the Baga back road to Anjuna. After paying the deposit, we moved into the big double room at the back. After Carmen and Marcus arrived, Carmen claimed the big room for herself and threw our bags into the smaller rooms, mine being the size of a broom cupboard. I didn't mind because I didn't plan on staying in or sleeping much. Rachael and the Fluffies then arrived and rented out most of the Bonanza Hotel in Baga. The illegal jungle dance parties were the order of the day, and after one all-nighter I offered Rachael a lift back on my motorbike. Earlier we'd split an acid tab, so as we drove home through the jungle, we felt like characters in a video game, except this time we would only get one life instead of three. Back in my broom cupboard we took some Valium to come down but, when we woke the next day, we couldn't remember if we'd had sex or not. We began to spend more time together and would get up around 4pm, get on my bike and ride to the German bakery to grab some fruit and freshly baked bread for breakfast.

Rachael remembered…

"Our existence was rooted in the nightlife and searching out illegal techno parties hidden in the jungle. With fading tans and black circles appearing around our eyes, we'd become nocturnal, while everyone else was bronzed, glowing and enjoying their days by the beach."

We used to hide our drugs and money in our underwear in case we were stopped by the dodgy Goan police, who would pay to be stationed in the province to profit from the bakshish they could make by extorting money from foreigners. They would step out from behind bushes to stop you, brandishing large bamboo canes and crossing them in front of your motorcycle.

On the way to breakfast one afternoon, we were stopped and searched. They found one dirty screwed-up old five rupee note (worth around 5p) in my shorts' pocket and promptly threw it to the floor in disgust before quickly waving us on as they spotted two fleece-able overweight American tourists approaching on a wobbly scooter.

On returning to London we continued to see each other but we had to break the news to our current partners that we had 'met someone else'. D'aw. If that sounds sappy, that's because it is.

More recently, Rachael suggested taking another trip to India, including a stop at the ashram where the Beatles stayed, followed by a visit to the Rishikesh Palace, the birthplace of yoga in the Indian Himalayas. The idea of breathlessly trekking through the jungle, covered in mosquito bites, squatting behind a palm tree with diarrhoea and then wiping your arse with giant red ants had lost its appeal.

"But that sounds wonderful!" replied Rachael disappointedly.

Not for me, my days of swimming with dolphins and dancing with squirrels were over.

Rachael reflected on that time, first getting to know each other…

"When I first met Del, he was playing with Flesh for Lulu and hanging out at the Earl of Lonsdale and the Portobello Gold in Notting Hill Gate and we were introduced via some mutual friends. Those times were hedonistic and to be honest I only have vague recollections of times and places but what I knew instantly was that Del was a genuine character and someone who you could trust in a world where I could only trust a few. Our friendship started when we were put together to help organise our mutual friends Carmen and Marcus's wedding. Carmen was a good friend I made when I was working at Tootsie's in Holland Park Avenue, and she was responsible for getting me a job with David Harper who was at the time Marcus's manager. Mine and Del's friendship grew and five years later turned into a romance while we were on holiday in Goa. That was 30 years ago, and we are still going strong. Back in those days, I lived life to the fullest and was wrapped up in the music scene where life was fast and cut-throat at times. Del became my rock and in a way my saviour. I had finally found my soulmate, my lifeboat, someone I could completely trust, who would never let me down. This statement remains current to this day."

Blimey. Thanks Rae. I felt like a ghost at my own funeral reading that.

Also on my return from India, I discovered that Nick, Hans and myself were about to be evicted from our squat in Chalk Farm, so together with Hans' girlfriend Ylva, we found and rented a house in Willesden Green. Most of our money was taken up by having to pay rent so Hans' Dad would send over emergency food parcels from Sweden, which meant that if I got the munchies in the middle of the night and raided their shelf, I would end up with a salty haul of pickled herring and liquorice fish sweets. Yum!

I had more or less given up clubbing, but Rachael and the Fluffies partied on and she would usually show up in the early hours of Sunday morning and sleep through until Monday night after phoning in sick.

Ylva would ask...

"Is she actually here? How come I haven't seen her?"

Sometimes we stayed over at Rachael's flat in Acton and, as we left in the morning, she would pick up her ever-increasing pile of red bills, rip them in half and toss them in the bin on the way out. Occasionally, we'd be met at the front door by the bailiffs...

"Rachael Chappell?"
"No. She moved out."
"May I ask your name, Madam?"
"No you may not and I'm late for work so get the fuck out of my way."

Rachael was consistently late for everything and wasn't a fan of hanging around at airports, regularly making flights two minutes before the gate closed by the 'skin of her teeth' (which would later become her catchphrase). If we ever went to see a movie, we would miss the first 10 minutes and have no idea what was going on. Not a great match-up for 'Mister Pedantic Pants' or 'Sergeant Major' as she had recently started calling me. Most relationships are like that, yin and yang. There is the bill payer and then there's the scatty one with the screwed-up unposted mail in the bottom of their handbag.

As she was always running late, I used to give her a lift to her office in Hammersmith Road. One morning, on the way through Holland Park, I pointed out an abandoned Fiat parked in a tow-away zone as we drove past.

"What idiot would leave a car there?"
"It's mine!" she replied.

"I don't want it. You can have it if you want?"

Another morning she was late once again, so I reluctantly lent her my beloved Citroen Diane 6. That night she returned it with both headlights hanging out of their sockets on their wires.

Rachael and I moved in together with her sister Debbie, who generously let us have a room in her two-bedroom, third-floor flat on Ladbroke Grove, next door to the Earl of Percy pub. It was a busy abode with many parties and visitors but as our room was a little too small for the both of us, I decided that it was time to buy my first property. This was going to be a tall order as I was back signing on at the dole office claiming unemployment benefit and I needed to raise at least £5,000 for the deposit on a dodgy mortgage.

I bought Carmen's old motorbike, passed my motorcycle test and Marcus recommended me for a job at Rising High Records in Westbourne Grove, a British record label specialising in ambient chillout music. My new job was to pick up and deliver master tapes and finished mixes. I survived a year of London traffic, only getting knocked off three times with relatively minor injuries. One time in the pouring rain, an idiot pedestrian decided to dash across the carriageway even though the traffic light was green, causing me to brake suddenly as the bike skidded and flew out from underneath me. Another time, someone opened a van door directly into my path, and the third accident was when I was lifted clean off the bike as two trucks converged into the middle lane on the busy Marylebone Road.

With a lot of abstinence and staying in, I finally managed to save up enough for the mortgage deposit and purchased a ground-floor flat with a large back garden in Hanover Road in Kensal Rise for just £72,000. The general Notting Hillbilly and Fluffy consensus was: Why the hell is he buying a house up there in the sticks?

A couple of years later, Notting Hill and Ladbroke Grove's house prices skyrocketed, and everyone started looking for homes further north. Even neighbouring crime hotspot Harlesden, with its high number of murders and crack dealers, became a target for trendy West London property hunters.

We'd only just settled into our new home when Rachael was asked to work for Swedish singer and rapper Neneh Cherry. She agreed to accept a year's contract as Neneh's personal assistant. One small problem however, her office was in Malaga, Spain. This turn of events meant it was 'decision time' again, should I stay or should I go? Which was it to be? The beautiful countryside of Andalucia, enjoying a daily routine of golf, tennis and swimming… or standing around in a stinking claustrophobic rehearsal room looking at people I hate?

Meh… The choice was easy.

As Rachael flew to southern Spain to start her new job, I stayed behind to tie up all the loose ends. I decided to drive over so Walnut, who was living with us at the time, decided to tag along and help me with the move. We strapped our pushbikes to the rack, stuffed as many of our belongings as would fit into Rachael's Peugeot 405 and took the overnight ferry from Portsmouth to Santander in northern Spain.

I don't know what it is about ferries but this one again had the usual effect on us, as we ended up pissed out of our heads in the disco doing the dance routine to 'Saturday Night' by Whigfield.

In the morning, we were about to disembark but Walnut still hadn't made it back to the cabin. As the other drivers started their engines and began to drive off, I waited patiently in the car. I had intended to follow the other cars on to the motorway and head south but ended up driving off alone and having to park up in the port on the other side of customs. The last of the other passengers were long gone when I spotted Walnut in the rear-view mirror stumbling towards immigration on foot. It soon became clear he was in no fit state to read a map, at one point looking at it upside down. We ended up driving around in circles, eventually coming to a dead-end in some dodgy barrio block. We still had no idea where we were, so I had a right moan up. Walnut promptly rolled down the window and threw the map out. So there we were in a packed, overladen car, lost on a B road in the middle of the desert.

Well into the early hours of the morning, after 16 hours of driving, we eventually arrived in the small village of Alhaurín el Grande. We pulled up outside the flat that Rachael was renting but inevitably, no one was home. Back then, there were no mobile phones of course, so we parked up and walked down to the main strip only to find it deserted with everything closed. Walnut and I wandered around aimlessly for a while until we heard some party noises coming from one of the closed bars named 'Blamne'. Out front the tables and chairs were stacked away for the night so we crept around the back and peered through a crack in the curtains only to see Rachael laughing, joking and playing pool in the middle of a party. We banged on the window and they let us in.

The town of Alhaurín is located in the province of Málaga in Andalusia. It was given its name by the Arabs, 'el Grande' was added later to distinguish it from the neighbouring town of Alhaurin de la Torre. Rachael had rented a three-bedroom apartment there for next to nothing and we became the only two British people living there, apart from Danny the gay, as he was known locally, who owned an antique shop. He really was the only gay (and ex-pat) in the village. The coastal town of Fuengirola was a 20-minute drive away and, if you knew where you were going, there was a shortcut to Málaga Airport, past the prison, where you ended up at the end of a runway with planes bearing down as you navigated your way through the mud and around potholes. It was the back of beyond, where no foreigner would dare to venture, much less live. Where would we get our Heinz baked beans and PG Tips tea bags? Ironically, that became its appeal.

Since no one spoke English, if we wanted to survive and get supplies from the local shop, we had to dig deep and learn some Spanish fast. I used to hang out at the Finca la Mota, a nicely tucked away quiet and unassuming bohemian hotel with a swimming pool, stables and a tennis court. The Indian owner and chef, Arun, would go to bed early and tell us to help ourselves to the drinks and just write down what we'd had. After a late night at the free bar, I would head into the town with Andre, the waiter. Andre couldn't speak a word of English either, so we used to get even more hammered and shout at each other using sign language. The more intoxicated we became, the more our communication skills improved. A great way to learn!

I thought I'd visited every bar on the Alhaurin strip, but one night, after a long session, he took me to a strange pub I'd never visited before. It was a bit of a walk into the campo (countryside) and when we arrived the place was packed with unfamiliar good-looking women. We sat at the bar and had a drink until Andre disappeared upstairs with a scantily clad lady. As I sat alone looking around, it suddenly dawned on me that I was in a whorehouse. Paying up quickly I tried to leave, but the door was locked from the inside. I managed to get my point across to the barman that I needed to go home. Therefore, he unbolted the two large wooden doors so I could stumble back into town. It's nice to get out!

I had brought my recording equipment with me to Spain so between leisure activities, and with plenty of spare time on my hands, I started writing again. I sent a few of my new songs to Henry. Peter described them as *"a breath of fresh air."*

Oh no!

What have I done…?

CHAPTER 20 – 36 ARSEHOLES

On my 36th birthday, I went out on the Alhaurin el Grande strip again with Andre the waiter. After a few drinks, I decided to show off my newly acquired drunken Spanish by telling everyone…

"Tengo treinta y seis anos."

Believing that I was telling everyone…

"It's my 36th birthday" which in Spanish scans as *"I have thirty-six years"* (Tengo treinta y seis años).

I then discovered, to my horror, that what I was actually telling people was:

"I have thirty-six anuses!"

While Rachael was working for Neneh in Spain, Neneh's best friend was British television presenter and singer Andi Oliver, they'd sung together in English post-punk band Rip Rig + Panic. Andi's 10-year-old daughter Mikita's best friend was soon to be singer Lily Allen, and Lily would often visit her in Spain. While hanging around waiting for Rachael to finish work, Neneh's driver Eric and I used to take turns chasing the soon-to-be celebrities around the swimming pool, catching them and throwing them in by their arms and legs.

Mikita later went on to become a television presenter, also hosting Channel 4's Popworld and T4 on the Beach. Fast forward a decade and while I was working for Lily Allen and partying on the tour bus, I mentioned to Mikita…

"You don't remember me do you?"

"Oh my God, I haven't shagged you have I?"

Eric also looked after Neneh's father, American jazz trumpeter Don Cherry. Unfortunately, Don had been diagnosed with liver cancer and was feeling unwell. One night Don wanted to go out for a pizza so Rachael piped up saying:

"We'll take you."

Don got excited, but Eric wasn't happy and told us firmly…

"If you take him then he's your responsibility. I want nothing more to do with it."

Despite Eric's reluctance, we went into town and the three of us shared a couple of pizzas. We enjoyed his company, especially when he told stories about his early days as a jazz musician and his involvement with the punk movement, including when he played with Ian Dury. In addition, Don told us that he missed driving and asked if he could drive the car home even though he could barely walk. Rachael didn't let him. Sadly, a few nights later we heard that Don had passed away.

Walnut, Ogs and his then-wife Karen came over to visit us one Christmas. Neneh Cherry and her husband and manager Cameron had invited us over to their house for New Year's Eve. Walnut, Ogs and I sat around the dinner table at the Finca La Mota telling jokes, drinking wine and laughing our heads off at some great memories, while the girls were getting ready upstairs. One of them came down and invited us up, where we found three lines of cocaine laid out on the coffee table. After we had partaken, we returned to the dinner table.

The laughing and joking had stopped and, after a few minutes, Ogs broke the silence with the declaration.

"Feel shit now!"

Henry also came over from Germany to visit us, so I took him out for a round of golf on my local course. Situated between Mijas and Coin, 'Alhaurin Golf' hangs on the side of a mountain, surrounded by picturesque landscapes with stunning views. It was designed by ex-World No.1 Spanish golfer Seve Ballesteros and Henry absolutely loved it.

"…I can't believe it," he marvelled… *"it's like a giant green carpet."*

According to a popular rumour, Seve Ballesteros attended the grand opening of the course only to discover the builders had cut some corners with his designs so, filled with rage and resentment, he got completely drunk and had to be physically thrown out of the 19th hole.

To this day, Henry is still an avid golf player and always tells me:

"Del, you are the one who brought me to the golf."

My new life in Spain had given me a more relaxed perspective in my approach to songwriting with tracks like 'Let's Do Lunch', 'Jetsetter', 'U Bore Me' and 'Busy Doing Nothing' (my reworking of a 1949 Bing Crosby song from the film 'A Connecticut Yankee in King Arthur's Court'). With these results, Henry had managed to secure a potential record deal with Stuttgart based record label 'We Bite Records', who also loved the new tracks. As an added incentive, and for a bit more cash, we would let them put out all the old Trapper Records and Hairy Pie stuff on the proviso that they paid for us to record two new studio albums.

Henry had arranged for us to meet with new record company boss Thomas Issler and his partner Margit, to sign the new record contract before a show in Strasbourg, France, near the German border. Before Thomas arrived, Peter went off to meet with a girl that he'd had sex with on a previous tour. In the faint hope of scoring again, he showered for an hour, greased back his hair, sprayed his face with perfume and lay on the floor trying to squeeze into his leather pants. Hurriedly, he made his way out of the venue and off to the bar for the pre-arranged meet up but, on arrival, she introduced him to her new boyfriend. Oh, dear. A moment later the backstage door flew open - it was Peter in a murderous rage. Grabbing a beer from the fridge, it almost toppled over as he angrily slammed the door shut.

A friend named Gary Bacon was filling in on drums due to Ogs leaving the band to focus on becoming a roadie, because as everyone in the music industry knows, the further away from the centre of the stage you work, the larger your pay packet.

We Bite Records' German lawyer had asked for our names and consequently put them alphabetically on the new contract, so it read 'Bacon, Gary' followed by 'Bywaters, Peter'. Thomas had never met us before and must have assumed that 'Peter' was Peter's stage name, so, after introducing himself and offering to shake hands, his first words to a still fuming Peter were…

"Hello, Gary."

"WHAT DID YOU JUST CALL ME?" Peter shouted.

Thomas' timing couldn't have been worse as Peter declared that he wasn't going to sign any contract with a record company who didn't even know the name of the singer. Fair point.

Additionally, Peter insisted that the new album had to be released on vinyl, forcing Thomas to plead the commercial logistics since no record stores were stocking vinyl at that time.

"Call yourself a RECORD Company, you don't even make fucking records!!!"

Another fair point.

Peter was now at his most contentious, pointing out that he didn't bloody own a CD player, so what was the point of releasing an album if he wouldn't be able to listen to it. He also demanded to know about the video budget. Thomas said there wasn't one. Peter was irate again:

"The Offspring and Green Day make fantastic videos."

"Yes, but they sold twenty million records, who's going to watch your video, you alone in your bedroom?" Thomas replied.

Diplomatic relations were at an all-time low as Henry watched on in exasperation as all his hard work started to circle the drain. Don't ask me how, but we eventually signed the recording contract and Thomas reluctantly agreed to press up some unsellable vinyl, pay for a small video budget and send Peter a CD player as a Christmas present.

Now having put pen to paper, it was time to plan the production of the next record. Gary Bacon had ruled himself out by refusing to rehearse the new songs during soundchecks in case his T-shirt got 'all sweaty'. We had also done a few tours with another drummer friend of mine - Steve Wren, a former member of Eighties English rock band Then Jericho - but he wasn't available. So I asked Hans, my old Flesh for Lulu bandmate, to come along to rehearsals in London.

Peter, Trapper, Hans and I recorded the backing tracks at the 'all analogue' Chiswick Reach Studios, which is located between Fuller's Brewery and the old Cherry Blossom boot-polish factory in Chiswick. At the time, it claimed to be the only commercial all-valve 24-track studio outside of America. We used the same mixing desk Bob Marley had used to record 'Exodus', and when we turned it on, it lit up like a Christmas tree and smelt like cannabis. Disappointingly, after an extensive, forensic search, we failed to find any of Bob's weed stuffed down the back. Harvey Birrell, who had previously worked with Therapy and who we'd hung out with on the Reeperbahn in Hamburg, came on board to help with production and we returned to Southern Studios in Wood Green for the mixing. The time had come for Peter to make his way from Brighton to do some shouting. Harvey and I waited for him for several hours until the studio door finally opened and a sweaty, out-of-breath Peter slammed his oversized bag on the floor and shouted:

"ONCE AND ONCE ONLY!"

Not being too familiar with the London Underground he had got lost.

"I'm not fucking doing anything until I have a pint."

We took him to the nearest boozer where he immediately ordered four pints of beer. Harvey and I looked at each other slightly puzzled. Four pints for three? The barman handed him the first pint, and he downed it in two seconds flat and picked up the next one.

"Where shall we sit?"

Once the new album was mixed and finished, I went back to my leisurely life on the Costa del Sol. Later in the summer, Peter decided to visit our apartment, convincing the record company to pay for his flights on the pretext we needed to finalise the artwork and come up with an album title. One night, we took him clubbing in Torremolinos or 'Terrible Torri' as we used to call it. At one nightclub, he was rolling a joint on the bar when the bartender smiled, beckoned him over, and asked him to come behind the bar. He thought he was being invited into the office for a line of cocaine, so he eagerly followed him, only to be unceremoniously shoved out the side door of the club and on to the street. The coast has a far stricter drug policy compared with the mountain villages where people look the other way.

We managed to lose him again at an all-night dance event near the village of Coín, staged on the set of British TV soap opera, Eldorado. The ill-fated show followed the fictional lives of expats from the UK and Europe and was supposed to build on the success of EastEnders and Neighbours, but it was cancelled after just one season. The producers had financed the construction of a complete town on the site but unfortunately, the Spanish builders didn't plumb in any water so the houses couldn't be sold. It was surreal walking around the set of Los Barcos, listening to banging techno. At one point the swimming pool, which had been boarded over to make a dance floor, collapsed with all the clubbers falling into the water below.
The place is still there to this day.

Early the next morning, Peter managed to track us down back at the Finca La Mota, where we were enjoying a sangria breakfast. He had taken a trip down Amnesia Lane as all his memories of the previous night had been completely wiped.

Rachael remembered that sangria breakfast…

"Within a few minutes, Peter had fallen asleep in his plastic chair with

his head back and mouth wide open and he was snoring so loudly it was disturbing the horses in the nearby stable. The owner Arun and the whole bar found it hilarious and took turns having their photos taken with him."

Back to the job in hand, the opening track on the album was 'Supermodels', so that was the title sorted, due to the fact that the only reading material in our apartment was a load of Rachael's old Vogue and Cosmopolitan magazines. An evening with the scissors and a Pritt Stick saw the artwork completed with 'Supermodels' turning out to be one of Peter's favourite albums and the reviewers agreed:

'Peter and the Test Tube Babies are just as stupid and obnoxious as they've always been and for punk rock fans that is a definite plus as the band continue in the vein of the classic-era 'Banned from the Pubs' style nastiness like they haven't missed a beat. They offer the world 'Supermodels'. From the title track (an indictment of glamour girls) to the pro-alcoholic 'Giving up Drinking', it's an album chock full of booze and guitar-fuelled fury that shows that the boys haven't lost their touch. In a modern era of poseurs, the Test Tubes show us the correct way to rip the house down.' ****

Rachael and I loved our lives in Andalucia, so when Rachael's contract with Neneh was up, we tried to stay on for as long as possible living off what little money we had managed to save. Fortunately, the cost of living in the local villages was cheap as patatas fritas, but sadly, so were the dismal local wages.

Rachael took on some waitressing work to keep busy and we became friends with Mike and Sue Dring and their daughter Rachel, the owners of the Santa Fe Hotel near Coin. On quiet weekday nights, if there were no customers, she'd get paid to play Scrabble with the family. Mike and Sue were looking to buy another hotel a bit further down the coast in Gaucin, so the two Rach(a)els and I went on an adventure to discover hidden Andalucia, staying the night in the ruins of the soon-to-be renovated Hotel Casablanca.

Later, Rachel Dring went on to buy and renovate a hotel of her own; The Hotel el Gecko, in La Cañada del Real Tesoro (also known as Estación de Cortes) which stands on the banks of the Guadiaro river. On our first visit to the village, we decided to go on a bar crawl to see whether the natives were friendly. There were only three bars so we went to the first one which was empty apart from two old men playing dominoes in the corner. The next bar was closed, so we decided to have one last drink in the third and final bar. This was also empty, except for the two old men who had been playing dominoes in the first bar, who had now moved along and were in the process of setting up a new game.

This place was hap-pen-ing, I loved it so much I got drunk and bought a house there.

The Hotel el Gecko was our favourite place to stay whenever Rachael and I travelled back to Spain. One morning, Rachel hammered on the door of our room and woke me up…

"Come on, you've got to go to the lawyer's office in Gaucin to complete your house purchase."

I was still drunk and couldn't even remember buying it. I ended up reversing the hire car into a concrete post outside the lawyer's office.

My new requisition was a traditional three-bedroom townhouse surrounded by a verdant valley with views of the Serrania mountains. In the summer we can see our neighbours picking fruit from their orchards irrigated by the Guadiaro river that runs alongside the village and the people are so friendly, always taking the time to stop for a chat, usually about the weather.

How often have you visited somewhere on your summer vacation and by the time you've found the right restaurant or bar and started making new friends, it's time to go home? Whenever we arrive in Andalucia, we jump right into the action, already knowing the best places to swim and hang out. Our children Liam and Sean can safely wander the streets to get ice creams or drinks with the local bar owners just putting it on our tabs.

My family, myself and my 36 arseholes spend every summer in our new second home in Canada del Real Tresora and visit whenever we can throughout the year.

Olé.

CHAPTER 21 – A TALE OF TWO DINNERS

I've always wanted to write a classic Christmas song. 'Wasted Christmas' is my Yuletide tale of a man who goes on a five-day pre-Christmas bender and ends up languishing in jail. On a cold, bleak Christmas Eve, he returns home to discover his wife and kids have left him.
Racked with guilt, he decides to hang himself but, as he kicks away the chair, the ceiling beam snaps under his weight. As the song comes to an end, Christmas bells begin to chime on the radio and we see him break down and burst into tears, kneeling on the cold kitchen floor covered in rotten sawdust - classic.

Continuing on with the Christmas cheer, Henry's 26-date mega European tour was looming menacingly, without a day off and smack bang in the middle of one of Germany's coldest winters. Was I ready for the pain? Of course not, but it was happening anyway.
Unbeknown to us, 'Supermodels' was to be Trapper's final album and, of course, we wanted him to play on the tour. He'd grown up with us, gone to school with us and formed the band with us, but had recently decided to follow in Ogs' roadie footsteps in search of more money, gaffer tape and hanging around all day at soundchecks. Having tried in vain to get in contact with him, Peter finally tracked him down in a hotel in Japan…

Peter testily recalled that telephone conversation:

"After much umming and ahring he said he was sorry but no, he couldn't make it, he had too much to lose. Too fucking right he had too much to lose... like being in a fucking band for a start! Thing is, Trapper was now in a position where money ruled his life, I best not elaborate further, so now we were in a right fucking mess."

During band interviews, the most frequently asked question is always:

"What happened to Trapper?"

Here Trapper answers that very question in his own words…

*"After leaving the band I became a roadie and worked for many different bands, some I liked and some I actively hated but you still smile and tell them the gig was fantastic, even if the keyboards/guitars went down.
My favourite thing to say if the keyboards go tits up is 'it's the output transformer and it can't be fixed'; surprisingly most musicians believe that.*

Of course, I hadn't a clue - not being trained in electronics and having spent the last 20 years drunk. I worked for Sam Smith before he went on to become mega-famous and back then the band and crew all travelled on the one bus. One day, we bought a load of nerf guns and masks and had a war against the bottom lounge who were trying to defeat the top lounge. We'd all had loads to drink and the attack became more and more heated and frantic. I was firing up the stairs when I saw my chance to grab a Dr. Martens-clad foot and dragged the owner down the stairwell on their arse. I then gave the masked victim some 'hard as I could' rabbit punches on the arms as he whimpered for me to stop. I was thinking I'd grabbed Pete the monitor engineer who I knew wore Doc Martens but I soon became unsure and asked, 'Pete? You're not Pete, are you?' That's when I realised, I'd just beaten up the Golden Globe and Academy Award winner Sam Smith. He used to like to wear the Italian wife-beater-style vests on stage but for the next two weeks of the tour, he had to wear long-sleeve shirts to cover his bruises."

Here's some more Trapper tour-tales…

"I also worked for a band called Sneaker Pimps. We had flown to the US on Virgin America and been invited to a pool party up in Beverly Hills thrown by Nancy, the wife of the guy who was head of Virgin America at the time. She liked to get her tits out and was famous for it, especially when she had a young band to entertain. The Sneakers' keyboard player and co-founder member Liam and I were play-fighting and knocked a massive great tree and an urn full of soil into the pool, which effectively finished the party. You can do virtually anything at these parties but trashing the pool is the ultimate sin. It took the pool guy two weeks to clean it up, not to mention replacing the $2,000 urn. Earlier at the party, we spotted a very well-known pop singer and overheard that he had some ecstasy in the pockets of his leather trousers. It was a bit of a job getting the pills off him, but with a mixture of drunken persuasion and force, we managed to secure them. Later on in an upstairs bedroom, we were off our tits when the pop star came in with a girl and went into the en-suite bathroom. About 10 minutes later a guy comes in and asks if we've seen them? We just stared at him as he pulled the bathroom door open and there he was getting fellatio from this bloke's girlfriend. With a view to a kill, the guy's first reflex was to pull the girl out and punch the singer on to the bed with his trousers down and still with a big lob on (I can confirm he is well hung). Mr pop star pulls himself together and stumbles out the door. We were all tripping off our heads and after a prolonged moment of silence, someone turned around and said…
'Did that really just happen?'"

Following the departures of Ogs and Trapper, Peter was now a single mother with a test tube baby and a new album to support. A local Brighton band, DV8, were about to break up, so 'Peter and the Test Tube Baby' quickly moved in for a double transfer swoop. In came Peacehaven Wild Kid, Steven Philp (bass) and Adrian Harris (drums). The nickname 'Rum' was given to Steve because his ears were shaped like those of the inept and bumbling floor manager Mr Rumbold in the 1970s British sitcom 'Are You Being Served?'

Rum and AD (or 'Aidsy', as Peter side-splittingly nicknamed him) were young, ambitious, and too naive to see the heartache that lay ahead.

AD mulled over the offer...

"When I was thirteen, I used to come over to Brighton and see the local punk bands with my mates. The Test Tubes were always the best, much better than the rinky-dink shit sound of most of the others like Nicky and the Dots and the Piranhas. I liked the Subs and The Clash and the Test Tubes sounded more like that, even though they looked weird and seemed deeply stupid. I soon got a drum kit and started playing in little punk bands. I even auditioned for the Test Tubes in 1980 when Ogs did one of his regular resignations. I didn't get in as I think Trapper didn't like me... (I was also going out with a bird he fancied!) My band had just been dumped from the record label and split up so I was moping around Brighton playing gigs with a big function band and a gypsy jazz swing trio when I got a call from Peter who said... 'You've got to help us, we're desperate and you're the only one that can save us now...' I decided to help out my old mates, quickly breaking off negotiations to mount the stool for Dire Straits."

New bassist, Rum, was expecting to enter a world of glamour, limousines and Jacuzzis filled with topless models, so he brought along his golf clubs and weights to stay in shape. It hadn't occurred to him that groupies had become extinct since 1982 due to the emergence of the AIDS virus.

Sightings of the species at a Mötley Crüe reunion concert in 2004 have recently been ruled out by conservation experts.

In 1995, our new line-up played a warm-up gig in Chelmsford and then flew out to Germany, where Henry was to meet us with the new sleeper bus. We walked out of the airport after clearing immigration and customs to find a brand new, luxury double-decker sleeper bus waiting for us. While we hustled towards it, dragging our cases, hoping to secure the best bunks, it pulled away... revealing a single-decked luxury sleeper coach parked behind it. Oh well, we continued to hurry toward that one instead, but that also pulled off… revealing the worst rust bucket of a bus you might ever have the displeasure to clap your eyes on.

It was a Mercedes prototype tour bus, possibly the first of its kind.

As we boarded, we found there was no internal lighting, the mattresses were wet from condensation, there were four seats for nine people, plus, as you sat on the bus toilet, you could see the autobahn whizzing by between your legs through a large rusty hole. Overall dissatisfaction was expressed in a variety of ways, before the bus was replaced the next day.

A film shoot for the soon-to-be-released promo video 'Busy Doing Nothing' provided a brief respite from the tedious trudge towards the end of the tour. For some reason, the filming had been cancelled, but the hotel rooms at the location had already been paid for in advance, which was a godsend, as we hadn't had a day off in over two weeks.

Amongst the travelling crew was our French sound engineer at that time, Tico. We had been sleeping on the tour bus for so long he thought the news of a five-star hotel was some sort of hilarious wind-up so decided to remain overnight on the freezing cold coach amongst the dirty laundry and empty beer bottles. He sure wasn't laughing the next morning when we all came down shaved, showered and refreshed.

To this day, we still laugh about that.

Every time we go for a beer in Berlin, Henry always reminds me of… 'The Tale of the Two Roast Dinners'…

As we checked into the hotel, Peter was feeling hungry and spotted that the restaurant in the lobby was still open. He promptly sat down and ordered a full roast beef dinner, gobbling it down quickly before, incredibly, ordering a second. When the hotel receptionist went off to attend to something in the office, he sneaked off to his room without paying. Henry had put his credit card on all the rooms as a deposit for any extras, so when he checked out the next morning, the hotel charged him for the roast beef dinners.

Later on, aboard the tour bus, Henry grilled Peter about the two unpaid meals.

"Peter, you owe me fifty Deutschmarks for those two roast dinners."

"I never had two roast dinners."

"Yes, you did. I saw you eating them when we were checking in."

"Ah! But! I was far too clever for them and managed to sneak off without paying."

L - R: Hans Perrson, Derek Greening, **Nick Marsh**, Rocco Barker, Mike Steed

FLESH FOR LULU

Flesh for Lulu - Before
Photoshoot, London 1990.

Steedy farts - After
Photoshoot, London 1990.

Demoted
Back to basics, London 1990. (Photo: Graham Trott)

We're not going through with it, are we?
The SAW phase. L-R: Marcus Mystery, Trapper, Peter, Del & Ogs.
Marquee Club, London 1990.

The Booze Brothers
Walnut & Del, Brighton 1991.

Feral
Rachael & Del, Arambol, India 1992.

In England we have Pies
L-R: AD, Del, Rum & Peter, Tokyo, Japan 1997.

First Contact
Alien Pubduction L-R: AD, Del, Peter & Rum.
Hazelwood Studios, Frankfurt, Germany 1998.

"But my credit card was on all the rooms. They saw me check you in and hand you your key, so they added it to the bill."

"Well, you are the one who will have to pay, because you are the idiot that got caught."

Walnut continued the story in his own book 'Diary of a Punk Rock Roadie'...

"After that, we started calling him 'Peter Two Dinners', a name he did not like. In Vienna, Del, Peter and Rum went to find a bar with Sky Sports to watch the football. During the match, Peter had a meal with his beer. When they arrived back at the venue it was pizza for dinner. I didn't fancy pizza, so I ordered lasagna but, when the food arrived, they had forgotten Peter's. To say he was gutted was an understatement, so to avoid another major sulk I offered to share some of my lasagna. He quickly shovelled in as much as he could, including all the sauce from the top, leaving me just a couple of dry bits of pasta at the bottom of the bowl. Then about 10 minutes later his dinner arrived, which he also ate. So we now call him 'Peter Three Dinners'! If he continues like this, by the end of this tour he will become 'Peter Five Bellies'."

'It was the best of times, it was the worst of times, it was the age of foolishness… it was the age of greed.' - Charlie Dick 'ead!

CHAPTER 22 – DIE AGAIN TOMORROW

KAPOW!

Big Vern is a heavily built, square-jawed, short-haired character who wears a large sheepskin coat and appears in the popular British comic, Viz. He is also paranoid and mistakenly believes himself to be a '70s blagger. Peter arrived at the airport one morning wearing an oversized sheepskin jacket so his nickname for the rest of that tour became 'Little Vern'.

After the show in Würzburg, we were on an overnight drive on the sleeper bus and about to arrive in Munich. When I awoke, I knew something was up as my spidey-sense was tingling. I stuck my head through the curtains of my bunk and could see there was some sort of drama unfolding, so I got up to investigate…

Henry had received a phone call from his father.

"Peter is left behind at a service station."

Henry brought me up to speed, saying that while everybody was sleeping, Peter had got off the bus in his T-shirt and shorts to go to have a shit but the driver, after refuelling, had driven off and left him behind. It was below zero outside and as I peered down the long corridor of the bus into the back lounge, all that remained was Little Vern's sheepskin coat swinging from side to side on its hanger.

It was fortunate Peter still had his tour pass around his neck with Henry's office number on it, and even more fortunate that Hans, Henry's father, was in the office to answer the phone.

"SEND ME A FUCKIN' HELICOPTER!"

Henry then paid the local promoter in Würzburg to send someone in a car to get him and bring him back to the bus. After four hours, he walked back on with a face like thunder and of course, everyone else was to blame.

"YOU BASTARDS LEFT ME!"

WHOOSH!

Peter later recounted his own version of events…

"Once again, we were in Germany doing the annual Christmas tour. We were on the nightliner and travelling overnight from Würzburg to Munich. As usual, it was snowing.

I was in the upstairs lounge having a drink and a smoke with AD, Rum and Walnut. We hadn't been travelling long before the bus pulled into a service station - which was my cue to put on my trainers and go out for a shit. I was dressed in just my shorts and T-shirt. I decided against putting on my 'John Motson' style sheepskin coat and left the bus. I met the driver and we walked into the service station together. I think he went off to get a coffee and something to eat, so I went and found the toilet.

When I came back out, the nightliner was nowhere to be seen so I just assumed they had parked up around the corner. So I set off through the snow (now regretting the decision not to take my coat) to look for the bus. It was bloody cold and still snowing. I couldn't find the bus so I reasoned that it must have gone a bit further and was now parked in the area reserved for coaches and lorries etc. Even at this point, I was not worried. After all, the driver had seen me get off, so surely, they were not gonna leave me behind? I got to the coach/lorry park and the bus was nowhere to be seen. However, I still hadn't explored the area fully (it was massive) so set off to do so, dressed of course in just shorts and a T-shirt. Anyway, as I trudged around in the snow looking for the bus, getting increasingly cold, a police car pulled up alongside me. Hardly surprising really. Quickly realising that a night in a warm police station was preferable to my current predicament, I tried, in my not so fluent German, to explain my situation and persuade them to take me with them. They must have thought I was a right nutter and just sped off.

(A sad slow-motion musical montage would be fun here, but that will just have to exist in my imagination - Del.)

It was around this point that the penny dropped. The fucking bus was gone, and those cunts had left me. I trudged back to the service station to take stock of the situation. You are probably reading this and starting to think, why not just call someone on the bus with your mobile? Well, it was 1997 and not everyone in those days had a mobile phone. Certainly, none of us in the band did. I went to the cafeteria, searched through my pockets, and found a few Deutschmarks in change, my tour pass, my passport, a lump of hash (just as well the cops had fucked off) and not much else. On the tour pass was the mobile number of Henry, our tour manager. So, no problem, I thought. I'll just find a phone, and call Henry's number as he is still on the bus. Fortunately, the people working at the cafeteria took pity on me and let me use their office phone. I called Henry, the only one on the bus with a mobile. It was switched off. What The Fuck?

What's the fucking point of turning your mobile phone off when you are the fucking tour manager? Aren't you supposed to be ready to react to any eventuality? Aren't you the person who should be continually contactable in case there are any emergencies – LIKE LEAVING THE FUCKING SINGER AT A SERVICE STATION IN THE MIDDLE OF THE FUCKING NIGHT?

Up until this point, I hadn't really gotten angry. In fact, for a while, I had still half expected one of the band to suddenly appear and tell me it was all a joke. To be honest, I hardly ever get really fucking angry. Yes, I get pissed off sometimes and I have been accused of being a moody bastard, but you will never see me blow my top. However, as the hopelessness of my plight, mixed with the disgust at the unprofessionalism of our tour manager, started to sink in, my blood began to boil. I was also beginning to feel hungry which didn't help, especially as I only had enough money for a bottle of water. But what could I do? I was fucked. So there I sat, alone in the service station (fortunately it was warm) with just a bottle of water and my festering anger, FOR NINE FUCKING HOURS!!!!! Even today, 24 years later, I know that was the angriest I have ever been in my life. Every now and then I'd try Henry's number, but it remained turned off. Eventually, around 8am, I managed to get through to Hannah, Rum's girlfriend, back in England. She then somehow got hold of Henry's father, who in turn got hold of the bus company, who in turn got hold of the driver. The phone rang, and it was for me. It was Henry. I remember the phone conversation well.

Henry – 'Peter, don't you have enough money to get a taxi to Munich?'

Me – 'A fucking taxi? If I had enough fucking money for a taxi, I would have fucking got one to the fucking airport and gone home you cunt!'

A few hours later a woman turned up at the service station to collect me and I was eventually reunited with the bus, which had come back some of the way from Munich to meet us. I was still apoplectic, and I think I probably said something along the lines of had I been James Brown, then I would have sacked all the band and crew and that for revenge I was gonna have the smelliest dump ever in the bus toilet. To my surprise, instead of being apologetic, they were all angry with me! What The Fuck? Again!

Of course, what had happened the night before was the driver had assumed I was back on the bus and Rum, AD and Walnut believed I had gone straight to my bunk."

If only Peter had heeded this important piece of advice from the late, great, Brighton tour manager and security chief Derrick 'The Perv' Furnival…

"If on a tour bus and it's stationary in the middle of the night and you fancy a bit of fresh air or whatever: Tell someone what you are up to and put on some clothes. Otherwise, you will more than likely get stranded in your now grubby underwear, and if you think anyone is going to pick you up other than the local police, who will more than likely section you, think again."

BIFF!

The comic tour capers continued…

We only ever used a sleeper bus when Henry was tour managing so on the next tour it was back to being squashed up in the back of a transit. We arrived in the Swiss city of Geneva where the venue was called 'La Cave d' Lilot'. We quickly renamed it 'Cave of Idiots'. It was bloody freezing down in the cave, so it wasn't long before we came to the usual decision to blow out the soundcheck. Come showtime and the place was packed. A girl kept shouting to Peter, in a sweet French voice, 'YOU ARE UGLY!'… which childishly became the tour saying for the next couple of days. She then made her way to the front of the crowd and pulled Peter's shorts down. He returned the compliment by pulling her dress up over her head. Can you imagine the fuss if that had happened in the age of social media? There would have been telescopically trained camera phones ready to snap and publish that 'out of context' moment.

After another surge in the crowd, Rum's mic stand hit him square in the face, causing him to have a large cut under his eye which started pouring blood. Apart from that, it was just another day at the office and business as usual.

SQUISH!

Still in Switzerland and the following night's show was to take place at an old anarcho-hippie punk squat. Dogs, of course, were largely in attendance and just as we were about to walk on stage one of us noticed a huge steaming pile of shit in front of the drum kit.

"Waaaalnuuut…?!"

Walnut firmly drew the line in the (kitty litter) sand…

"I don't mind changing strings or setting up the equipment but there's no way I am cleaning up animal shit. I'm a roadie, not a fucking zookeeper!"

THWAPP!

The next day we arrive in Montbéliard in eastern France, which is about eight miles from the Swiss border. The town seemed quite small and, once again, we weren't sure where we were going so we just aimlessly cruised around the city centre for a while. All of a sudden, the car next to us started blasting its horn and an irate red-faced driver began shouting and pointing at us. We must have cut him up or something... He kept following us...

BEIGE ALERT!

Walnut relived that colourful incident...

"AD was sitting in the front passenger seat, so he wound down the window, started making rude gestures and hurling abuse back at the other driver. The bloke is now right on our case, he's flailing at us and honking his horn. I think he has a bad case of road rage. He keeps trying to overtake, but we won't let him. Finally, we are forced to stop at some traffic lights, so he jumps out of his car and starts running towards the van. He must be mad because there are seven of us and only one of him. AD quickly winds up his window to avoid getting a fist in the face. The bloke then presses his face up against the windscreen and shouts...

'Are you Peter and the Test Tube Babies?'

We couldn't believe it; this guy was the promoter for that night's show. We felt like a right bunch of moronic gammons but fortunately he saw the funny side and told us that he had been waiting for us outside the venue when he saw the van drive past, so he got in his car and had been trying to get us to turn around for the last 10 minutes."

CRASH!

During the show, Peter was attempting to do his best Iggy Pop impression by scaling the P.A. stacks and standing on top of the sound system. Walnut, who had followed him up to make sure he was safe, then decided to pull Peter's shorts down just as he was about to start singing. Taken by surprise, Peter stumbled and pulled down half the P.A. and lights on to the audience - comedy moment of the tour.

FLRBBBBB!

The predictable pointless painful slog towards mental breakdown showed no signs of abating as we arrived in the German city of Osnabrück. At the venue, it was time for dinner again, so we sat down at the makeshift table on the venue dancefloor while the staff brought out bowls of chicken pasta. Since I don't eat anything dead, I complained and returned it. In the kitchen, they removed the chicken pieces from the top and brought back the same bowl of pasta still covered in chicken gravy. I was smouldering with mid-tour discontentment and instantly became uninterested in making the night a success. I took out a handful of magic mushrooms I still had in my pocket from the night before and sprinkled them where the dead chicken pieces once sat. Later that night I was stretchered on stage and put in, arguably, one of the worst performances of my career... mission accomplished... How you like me now?

That'll learn 'em.

DICKHEAD!

Later on that tour, the singer from a local support band came into our dressing room to tell us his band were going to cover our song 'Banned From The Pubs' in their set. He then hassled Peter to come up and sing it with them, to which he reluctantly agreed. After Peter's performance, we found out that the band were called The Dickheads, so obviously, soon after that, Peter's latest nickname became 'the fifth dickhead!'

GASP!

The non-stop conveyor belt of disappointment then transported us to the mediaeval town of Bratislava in Slovakia. Once again, we were lost as a gaggle of expert map readers offered up unhelpful directions. We drove around an old castle a few times until we eventually spotted a door on the side of a hill with the name of the venue graffitied on it, 'DK Lúky'. It was a dark, damp underground bomb shelter in which the wealthy residents of the castle above would have taken shelter during the Second World War. After passing through the door, we walked down a dark dusty tunnel for a few minutes before we reached a room with a small stage. There were no windows, no air conditioning, and even more frightening from a health and safety perspective, no fire exits.

Walnut went on to describe the rest of the evening's ordeal from a cross-eyed roadie's point of view...

"Before I'd had a chance to unload or even think about sound-checking, the promoter insisted on taking us straight to a bar called the KGB. Bad move. I told him to make sure the doors don't open, or it will be impossible to load in. Of course, when we returned at about 9pm they had already started letting people in and the place was chockablock.

So now I had the impossible task of getting the equipment in. We couldn't back the van up to the doors as there were too many people outside and the long tunnels were just a solid mass of heaving bodies. Inside, all the oxygen was getting used up, so it was almost impossible to breathe. The band helped me, but the only way to do this was to carry the gear above our heads and barge our way through the crowd shouting at people to let us pass.

Each trip took about 20 minutes and the place was like a sauna with condensation dripping off the walls and ceilings. My head had steam coming off the top of it like a dry ice machine and I thought I was going to lose consciousness. We got everything to the side of the stage, both support groups had now finished so I started to get the gear set up.

Then the biggest nightmare began... We had not played in this country before, so I did not have the right power adapters to fit into the plug sockets and even if someone had given me the correct plugs, I don't think I would have had time to rewire them. The sound system then blew up, probably due to the moisture in the air. Finally, I got it sorted as the sound engineer found a couple of German/Slovakian adapters. I had English/ German so together we taped them all together and made an excellent but potentially lethal bodge."

It was all hands to the pump for the load-in, so while we were sweating our bollocks off unloading the van and pushing our way through the crowd, Peter went for a snooze in the back. As he lay there in his underpants, punks surrounded the van with their faces squished up against the windows staring down at him. Poor old Peter, I bet Lady Gaga doesn't have to put up with that before a show.

Inside, the place was hotter than a smackhead's spoon on giro day, and with no working monitors, all I could hear during the show were drums without any vocals or instruments. Through the condensation, I could see our drummer AD suffering, his body drained of energy, fighting for breath between songs with his heart beating fast beneath his sweat-sodden vest. At one point, Walnut poured a whole bottle of water over AD's head to try to cool him down while the promoter spent most of the set dancing with Peter, with his trousers and pants down - Helpful!"

ZONK!

After surviving the World War 2 bunker we arrived at that night's venue, a reggae club in Montpellier in the south of France, where AD managed to secure a large family-size bag of skunk from one of the Rasta guys who worked there. The next day, our old friends the French police stopped us again. This time, it was two motorcycle cops who flagged us down on the motorway. As they were dismounting, AD managed to stuff the bag of weed down between two of the van seats.

As they removed their helmets, we could see that one of the cops was a young recruit in his early twenties, wearing mirror shades with black slicked-back hair, while the other was a balding, portly, older man who looked like he'd seen it all before and would have much preferred to have spent the afternoon at home with his family. The younger cop, noting the state of us and thinking he was on to a winner, slid open the side door and told us all to get out. He then searched the bus but soon returned empty-handed, at one point asking us to lift the bonnet, so he could check the engine (...as if we'd hide anything in there!) The older cop remained slouched on his bike during his colleague's endeavours and began to roll a cigarette.

The younger cop then walked over to where we were waiting and gave us an ultimatum…

"TELL US WHERE THE DRUGS ARE NOW AND YOU WILL BE ON YOUR WAY WITH A FINE. IF YOU DON'T TELL US, WE WILL CALL THE DOG UNIT, THE DOGS WILL FIND THE DRUGS AND YOU WILL GO TO JAIL. NOW TELL ME, WHERE ARE THE DRUGS?"

We weren't falling for that old trick, so we all shook our heads and replied… *"We don't have any drugs."*

Sam Burlot, the French promoter who was travelling with us, spoke with them for a while and then returned to tell us there was an issue with the dog unit, and we would have to drive to them since they would not come here. A heated debate began between the two cops as to which one was going to travel with us in the van to make sure we didn't dispose of the drugs, and which one of them was going to leave behind his beloved motorcycle.

Sam translated the cops' new plan to us…

"They want us to drive to the dog unit which is situated by the toll booths at the end of the motorway but neither of them wants to leave their bike… Therefore, they are going to both ride in front of the van and we all

have to put our hands on our heads as they will be checking their rear-view mirrors until we reach the dog unit."

We all got back into the van and set off following the two police motorcycles. As soon as we pulled back onto the motorway, we yanked the family size bag of skunk weed from between the seats and stuffed as much of it into our mouths as could fit, swallowing it and washing down the evidence with a two-litre family size bottle of warm cola.

The young cop saw what we were up to in his rear-view mirror and turned around in his seat, angrily waving his finger. In our rushed attempt to consume it all, tiny sensimilla crumbs and dust became scattered all over the back seats. We reached the end of the toll road, and pulled up alongside the dog unit, where a large white Alsatian was unleashed on to our bus. On smelling the scent, the animal went ballistic, barking, wagging his tail, and spinning in circles. Nothing of any substance was found and the already agitated dog unit guys weren't too happy to have had their time wasted and loudly reprimanded the young mirror-shaded cop as we drove away laughing.

At that night's show, we were very, very... very stoned.

ARRGH!

A possibly still stoned or hungover Peter came up with the idea to dress up as ballerinas for the following year's Christmas tour 'theme'. The connection between ballet and our latest release 'Supermodels' was lost on me, but I reluctantly went along with his plan and suggested that we use Tchaikovsky's Swan Lake as the intro music. When we arrived at the Feierwerk in Munich, Henry and I had a wander around the building before the doors opened and discovered a fully functional 24-track recording studio behind the stage. The band were performing solidly enough and we were also debuting songs from the new 'Supermodels' album so Henry and I decided to record the show. We talked to the house engineer about placing a second microphone on each mic stand and completed the soundcheck. When I returned to the UK, I listened to the Munich recordings and they sounded excellent, beautifully capturing the atmosphere of the tour. In January, Harvey Birrell and I fixed a few glitches and mixed the 18-track live album. As for the title, I thought... swans/fat pigs in tutus/Germany... and came up with the nonsensical award-winning title 'Schwein Lake'.

'Schwein Lake Live', the second album on We Bite Records and the first official Test Tube Babies live album since 'Pissed And Proud' was released with Peter enthusiastically giving 'Schwein Lake Live' a rave review on the band's website...

"I've never heard it. I expect it sounds great and everyone says it does but as I've mentioned before, I hate live albums and I hate listening to ourselves live."

Th-Th-The, Th-Th-The, Th-Th... That's all, folks!

CHAPTER 23 – LAND OF THE RISING PIE

There is something very special about Japan, its food, its people, and its timeless culture. I'd visited a few times working with various bands, usually to perform at the Fuji Rock Festival, a three-day annual event held in Naeba Ski Resort, in Niigata Prefecture.

At Fuji Rock, everything is neat, clean, and tidy. No trouble, no drunks, no fights and people would even carry ashtrays around their necks so as not to flick any cigarette ash on to the grass. There are rope fences that are so low you could easily step over them but, since that would be considered dishonourable, everyone just bows and joins the queue. I did see one kerfuffle but, as Japanese security wrestled the troublemaker to the floor, I could see a white overweight bum crack sticking out from a pair of Union Jack shorts!

After the traditional party on arrival, we would wake up at the ski resort lodge and get driven down to the festival site on golf buggies for a soundcheck. Our Fuji stage crew would have studied our specs in great detail and scoured YouTube for live footage so our stage equipment would always be perfectly positioned to within a millimetre of perfection. They would clean, repair and replace any missing parts, even the tiniest of screws. The most efficient country on earth and that's why I love it.

When I toured there with North London band South, all the shows were at the same purpose-built venues, but in different cities. On arrival, the local crews and venue staff would carpet bomb us with friendliness. At the first show, I removed the protective cargo tape from all the equipment, crushed it into a large ball and attempted a basketball shot into the furthest-away bin. Immediately, one of the local crew members leapt to his feet, jumped in the air and made an incredible goalkeeping deflective punch to guide the wayward shot into the correct bin before landing back on his feet and bowing.

At Fuji Rock again, this time with singer Lily Allen, Japanese alternative all-girl rock band Shonen Knife were on the same stage. In my excitement to meet them, I bounded into their dressing room for a chat but ended up doing all the talking while they giggled and bowed. Later that night, I took Lily's saxophonist Nik Carter and trumpeter Jack Birchwood along to see them but, after a few songs, music teacher Nik looked bewildered and commented…

"I can't understand how you can like this, they're not even in tune!"

On those occasions, I never got to experience much of rural Japan; I only saw the airport, the bus, and the inside of a very small hotel room with a very small bath. However, none of those trips was able to compare to when the Test Tubes visited in 1997, the difference being, we got to experience the 'real' Japan.

Earlier that year, we'd been receiving some indecipherable messages from a Japanese guy called Hiroki wanting us to go and tour over there. We couldn't make head nor tail of the deal, but he was paying for the flights, so we thought we'd go anyway. In addition to being the promoter, Hiroki was also in one of two Japanese support bands: Crikey Crew, a punk band of multi-colour-haired hobbits from Okayama; and Gruesome from Osaka, four Japanese skinheads who wore DM boots and green bomber jackets and tried their best to look mean. Shun, Gruesome's bassist, also had something to do with promoting the tour.

Flying Lufthansa via Frankfurt, we arrived on Friday, 4th of April. Rum was pleasantly surprised by the quality of his journey...

"Finally, I felt like a proper rock star. There weren't any non-smoking seats left so we were upgraded to business class. Comfy seat, fillet steak, a bottle of wine and my own TV – Bingo!"

Hiroki, Shun, and some of the others met us at the airport and we crossed the Sky Gate Bridge R, which connects the mainland with the artificial island in Osaka Bay on which Kansai International Airport is situated. Once in Osaka, we were summoned to a dimly lit private room to meet the boss of Crikey Crew and Gruesome's record label 'Bronze Fist Records'. He was appropriately named 'Boss' and the room was full of Japanese punks and punkettes. Lots of beer and sake were then consumed before karaoke was performed. As soon as we got hold of the microphone, 'Boss' quickly picked up the bill and left.

The next day we visited Shun's house, where Peter asked to watch some Japanese porn. Shun's wife kept coming into the room with beers and snacks for us, and then reversing out with her head bowed to go and sit in the kitchen. Strange. In Brighton, it's usually us male southern softies who have to do that.

Rum was more than satisfied with the impressive Japanese toilet…

"When we stayed at Hiroki's house, he had an amazing toilet with a control panel that heated the seat, squirted water and gave you a blow-dry."

We kicked off the tour with two sold-out shows at the Fandango in Osaka. The crowds in Japan can be very disconcerting. While you are playing, they go crazy, but being so polite, they are completely silent between songs. After the first song you could hear a pin drop in the hall, which took Peter completely by surprise, leaving him unsure as to what to say or do next. Thankfully, someone in the crowd broke the silence when they shouted…

"YOU FWAT BASTARD!" in broken English.

"I couldn't believe it! The other side of the world and I still can't escape it!" Peter declared after the show.

I, however, loved that and managed to track down a copy of Carter the Unstoppable Sex Machine's 'Surfin' USM', which starts with the chant *"You Fat Bastard"*, so that became the intro tape for the rest of the tour.

For the next show, we set off to play two nights at the Loft in Tokyo in a convoy of three little Suzuki vans. One with the drum kit, one with the bass rig and one with the guitars and amps.

When we were unable to stay with our new Japanese friends or their relatives, we spent the night in a capsule or pod hotel, which consisted of canisters stacked two high with communal showers. You climb in and pull a shutter across, sort of like a coffin but with a TV at the end so you can change the channels with your feet.

Peter described our arrival in Tokyo:

"We arrived in Tokyo at about 7am but our hosts were totally lost, and the convoy had got split up. By this time, I was starting to get a bit hungry. Much U-turning and mobile phoning later, we all met up at a coffee shop opposite the venue (the Loft) in the Shinjuku area of Tokyo. By now it was about 10am, so we all had some coffee and sandwiches for breakfast then went to a local park. I slept in the van. At midday, we checked into a cheap hotel so we could all get a few hours' sleep.

What a strange place that hotel was. In our 'room', there were about six very large canisters that looked like mini-submarines, they were stacked two high. These were in fact our beds; you sort of climb in and pull a shutter across. Actually, they were quite comfortable and I soon nodded off. At 3pm we had to get out and went to check into the next hotel, which was just up the road from the venue, the others then went off to do a soundcheck, I crashed out.

I was awoken at about 8pm and walked down to the venue, but for some reason, it stank of shit. It was packed and after a few beers and a weird speed drink, we went onstage at about 9pm. We played well and due to the fact that we were using some decent gear, it probably sounded OK.

The audience seemed to like it anyway. I got introduced to Billy from the band Laughing Noses who apparently is some sort of punk superstar in Japan, he certainly seemed like a nice bloke.

After the gig, we all went (along with half the audience again) to a nearby flash restaurant. I really thought my luck was in as the girl I was sitting next to started to fondle me. She was bloody gorgeous and her name was Middle. One thing led to another and she asked me if I would like to stay with her the night at her house. Unfortunately, she was also putting up most of Crikey Crew and Gruesome, still why not? Trouble was, by the time we left the restaurant, after much saki and beer, she was absolutely legless and couldn't stand up. Hiroki blamed me, and I was told to go to the hotel."

The shows always started early, at around 7pm or 8pm, and afterwards we were always taken to a restaurant along with the support bands, their girlfriends and guests. Japanese people eat and sleep close to the floor, so for reasons of hygiene and cleanliness, etiquette dictates that you remove your shoes and socks before entering a restaurant. One night, as we were about to leave a restaurant, AD couldn't find his shoes. Hiroki and Shun were stunned and couldn't stop apologising even though, of course, the theft was nothing to do with them. Shun even started crying. The next night they bought AD a £100 pair of sneakers to replace the ones stolen in Tokyo. Subsequently, Peter and Walnut sneakily hatched a plan to stash their cheesy old cheap trainers somewhere, so they could get a new pair as well. Their scheme failed. The Japanese crew were so over helpful, that in an eager attempt to carry my bag for me, one of them pulled the strap so hard it broke off. No new bag offer was forthcoming either.

On the next journey we stopped at one of their mother's restaurants, which was in the middle of nowhere in a tent. She came over and threw a blanket on the ground, which doubled as a dining table and a tablecloth. We puzzled over the menu, a single tatty piece of paper with handwritten Japanese symbols on it. Next, she brought us bowls of nameless bits of unrecognisable food; chicken gizzards being one of the loose translations.

Inevitably, I got the shits so I had to keep asking our minivan driver to stop at the motorway services so I could use the bathroom. After that, I didn't eat or drink anything for a couple of days before I started to feel a little better and was ready to party again. The next date was at Salon Kitty at a university in Matsuyama, Ehime, on the island of Shikoku. There was no alcohol allowed on campus, not even backstage. By now I was desperate for a drink so Walnut and I walked off campus to get a beer. There were many bars to choose from, so we settled on a small strange-looking one with a lot of old Japanese men hanging out. We sat at the bar and ordered a couple of beers. Some strange videos then started playing on a big screen with stills of traditional countryside and mountains. Some of the old men started singing and crying, and one of them walked over to us and began laughing at Walnut…

"Ha Ha! Hair on chest but no hair on head…"

Then his attention was drawn to Walnut's pierced eyebrow.

"Pain. Call that pain? This is pain…"

As he extended his hand, he showed us that half of his finger was missing.

"Could be time to drink up. Walnut?"

We paid the tab and scuttled back to the venue where Hiroki had been waiting, out of his mind with worry.

"Where have you been? We have been everywhere looking for you. This is very dangerous area."

We explained where we'd been and what had just happened. Alarmingly, the local promoter and Hiroki both turned white and began shaking their heads while making throat-slitting gestures.

"Very dangerous bar. Yakuza bar."

Having eaten nothing but rice and vegetables for a week, the rest of the band was in desperate need of some meat. Feeling their desperation, Hiroki took us to a Japanese version of an American diner, called 'The Sunday Sun', where we eagerly crowded into a booth to await our fried breakfasts. As Peter received his sausage and chips, his mouth watered and his eyes lit up, but as he plunged his knife into his sausage, his heart sank. It was stuffed with seaweed!

As for me, I love Japanese cuisine, rice, noodles, grilled seafood and sashimi or sushi. Rum not so much…

"All the restaurants had a strange smell of sweaty socks for some reason, and I also remember buying a bag of sugar-coated doughnuts that had lumps of octopus inside."

A little later, I overheard a conversation between Rum and Hiroki, which included one of the most culture-free opinions in the history of Anglo-Japanese relations:

Hiroki: *"Rum, I can sense you don't like rice or Japanese food. What do you eat at home?"*

Rum: *"In England we 'ave pies. Steak an' kidney, chicken an' mushroom and apple an' blackcurrant!"*

Ugh!

After Piemageddon, we played the final show of the tour at Pepperland in Okayama. During the gig I turned to look at Shun, Hiroki and the other bands standing in the wings and they were all crying. I had to do a double-take. A big Japanese skinhead in a bomber jacket and bovver boots, crying. Both their girlfriends were crying as well, and on the other side of the stage, two girls who had been with us throughout the entire tour, Punk and Skin (we chose those nicknames), were also crying. It was a right old blubfest. The songs couldn't have been that bad, could they? Happily, I found out later that they were all just sad because it was the last show, so it was a very emotional end to the tour.

The next day we all met up at a quaint Japanese tea shop in the Kurashiki Bikan Historical Quarter of Okayama before being driven back to Kansai Airport. We sat in the corner by the window so we could look out at the willow trees lining the banks of the Kurashiki River and enjoy our last moments of traditional Japan. The waitress appeared dressed in a kimono, politely bowed and served us each a large round cup of dark green Japanese tea with a square of green jelly balanced on the edge of the saucer. Rum was disgusted once again…

"In England, we 'ave biscuits, digestives, bourbons, custard creams…"

My cringometer started going doolally again.

Earlier that year I had travelled down to Brighton for the weekend with a newly written collection of songs. At Andy Aggro's home studio, Peter replaced my guide vocals and We Bite Records liked what they heard again so gave us the go-ahead to make the next record.

Henry then got us a deal at Hazelwood Studios in Frankfurt, Germany. This would turn out to be AD and Rum's first and only Test Tubes studio album. At the airport, they got upgraded to first-class while Peter and I remained in standard class. Peter was unforgiving and furious, which possibly planted the seed of their early demise. The flight time was only an hour so I couldn't care less. As usual, Peter employed a wide variety of tactics to avoid hanging around in the studio, spending most of his time at McGowan's Irish bar or watching Kickers Offenbach, Henry's favourite football team. I slept in the studio and, despite the small budget running out, I managed to wheedle some more time out of the studio owner and finished most of the mixing. Due to this race against time, I still wasn't happy with the record, so I managed to blag some extra money and mixing time from We Bite Records.

GBH's Colin, Scott and Pedro came down to Brighton to record some parts for my track, 'I'm Getting Pissed for Christmas' (a Christmas song at last!) Jock, GBH's guitarist, was supposed to put in an appearance but was hiding behind his sofa too afraid to answer his front door because he thought the TV licensing people were after him. The album also contained the track 'Big Disappointment', which featured Peter's and Rum's daughters singing about their fathers.

The Test Tube curse struck again when our 'Alien Pubduction' album was released in 1998. The opening track was a song about Trapper entitled 'Sour Grapes' but on the track listing We Bite Records managed to leave off the first letter of the song title and turned it into a song about collective haemorrhoids – 'Our Grapes'.

Rachael had come to the end of her contract in Spain so it was time for us to return to the UK, regroup, reassess and try to earn some bloody money. But then Rachael discovered she was pregnant. In October 1997 we celebrated a 'shotgun' wedding at Fremington Methodist Church in Barnstable, North Devon, where most of her family were now living. The vicar couldn't believe he had 60 people crammed into his little chapel and droned on about the importance of coming 'every week', even though most of us lived 200 miles away in London. Marcus Mystery played the guitar and sang Lou Reed's 'Perfect Day' and the church organist complained that she would have brought her flute along and played the solo if she'd only known in advance.

We held our reception at the Cedars Inn country house in Bickington, where punk rock Brighton stalwart Smelly showed up uninvited. Peter has recently begun paying Smelly £10 to prevent him from getting up on stage, where he would grab Peter's mic and shove it down his pants. However, shortly after Peter walked away, I would pay him another £10 to ensure that he did. At the reception, Smelly got drunk and fell asleep on the dance floor so the bridesmaids and other children formed a line to take it in turns to play 'kick the dead hippie'.

On the day of the wedding, England men's football team only needed a draw with Italy in Rome to qualify for the 1998 World Cup finals in

France. This resulted in a slow start to the reception since most of the men were glued to the television set in the pub next door. In spite of Peter's confirmation with the Cedars Inn that they had Sky Sports, it was on the unavailable Sky Sports 2, so he refused to pay his bill as he left. They had his credit card details anyway. The match (not the marriage) ended 0-0.

When your partner gives birth, it's awkward. You arrive at the hospital with flowers and then you sit around for pretty much the entire day watching your wife endure more and more pain until she finally relents and gets an epidural. A brief respite from the boredom is a trip down to the hospital shop to get fleeced for an overpriced copy of Vogue and some jelly babies. There is little you can do to speed things along and, upon returning to the ward, a joke is half-heartedly attempted to try and lighten the mood…

"Maybe I can help cut something?"

The midwives and hospital staff are too busy and glare at you, making you feel about as welcome as an overfilled bedpan, so you turn away, hold her hand tightly and timidly offer support.

In the operating theatre, you feel even more 'in the way' as a large blue sheet covers her lower body and the tension is ratcheted up another notch. On the 30th of January 1998, William Steven Greening arrived at St Mary's Hospital in Paddington, London.

Throughout the day, from the hospital window I had been eyeing the Fountains Abbey pub, which closed at 10:30pm on a Sunday. The selfish little bastard was born at 10:26pm, which only gave me four minutes to get to the pub… now I would have to drive home gasping.

That moment when it finally happened was surreal – nothing can prepare you for it. I almost fell off my stool backward when the doctor spun around and passed him straight over to me. What am I supposed to do with this? His tiny little black eyes started to open and as he looked up at me for the first time, he heard his new Dad's first ever words to him...

"Welcome to Planet Earth."

CHAPTER 24 – SOME TURTLES NEVER MAKE IT

Trapper always maintained the reason you have two double beds in your hotel room in America is so you can have a wank in one and sleep in the other.

We'd completed short US tours before, the first being in 1983, sharing a bus with British punk band The Adicts. The tour included the now-infamous sold-out show at The Grand Olympic Auditorium venue in southern downtown Los Angeles. Legend has it that at this gig, Fat Mike from NOFX lost his virginity – or so he recently told me at the Punk Rock Bowling festival in Las Vegas.

The Los Angeles Times reported:

'Question: How do a mediocre punk band get to headline the Olympic Auditorium?

Answer: When it's from England, that's how.

Peter and the Test Tube Babies are hardly a sensation in their own country, but the quartet's British passports seemed enough of an attraction to lure a few thousand spiky-haired Anglo-punk fans, Friday. With gruff Joe Strummer-like vocals on such innocuous topics as getting on guest lists, the band had little to offer beyond its good-natured swagger. Singalong anthems like 'Banned from the Pubs' are better heard in a small club since these Test Tube Babies are little more than a punkish bar band.
Even worse were The Adicts, another Brit quartet that preceded the Test Tube Babies. The group's singer sporting mime makeup and wimpy demeanour resembled a cut-rate Adam Ant.'

The 1998 'Alien Pubduction US Tour' was scheduled to be the longest tour we'd ever done in a van, 34 shows in six weeks as we set off like hapless cannon fodder full of hope and excitement.
Starting at New York's historic CBGB, we planned to circle the country via the Midwest, West Coast and Texas before finishing at The Stone Pony in Asbury Park, New Jersey. The problem with an America club tour is that all of the profits are made on the east and west coasts, but you spend it all on gas driving through middle America playing shitholes for next to nothing. In other words, a waste of time and money.
The Forgotten, an American punk rock band based in San Jose, California, were our guests on the tour with my brother Walnut being

our solitary crew member. The Forgotten had driven all the way from California to start the tour with us in New York City. It felt more like we were their guests as we were using all their equipment and travelled in the same van and, it has to be said, the reason this tour didn't fall at the first hurdle was the unbelievable tolerance of our four 'Forgotten' amigos.

Singer Gordy Carbone and guitarist Craig Fairbaugh met us at the gate at Newark Airport, while bass player Kenny Helwig (who was going to drive for the whole tour) and drummer Todd Loomis circled to save on parking fees. The blue 10-seater Chevy van seemed spacious enough until you crammed all nine of us in with all our amplifiers, guitars and suitcases. As normal, we were doing the tour on holiday visas because the price of a work visa would have made the tour financially untenable. Naturally, we were concerned about bringing the guitars through, but fortunately for us, British Airways lost them, and not for the first time.

Peter described the scene on our arrival…

"So here it is, the first major hurdle of the tour - US Customs. We'd already decided to do this tour 'under the counter' so to speak, that is to say, with no work permits thus not paying any tax etc. Thing is, would they believe us at customs, especially seeing as Del and Rum have both brought their guitars, and I've brought the backdrop? For me and AD it was no problem, and we breezed through. While we're waiting, some punk rockers saunter in and are also hanging around the arrivals gate. One has a big mohican and the other has leopard-skin hair… now where have I seen that before? Obviously, they are The Forgotten who have come to pick us up. We introduce ourselves, and it's immediately obvious that they are fucking nice blokes, which is just as well really seeing as how we're doing the whole tour with them, travelling in their van.

The other three still haven't made it through customs and I start to become concerned. The story of Boring John (GBH's roadie) comes to mind and I hope, unlike him, the others haven't been sussed out and put on the next flight back. Eventually we see them through the glass but instead of walking through they are being escorted in another direction and, worse still, they all look fucking pissed-off. Things are looking ominous.

By now, all that red wine on the plane had taken its toll, which doesn't mean to say I was drunk but just fucking gasping for a cold beer. This is where I get introduced to the harsh reality of trying to get a drink in America, something that really pisses me off for the whole tour. I am sure that it would be easier to get shot than it is to get a beer in this fucking country.

Anyway, after failing to succeed in the (seemingly) innocent mission of finding a cold beer, we eventually do find Walnut. It transpires that what has really happened is that they are not being deported but that the fucking airline company has lost the guitars. 'Not again' we collectively groan, this always seems to happen to us. In fact, I'm sure Del's guitar is the most lost guitar in punk rock history. Mind you, in hindsight, it was a bit of a blessing really. Now Del and Rum don't have to worry about awkward questions along the lines of 'Why have you brought an electric guitar with you when you claim you're just here on holiday?' It takes about another half hour for Rum and Del to report the losses and give addresses of where to send them on to. Things aren't made any easier by the fact that the dozy woman there can't even spell guitar! In fact, they're so fucking stupid that what has really happened is that they are still on the plane on the way back to London."

As I mentioned earlier, our first show was at the now defunct but infamous CBGB in Manhattan's East Village. We were so jetlagged and knackered we had to be woken up to go on stage. As I was attempting to tune Craig's spare guitar, I noticed two British Airways guys in full BA uniform making their way through the punk rock crowd carrying our guitars - what a way to beat customs and immigration.

Prior to the tour, Ken and I had spent a lot of time setting up the whole thing via our home computers. An American lady named Sue Blank was taking care of the East Coast and some of the Midwest, while Dave Wood was assisting us out west. There were several dates yet to be confirmed, but Sue assured us she would tie up all the loose ends when we met up in New York City. Prior to taking the plunge and flying over, Dave Wood sent me some un-reassuring e-mails:

'It's very frustrating at the moment as the tour is only weeks away and Sue simply won't return our calls or e-mails. I'm handling all the tour merchandising so we'll be sure to get you all the shirts, etc. Also, the new album "Alien Pubduction", will be released in the States on Pub City Royal, with a release date of Sept. 4th, to coincide with the tour. - Dave.'

Then…

'Again, sorry for the missing pieces. I would sack Sue right now if I could only get in touch with her. I'm pulling my fucking hair out! The issue with the Chicago show is crucial. It is on Sunday the 13th (I called the club), and I'm a bit worried about how you will get to Montreal on time the next day. - Dave.'

Eventually…

'Finally got a call from Sue, though just a message on the voice mail, to assure me that everything is all taken care of and looking good, and not to be nervous! The nerve! It's been three weeks since she was last in touch. - Dave.'

Here's Walnut's review of that first show...

"We hit New York at rush hour and arrived late. It was a bit chaotic as there were lots of bands and equipment all over the place, so we just said 'fuck soundcheck' and decided to go to the pub. I'd recently been to New York and remembered it was 'happy hour' between 4pm and 8pm at a bar just up the road called 'The Continental'. Tonight's gig was always going to be a shambles as we were all tired and hadn't got a clue what equipment we would be using. I don't think anyone gave a shit as everyone just kept drinking. At 9pm we returned to a very busy venue and when the Test Tubes started playing it was just as shit as I thought it was going to be. Del had a shit guitar sound (a bit like George Formby), Rum was really out of tune and AD kept breaking snare skins. Despite all that, the crowd were going mental, but I had no help with security and eventually, the whole stage got invaded and I gave up trying to push people off - very punk rock indeed."

Sue Blank hadn't shown up in New York and it wasn't until after the show, once Walnut and The Forgotten had loaded the bus, that we realised we had no clue as to where we were supposed to be staying.

We still had no contracts or itineraries so we ended up doing what would become a regular occurrence on this leg of the tour: got the fuck out of dodge, hit the freeway, and found a cheap motel. We stupidly prayed Sue would appear at the next show and provide us with the rest of the tour details.

After a packed show, downstairs at the Middle East in Cambridge Massachusetts, it was time for our first day off of the tour. A day off on a Test Tubes tour usually spells trouble - fights, arrests, loss of belongings or any remaining sanity – so, as we were in Boston, we decided to spend the day as tourists.

AD went to look at an old ship in Boston Harbour while the rest of us decided to visit the place where nobody knows our name – TV's 'Cheers' Bar.

This was one of the days Peter could remember…

"Del gave us $100 each so we could go and enjoy our first day off of the tour. Rather predictably, we headed straight to the pub to have some lunch. I had the Guinness and beef casserole which was fantastic. We'd arranged to meet John (a photographer) at TV's 'Cheers' bar in Boston at 4.30 to do a photo session. So at about 2pm, Del, Rum, AD, Walnut and I leave the pub to find a couple of taxis. The Forgotten's Craig comes with us. About 10 minutes later we are at Boston Common and AD goes off to see some old warship, the rest of us wander through the common and go to have a look at 'Cheers' with all the other sad tourists. The pub there is actually called 'The Bull and Finch' and, as you can imagine, it's heaving. Therefore, we decide to have a drink at another pub and eventually end up in a tiny bar appropriately called 'The Littlest Bar'. By now it's absolutely pissing with rain, so we settle in for a bit of a session on the Guinness. At some point we noticed some bloke standing on the steps outside trying to shield himself from the rain with a soggy newspaper – he looked like a nutter. A long time later he decides to come in and asks if he can use the restroom, which he then does. After about 15 minutes, people are beginning to wonder what's happened to him. Another five or so minutes later and one of the customers needed to use the bog, so starts knocking on the door."

Walnut continues the story…

"He'd locked himself in the bathroom and needed to be talked through how to unlock the door. When he eventually emerged, he was livid and started shouting at everyone in the bar, including us. The barmaid kept telling him to leave but he ignored her so she threatened to call the police. He shouted back at her 'Call them then. Anyway, I'm going to report you for having unsafe restrooms.' Then he shouts at the barmaid…

'Marry me?'
'No. Get out' she shouts back, so he replies…
'I prefer oriental women anyway.'

We are in hysterics."

Peter picks up the story again.

"Finally, he does leave, ranting and raving as he goes, everyone has a laugh about it thinking the little incident in the littlest bar is over. However, 10 minutes later a fucking great big fire truck turns up and two firemen come in, apparently the nutter has called them as part of some sort of revenge."

Despite the rain, we walk back to the 'Cheers' bar to meet AD and John the photographer. John is there but there is no sign of AD, so we go upstairs to Melville's for some more beers and wait. John tries to persuade us to pull our pants down in front of the Cheers sign for a photo. We refuse. Eventually, AD turned up an hour and a half late, and we decided to have the photos taken down an alley against a brick wall. Groundbreaking!

Walnut again...

"After the incident at the 'Littlest Bar', we went to visit the 'Cheers' bar. The Forgotten's guitarist, Craig, was only 20 and you have to be 21 in the States to enter a bar so he was devastated he couldn't get in as the doorman sussed out his fake ID.
He suddenly became possessed by 'the spirit of the nutter from the Littlest Bar' and shouted...

'Shove your crap tourist bar up your fuckin' ass' as he was refused entry and bundled out of the queue by security.

The band went off to do a photo session, so Craig and me went back to the 'Littlest Bar'."

The Sue Blank situation had become farcical as she hadn't bothered to contact us since we arrived. Despite having no information, Ken and I had done well to keep the tour moving along, having to rely on favours from friends and local promoters and, when offered, even staying at members of the audience's flats and houses.

In Boston we had been well looked after staying with promoters Tom and Victoria, who also played in the other band on the bill, 'The Showcase Showdown'. We felt at home in more ways than one as they lived in Brighton, Massachusetts. Walnut and AD went out for a stroll to look for some postcards as they thought it would be hilarious to send some postcards home to Brighton from Brighton. What you need to realise about America is that, apart from New York City, nobody really walks anywhere. If you check into a hotel and ask where the nearest pub is, they may say: 'Just five to ten minutes down the street.'
Don't start walking because, in reality, what they actually mean is 'five to ten minutes' by car. There is very little to discover just strolling around a suburban neighbourhood. As predicted, they returned empty-handed with a frustrated Walnut complaining:

"There's nothing out there... This town is a big insult to be named after

Brighton. We couldn't find anything. It's the biggest dump I've ever been to."

Despite the continued absence of Sue, the finances were back on track after the sold-out show at The Middle East, so we prepared to make tracks to New Haven (Connecticut, not Newhaven, East Sussex).

Before we left, Victoria checked out our list of upcoming dates and warned us the drive from Portsmouth (New Hampshire not Hampshire) to Cincinnati would take us about 17 hours, which seemed glaringly implausible. The only information we had was the name of the venue and the date, no promoter or box office details. I stopped at a phone booth and called the venue directly…

"Hello, please could I speak to the manager?"

"Sorry honey, there's no one here, I'm just the cleaner."

"Oh! I'm sorry to trouble you but I'm desperate, could you please take a look at any posters there and tell me who is playing tomorrow night?"

I could hear her shuffling about in the background and a few moments later she returned to the phone.

"There's a poster here for Wednesday that says the Twelve Angry Men are playing, is that any help?"

"Yes, it is. Thank you."

Thus, the nine angry men in the van decided to blow out the Cincinnati show rather than drive through the night to certain disappointment.

CHAPTER 25 – GIMME A DOLLAR

The day-to-day struggles of surviving the US tour continued...

After the show at the Elvis Rooms in Portsmouth, New Hampshire, Kenny and I were drinking at the bar when out of the corner of my eye, I spotted a heavily tattooed punk girl making her way through the crowd and into the dressing room. Sure enough, it was Sue Blank, she really did exist!

True to her name, she didn't want to talk to Kenny or me, I guess because she knew how pissed off we were, so she gave Peter a large office ring-binder folder we hoped would contain all the future information we'd need to successfully complete this leg of the tour.

Sue said goodbye to Peter and as she was leaving told him:

"Good luck and say hi to the rest of the band."

Peter replied…

"Say hi yourself, they're all sitting at the end of the bar."

Despite Peter's advice, she walked straight past us and out the door.

Peter handed me the new tour bible, so I expectantly started flicking through the pages, hoping to find exhaustive lists of PA, lighting and catering specs. My heart sank as I discovered there was hardly any information at all. Some pages just had the date at the top and nothing else. I did notice Cincinnati was cancelled… Good to know.

Here's how Walnut reported Sue Blank's eventual arrival in his journal:

"Sue actually showed her face. Everyone we'd spoken to so far (local promoters etc...) told us she had gone into hiding and was having personal problems and on the verge of a nervous breakdown. Well, I think she should have told us this before dragging us halfway across the globe. We later found out that she tried to get our fee from the promoter as her commission, but luckily it was already safely tucked away in Del's back pocket. She'd be lucky to get a free sticker if it was up to me. The contracts she gave us weren't even filled in properly, maybe that's why she's called Sue Blank!"

As satnav or Google Maps were yet to be invented, we were having to rely on the tiny tourist maps in AD's pocket-sized guide to America to get directions to venues. The motels and feeding everybody was eating away at the small amount of money we had left from New York and Boston. On some nights we could only afford two motel rooms, one for each band. There were five of us, so Walnut and I, being brothers, usually grabbed one bed, while AD and Rum claimed the other. Peter is the 'snorer' in the band so he would usually wander off to sleep in the van muttering something along the lines of…

"In James Brown's band if you play a bum note you get sacked, in this band, James Brown can't even get a bed."

We arrived at the Magic Stick, a theatre on Woodward Avenue, north of downtown Detroit. It was now Rum's turn to buy some postcards so I said I'd go along with him for a change of scenery. Outside the venue, we were waiting for the crosswalk light to turn green when an African-American homeless guy with his hood up spotted us and started to shuffle his way over.

"Gimme a dollar."

In anticipation of the light changing and to avoid any hassle I gave him a dollar. He must have thought, this is easy...

"Gimme another dollar."

Still the light wouldn't change and, if it didn't soon, we would have no money left to buy postcards.

The light changed, phew, but still wanting more free dollars, he followed us across the street. Fortunately, he was limping so badly that we easily outwalked him. On the other side of the crosswalk, there was a body lying flat out against a wall, with a stream of piss flowing down across the sidewalk and into a drain. Was he dead or just lying down having a piss? We didn't hang around to find out, turning to walk back in the other direction, only to see that the 'gimme a dollar' guy had managed to gain on us. We quickly turned the corner to avoid him, and stumbled across a big fat woman with an eye missing, no glass eye or patch, just a hole where her eye should have been. This was like a fucking George A. Romero movie; nothing like the TV shows Dallas or Dynasty we'd grown up with on our UK TV screens. Fucking off the postcards we sped back to the venue and locked ourselves in the dressing room. Once safely inside, Rum declared:

"I'm never going out there again."

I still needed to pay back the credit card that I had used to pay for the flights from the UK so, as we hit Chicago, I told Kenny I needed to find a bank. While the van circled to avoid paying parking fees, I was dropped off at a Thomas Cook travel agency with a sign in the window advertising 'International money transfers'.

After I told the camp employee behind the counter that I wanted to transfer $3,000 to my UK account, he suddenly became all flirty and helpfully showed me all the forms I needed to fill out. I had never been called 'sir' so many times, but his mood changed when I started handing over the dirty screwed-up $5, $10 and $20 bills taken by local promoters on nightclub doors.

Awkward questions followed, such as:

"Where did you get this money from?" and

"What was the purpose of your business here in the United States?"

Thinking I must be a drug dealer, pimp or worse, he then went in to the office to speak to his manager. He had left the door slightly ajar so I managed to overhear them deciding to alert the local sheriff.
Our cash was now on the other side of the glass screen and with us having no work visas it was starting to look like we might be about to lose everything. To add to the escalating stress, a stinking homeless guy who'd been begging outside kept opening the automatic glass door in the entrance and shouting…

"CAPITALISTS!"

About to become stinking homeless guys ourselves, I had to think fast… I dashed outside onto the sidewalk, flagged down the circling van and instructed everyone to search for flyers and posters. Kenny gave me whatever paperwork Sue Blank had provided, and I put it together into an almost convincing presentation. I rushed back into the bank and slid it under the glass to the Thomas Cook employee, who took it and went back into the office where the manager was still on the phone to the police. He explained to them that we were some sort of touring troupe and the money had come from the paying public. After some deliberation, they decided to accept my story and the FBI were stood down.

With a disgusted look on his face, the Thomas Cook guy started counting and smoothing out the dollar bills, and the transfer home was completed.

Exhale!

While all this kerfuffle had been going on, the stinky homeless guy had crawled in from the street on all fours and helped himself to the dish of complementary boiled sweets from the counter.

Ah, the American dream.

Having played Detroit and Chicago, it was time to make our merry way across the border into Canada to play Montreal and Toronto.
Being visa-less we couldn't take any of the equipment, merchandise or The Forgotten with us, so we piled them into a cheap motel room on the US/Canadian border. With Kenny driving and pretending to be our tour guide we made up a lie about wanting to see Niagara Falls from the Canadian side while doing our best tourist impressions by wearing crappy 'I Love USA' baseball caps.

As it turned out, we were able to enter Canada without any problems but were warned that US immigration and customs on the way back would be more difficult. It was an 18-hour drive to Montreal so Rum and I helped share the driving. The line was already stretching down the street as we arrived late at the venue 'Jailhouse Rock'. Yannick, the Canadian promoter, was extremely happy to see that we had made it to the show.

Montreal punk band The Ripcordz kindly lent us their guitars but, after driving all day and getting rushed into the venue to hurriedly prepare for the show, I was less than delighted to discover that tonight's guitar had all the strings put on the wrong way round so when you detuned you had to tune up and when you needed to raise the pitch you had to detune.

Unworkable, like the tour.

The next day, we played in Toronto at the El Mocambo.

Walnut summed up the venue nicely…

"This place was a right shithole. The dressing rooms had no locks and were right next to the public toilets, so people kept wandering in and out as there was no security, so it soon filled up with pissed idiots. The owner

came in and told us that his place was legendary as 'The Rolling Stones' had played there - so what? That doesn't make it any less of a shithole."

Yannick's band, 'Walter', provided support, and the next day he took me to the bank to exchange our Canadian dollars for US ones. We travelled back into the States with no trouble at the US border, picking up The Forgotten at the motel in South Holland. When we arrived, they were in a foul mood because we had dropped them off in a dry town and they had to spend what little money they had to get a taxi or train to Chicago to buy a beer.

Alcohol consumption and federal law had been a major cause of disruption on this tour as Walnut experienced first-hand:

"At one venue I was sitting in the dressing room with a bottle of beer when the manager came in and told me that, in this state, federal law prevented alcohol consumption in the dressing room and on the stage. I asked her why and she told me that it is an offence to consume alcohol in a place of work and, while a band is performing, they were considered to be working and the dressing room is considered an office. What a crock of shit. So it's okay for the audience to drink but as soon as the band step on stage they are breaking the law. I'm going to call this...
'The Shit Law Tour'."

This was heavily highlighted at our next show at the Concert Café in Green Bay, Wisconsin on Lake Michigan. Tom, the overzealous paranoid promoter, had been emphasising the fact that the local scene was on its knees, he was going to lose money and the local police were looking for a reason to close him down. He told us there could be absolutely no alcohol consumed on the premises, front of house, on stage or backstage.
Peter was now becoming more and more irritated with the ever-changing draconian alcohol laws that changed from state to state. He was also beginning to suffer from LSD (Lead Singer Disorder) and flatly refused to play unless he could drink beer on stage. We desperately needed tonight's 500 bucks guarantee to cover the next day's motel, gas and breakfast. I did everything I could to resolve the situation, eventually getting the promoter to set up a tab in the bar next door. However, they only sold domestic US beer, so Mr LSD was still not satisfied as he wanted imported beer. We then went to a liquor store and bought him a small bottle of Jack Daniel's and filled up a couple of Burger King Pepsi cups, so he could secretly drink JD and coke on stage. Meanwhile, Peter, being Peter, had attempted to walk into the

venue with some beers, and Tom, the promoter, had gone berserk and threatened to pull the show. Kenny and I were able to smooth out the situation when we returned and The Forgotten went on as planned.

But wait… The fun doesn't end there… As Walnut remembers vividly…

"The band were on stage and ready to start but Peter was still refusing to play unless he could have a beer on stage, so I went into the dressing room to see what was happening…

'Come on everyone's ready.'
'Well, I'm not.'
'Are you gonna do this fucking gig or not?'
'Not.'
'Right, so I'll go on stage and pack everything away, shall I?'
'Do what you like.'

This pissed me off big time so I thought, what's the fucking point, I'm just gonna get drunk. I switched off all the amps and I went for a piss in the back alley outside. As I finished, I heard a noise coming from the venue and when I went back in, to my surprise, the Test Tubes were playing.
Peter had eventually graced the stage with his presence but was still wearing his leather jacket, which was a bad sign. The first song was 'Keep Britain Untidy' which sounded shit. I soon realised Rum hadn't switched his amp back on. The band then went into their second song 'Up Yer Bum' with Peter making one finger salutes to Tom the promoter. Tom runs to the front of the stage and shouts hysterically back at Peter…

'NO. UP YOUR FUCKING BUM!'

Tom then comes around to the side of the stage to get on but I restrain him. I actually feel sorry for him as he is in a right state. I apologise but nobody gets on the stage while the band are playing. He then jumps into the crowd and tries to push everybody towards the door shouting

'GET OUT OF MY CLUB… SHOW'S OVER… BECAUSE OF ONE ALCOHOLIC WHO CAN'T GO ONE HOUR WITHOUT A DRINK!'

I tended to agree with him as I'm sure everyone else did."

After the last of the audience had left, Kenny and I attempted a half-hearted apology in a thinly veiled attempt to try to retrieve some fraction of the fee. At least then we would have some money to pay for some gas. No luck.

A solemn atmosphere hung in the air as we loaded out and soon everyone was ready to go except Peter, who never helps because he's 'the singer' who doesn't own any equipment... so *"why should I?"*

The line he most often uses when being challenged for not helping his band 'mates' is:

"I've got all the equipment I need in my trousers."

This time I eventually found the 'man with the equipment in his trousers' at the bar next door, still steaming into what was left on the bar tab swapping three domestic beers, meant for everyone, for something from the top shelf for himself. Normally I don't lose my temper, but this time I wasn't the only one who was about to suffer because of his attitude, it was all nine of us.

Hold my coat. AD and Rum had to restrain me but I'd had enough of his selfish behaviour, so Walnut and I jumped into Amy's car - who'd earlier been helping with the merchandise - and we sped off into the night.

I had left the tour.

CHAPTER 26 – MID-TOUR MADNESS

Like many, I often suffer from mid-tour madness – a condition in which your initial enthusiasm ebbs away and you realise that you're trapped in a psychological experiment in which disparate personalities are crammed into unbearable proximity. That's when you start to lose the plot, reverting to childlike behaviour such as smashing up hotel rooms and taking drugs. The mental struggle to maintain your sanity rages as you stare longingly at your return ticket, waiting for the light at the end of the tour bus to finally appear...

Now, where did I put my passport?

Amy was driving myself and Walnut through the night but had started to tire so we stopped at a dodgy looking run-down motel in the middle of nowhere, paid some cash to a man in a glass booth and traipsed off to our rooms to be murdered.

Walnut remembered surviving that night at the Bates Motel...

"I woke up and watched MTV for a while, then Del suggested finding a bar. He's obviously on a mission to get pissed again but sounds like a good plan to me. We drive to the nearest town and have a few beers and a game of darts. It gets to about 2pm and we ask the barman how long it will take to get to Minneapolis, and he tells us about five hours, so we decide to make a move to see if we can make the show.

We halt at a truck stop to get more beer. Del opens a beer in the store and starts drinking it. The storekeeper freaks out and throws him out.

After Amy has been driving for about another three hours we decide to stop for more beers. We found a gas station and there must be a bike rally nearby as there are hundreds of bikers here. On the way out Del asked one of the bikers how much further it is to Minneapolis. He tells him we're going the wrong way. We were heading north when we should have been heading south. Maybe we should have concentrated on navigating instead of drinking.

We eventually arrive at around 9pm and finding the venue is pretty easy as Del has played there before. It's owned by Prince or the Artist or whatever he called himself at the time. Amy takes over the merch while Del goes to find Peter to either kill him or make peace before the show."

That evening, Walnut, Amy, and I resurfaced at the 7th Street Entry in Minneapolis, where I was told that as they hadn't been paid for the previous night, the two bands could only afford one motel room between the seven of them, with Peter having to sleep on the floor.

While Walnut set up the equipment, I wandered across the street to smoke the pipe of peace (not the pipe of Pete) in O'Donovan's Irish pub.

Walnut continued...

"Del was so drunk by now he got up on stage and introduced one of the support bands, which made us all cringe with embarrassment. Even The Forgotten's drummer Todd was starting to lose it as I saw him dancing at the front, even though the show was awful. He'd hardly spoken for the whole tour but, after last night's show cancellation, he went up to Peter and said 'HEY MAN YOU'RE A PRIMADONNA!' - I think that was the first thing he ever said to him."

AD filled in some alcohol-induced gaps in my memory from later that night...

"Del got SO pissed 'smoking the pipe of peace' that, although he managed to stay upright for the first bit of the show, he then fell face down unconscious on the dressing room floor in the two-minute gap before the encore. Walnut had to take over for the last three songs!"

Our journey continued across the Midwest and took us to shows in Rapid City, South Dakota, and Great Falls, Montana, where Rum witnessed some shocking scenes through the bus window...

"I remember driving through Montana and seeing American Indians, no longer proud people but homeless drunks laying in doorways and begging at gas stations. God bless America - the ex-home of the braves."

Most of these shows were attended by gormless teenagers with braces on their teeth, carrying skateboards under their arms and between songs they would go outside for a 'skate'. During one soundcheck, I asked when the stage lighting would be arriving only to be told that there was only one house light and would we like it ...

"On or off?"

File under 'U' for Underwhelming.

We eventually arrived on the Pacific coast, playing both Seattle and Portland. By this time, Kenny and I had begun floating the tour on our credit cards again and were hoping to make some of our money back when we hit San Francisco.

Once we had arrived in San Francisco, I happened to meet a well-known tattooist, Patrick, on a night out. As a kid, I'd inflicted myself with some homemade crappy Indian-ink tattoos while skiving off school, subsequently having them covered up while drunk with a large depiction of the Grim Reaper giving the finger. Everyone used to ask me why on earth I had such an evil tattoo when I was the least evil person they knew? Patrick turned out to be a big fan of the band, so he grabbed my arm, looked at my tattoo and told me it was shit and asked if I would like a free cover-up. I was drunk again, so I said yes and arranged a time early the next morning. As soon as the alarm went off, I changed my mind, turned it off, and went back to sleep. The front doorbell rang and it was Patrick waiting to take me to his tattoo parlour. Yikes! Walnut and I quickly got dressed, hurried downstairs and followed him. In order to decide what to have done, I flicked through his illustration books.
I needed something more in character with my personality rather than the Grim Reaper, so I suggested Homer Simpson.

"That's no good. He's yellow, you would see straight through it."

Doh! The only design large and dark enough to cover up the fearsome Reaper was a Japanese coy carp.

Patrick the tattooist was full of enthusiasm…

"Once you start with a Japanese sleeve you'll be addicted and won't be able to stop, you could have a sea serpent across your back, a mermaid on a rock on the other sleeve, sharks, crabs, starfish and so on. I can hook you up with some buddies across the States for the rest of the tour."

I didn't have the heart to tell him I didn't actually like tattoos.

Despite my reservations, Patrick did a great job and finished it in one sitting. He drew it freehand, it took several hours to complete, and he used some of the brightest new colours I'd seen around at that time.
I was told later it would have cost around $400.

During our time in LA we met up again with my 'worst man', ex-Wanker and illegal US immigrant Mark 'Skweeech' Verrion. After the soundcheck at the Whisky a Go-Go, it was Skweeech who spotted Lemmy from Motörhead sitting at the bar in the Rainbow Rooms next door.

I overheard Skweeech say…

"I'm gonna ask him if he's coming down to the gig tonight?" as he hastily made a beeline towards him.

After the enquiry was delivered, he eagerly awaited Mr Kilmister's reply. Jack 'n' Coke in hand, Lemmy took a deep breath and replied:

"THOSE BASTARDS AREN'T STILL GOING, ARE THEY?"

We stayed at the house of Bill and Crystal from Dr Strange Records for a couple of days and, while enjoying a sunny barbeque in the local park, managed to strike a deal to release a live video 'Pissed And Loud In Hollywood', a recording of the show at the Whisky a Go-Go, adding an extra $100 to the dwindling tour budget. Kerching. Bonus!

In an attempt to make the van less excruciatingly uncomfortable, Walnut and Kenny tried to rearrange 'the pack'. Then Peter decided to invite his girlfriend and Little Mark, a friend from Brighton, along to join the tour. What fresh hell is this? We now had 11 people in a nine-seater van plus equipment, new boxes of merchandise and guitars wedged between seats. Skweeech also wanted to squeeze aboard the sardine express, but an attempt to shoehorn him in proved unsuccessful. Thanking our various gods, we crammed aboard and waited for deep vein thrombosis to set in.

We wound our way across Arizona and Texas, only stopping occasionally to have pisses behind giant cacti. It took us around 17 hours to reach Dallas, or 'Dullarse' as Peter later dubbed it and, after staying at 'Bones' the promoter's house in Houston, Rum had another eye-opening experience.

"In Texas, the promoter had a stash of weapons. Peter thought it would be funny to go around waving an AK-47 in people's faces, he was smiling like a maniac, and it was the only time on the tour I remember him being happy."

Peter wrote about this in his tour journal…

"The others all crawled into their sleeping bags and I went off to find myself somewhere to crash. I hadn't realised the house was so big and that there were another seven or eight people still partying. I, of course, joined them. Mind you, by now I was pretty stoned and pissed... just for a change.

We all had a few more beers and smokes and I can't remember how, but the conversation turned to guns. The next thing I know I'm holding a real AK-47, fucking wow. This probably isn't such a big deal to most

Yanks, who have relatively easy access to guns, but to us Brits living in our namby-pamby 'Nanny State' holding an automatic weapon is close to impossible. I've got to admit it felt incredible, but better was to come. A minute later someone gave me what I think was a Mossburg Tactical shotgun. Do you remember Linda Hamilton in Terminator II when she's got the black shotgun which she keeps reloading just by one up and down jerk of the arm? It was that fucker! Fucking double wow. A big fucking handgun appeared as well and for the next hour I was Linda Hamilton, Sly Stallone and Arnold Schwarzenegger all rolled into one. It's a bloody good job they never gave me any ammo because the power I felt was incredible. Do you know what? It was more than incredible, it was sexual. I'd always suspected that I'd get turned on by guns but I'd never had the chance to find out. Now though, I had a super executive first-class hard-on and I'm not embarrassed to admit it. If my girlfriend had walked in and demanded that I make love to her she'd have to wait. Mind you, if Cindy Crawford was my girlfriend, I might have changed my mind. The thing is, it was a real eye-opener because up to this day the only time in my life that I would get sexually aroused would be by having, or thinking about having sex with a woman. Now though, a whole new side of my sexuality had presented itself to me. I'd always suspected it, but what knocked me for six was the strength of this new arousal, I could have knobbed every supermodel in the world and given them ten orgasms each I felt so turned on! It's not every day you find out something new about yourself, especially at my age, but this just blew me away. I couldn't believe how excited I was. I remember I went and woke Rum, mistakenly thinking he'd be into guns as well because he's a big Rambo fan. He followed me, I showed him the old Linda Hamilton with a shotgun movement, he looked at me like I was a fucking idiot and went straight back to bed. Judging by the comments of the rest of the band the next day they would have agreed with him, but what the hell, fuck 'em, I was in a world of my own and no-one was gonna take this moment from me."

We managed to make it out of Texas without being terminated by a now certified insane Peter and headed on to New Orleans. Hurricane season 1998 was among the worst in history. Our West Coast tour profits were rapidly declining, so we desperately needed to make this show. In between dodging fallen trees and overturned trucks, I thought I'd better call ahead to make sure the gig was still going ahead. It was too dangerous to get out of the van for fear of being blown away or hit by loose debris, so I made Kenny pull up as close as he could to the phone booth on a gas station forecourt. As I leaned into the driving rain out of the bus window, I managed to reach the local promoter who said there was still a long line around the block. All of the roads ahead were now closed, so despite our best efforts, we were unable to continue. Pub anyone?

AD recounted one particular highlight of that trip...

"By the time we got to Atlanta, I'd come down with what the Yanks called 'strep throat'. I had a soaring fever and was also suffering from malnutrition, probably caused by the previous four weeks' vitamin-free diet. One night, after being forced to carry the show as usual (Peter and Derek squabbling and Rum playing with his volume down so you couldn't hear his mistakes), we rocked up at that night's money-saving sleeping arrangements, a dogshit-strewn squat.

I managed to fall into a delirious sleep in a manky double bed and woke a few hours later with the crusty bird whose house it was snuggled up next to me. A snot-covered toddler wandered into the room, stared me in the face and in a southern drawl asked...

'Mommy, is that Daddy?'

I thought, is this really my life right now...?"

On the way back up the East Coast we played another couple of shitholes and then, unbeknownst to us at the time, the show at the 'Phantasmagoria' in Washington was to be our final show of the tour...

We went directly to the promoter Richard Gibson's house, where we were staying the night. Richard was a guitar freak and played in one of the opening bands, United 121, named after their section of seating at the DC United soccer ground. The show was great, and the next morning Richard's wife, Sherrill, cooked for us as we lay in our sleeping bags. During breakfast, we were about to make a very easy decision...

As we were back in Sue Blank territory, I blew away the cobwebs from her book of evil spells, ahem, itinerary. Rather unsurprisingly, there was no information for the next two shows. Things were starting to look shaky again but luckily, Richard had the phone number of Mary, the local promoter in Philadelphia. Mary told me the club had cancelled the show three days earlier but, not to worry because she had a great idea... we could play in her friend's basement. I could hear the sound of many barrels being scraped as she calculated how many people we could fit in at $2 per head. We had been to hell and back and now we were about to take another trip back down there.

That was it. We decided to cut our many losses, bring our return flights forward and head back to New York. The cost of changing our flights with American Airlines would be an extra hundred dollars each, and I was told we could pay at the airport after we checked in. Even though that was about all the money we had left, everyone's faces lit up at the prospect of sleeping in their own beds, in their own houses and within seconds we had smashed the tour record for getting ready and jumping in the van.

By chance, when we arrived at Newark Airport the American Airlines check-in clerk forgot to charge us the extra $500 for the flight changes.

Hooray for American blue-collar workers... Hip Hip...

Thanks to that clerical error, we were now in profit. I finished the accounts on the plane, and it turned out that we were due the considerable payout of $88 each for the whole six-week tour. At least that was better than the $12 we got for the 1983 tour. It was Peter who presented AD with his $88 at the Heathrow Airport luggage carousel. He immediately threw it on the floor and shouted *"SHIT!"*

This signalled the beginning of the end for AD - and who could blame him? The lengthy touring for very little return had become too much as AD later revealed...

"I was too depressed to talk by the end of that tour and just wanted to go home and soak in a deep Prozac bath."

Rum enjoyed the tour. Mind you, he also enjoyed his colonoscopy scan.

"Unlike the others, I enjoyed the US tour and would happily do it all again, but with a different band, of course! One memory that sticks in my mind was in Atlantic City. AD was so hot on stage he threw a jug at Walnut and ordered him to fill it with water. I've known Walnut since we were kids and that was the angriest that I'd ever seen him. If he had got hold of AD there would have been blood. Furthermore, I think during that tour AD had a chip on his shoulder as he was just the second-best drummer in the van. It was a bloody long tour and I relished my role as bass hero and poster boy of the band. I was the missing link between Del's drunken intros and AD coming in at twice the speed with Peter's shouting. Still, I guess that's punk rock and I love them all and miss the good times we had."

Peter was always quick to remind them:

"You came as a pair - you can go as a pair."

In one of AD's last shows in Switzerland, he was in such a bad mood that at various points during the set, he played the fast bits slowly and the slow bits fast. Peter no longer wanted him in the band, so he called me up and told me. I then phoned AD to give him the bad news. In response, he said he would call Peter and smooth things over. Peter then phoned me again to ask if I had 'done it'. I told him to expect AD's call, to which Peter responded by saying he was switching his phone off. Courageous.

I also hoped AD was joking when he told me he was coming round to collect a wheel as his share of the van. Rum also hung up his bass, collected his golf clubs and left the band to concentrate on his painting and decorating business. (What is it with bass players and decorating?) He moved back to Peacehaven and into a bungalow, so he could get his ladders down the side of the house. Rum's last gig was at the Free Butt in Brighton and, about six songs into the set we did an official bass guitar handover to new masochist Paul 'H' Henrickson.

AD recalled his last moments before freedom…

"Two weeks before my first son was born, Peter fired me, I think for not knowing enough about football." (AD had once asked what time 'Kick Away' was, after being forced to get up at some ungodly hour to get to a match - Del.)
"I still quite like them though, and Peter now lives in a derelict caravan at the bottom of my garden."

The Alien Pubduction US Tour 1998: Nine men packed into a small van for six weeks, performing 34 shows. It certainly was a transformative campaign and a catalyst for the breakup of that second Test Tubes' line-up. The experience was certainly one that I will never forget, but I'm glad I did it because now I know for certain…

I would never do it again… never a-fucking-gain.

CHAPTER 27 – REASONS TO BE CHEERFUL

As someone who has been in the music 'business' since leaving school, touring and recording music was the only thing that I really knew how to do. Forget painting and decorating, bricklaying or astrophysics, it was now time to cease shouting abuse at the audience from the front of the stage, to sniggering at the band from behind the stage curtain.

I loved 'New Boots And Panties!!' - the Ian Dury and the Blockheads album, not the articles of clothing - so I was thrilled when Trapper offered me the job of looking after their stage. Without a doubt, the Blockheads were the finest musicians I had ever worked with.

It was 10am on a Tuesday morning on 24th February 1998, when I arrived at West London's Nomis Studios in Sinclair Road and dragged their equipment out of the storage space and set it up in the rehearsal room. Around mid-afternoon, one by one, the band members started showing up. This was the first time that I'd met them and to be honest, I was expecting Ian and a load of 'A. N. Others', so I was delighted when original Blockheads Chaz Jankel (guitar and keyboards), Norman Watt-Roy (bass), Mickey Gallagher (piano and Hammond organ) and John Turnbull (vocals and guitar) arrived. Dylan Howe (the son of Steve Howe from Yes) was playing the drums, with jazz saxophonist Gilad Atzmon on tenor, baritone sax and piccolos. Setting up a piccolo stand was a first.

A journalist once remarked that the Blockheads looked nothing like a band, more like six people waiting at a bus stop. I liked that.

A lot of bands I've worked with would flap around testing and retesting the equipment and complaining, Ian and the band just sat around on the empty flight cases, smoking joints and catching up on old times. Dylan eventually wandered over to the drum kit and began to tap out a quiet beat so as not to disturb anyone. Norman picked up the bass and started jamming along, then one at a time the others joined in. It sounded exactly like the records, no faffing, no fiddling, full of humility and arrogance-free. It came as no surprise to discover the upcoming shows were all sold out.

They carried their guitars in soft cases with a curly guitar lead tucked inside the zipped pockets on the front. Before one show, Chaz Jankel was upset that someone had lost his one and only guitar pick. Once he had shaken out his guitar case, the panic was over. Phew! One of my high-tech jobs was to scour each venue for a wooden chair so he could have his tiny guitar combo high enough to be able to hear it.

Norman's Fender Jazz bass never left his side. Having a closer look at it one day, I felt a hole that you could drop a golf ball into, which had been gouged out by Norman resting his thumb on the wooden body while playing with his fingers.

Trapper on Norman:

"In my opinion, Norman Watt-Roy, when he played, was the best white funk bass player in the world. He wore an old grey suit that gradually turned black with sweat during the gig, he also wrote the Frankie Goes to Hollywood 'Relax' riff and took a £500 one-off payment for the biggest tune that year; the pitfalls of the music industry."

Johnny Turnbull was also one of the best guitarists I had heard and as I dropped them off at their various humble abodes across London, I couldn't help but feel they deserved to reap more of the benefits from their immense talents.

The late Derek Hussey, nicknamed 'Derek the Draw' for obvious reasons, was Ian's assistant and helper. If Ian needed something during the show he would shout *"Del!"* and we'd both mistakenly run on at the same time!

Sadly, Ian was found to have colorectal cancer and had been told that his condition was terminal. It was always touch-and-go the night before an event, with many shows being called off at the last minute. I remember the band sitting around in the rehearsal room when the agent arrived and began going through a list of possible upcoming dates. After he'd finished, there was a long awkward silence, interrupted eventually by Ian:

"Well, if I'm alive, I'll do 'em."

I certainly enjoyed some great shows with the Blockheads, one in particular at the Blackheath Halls in South East London. The band were onstage performing 'Reasons To Be Cheerful, Part 3'. The track has a long section where everyone grabs a percussion item and plays along. Mickey Gallagher beckoned me over while sitting at the keyboards and whispered…

"Del, I've left me cowbell in the glove box of the car. Could you take my keys and get it for me, please?"

As I began my descent in London's slowest elevator, I could hear the song rapidly progressing. In the car park, I quickly retrieved the cowbell, locked the car and rushed back up via the stairs before hurrying onstage to pass it over. As Micky raised the drumstick to hit the cowbell, the song finished!

TV presenter and pianist Jools Holland was standing behind me at the side of the stage and asked if he could 'squeeze' past and get up to play along on the spare keyboard. Earlier, Ian had given me strict instructions…

"Don't let the dwarf on."

I therefore stood firm and didn't let him pass, but he must have managed to sneak around the back to the other side of the stage as I later saw him dash on to sit up beside Mickey to tinkle along to 'Sex & Drugs & Rock & Roll'.

In Paisley in Scotland, the band were getting ready in the dressing room downstairs when the house manager started shouting in my face in a thick Scottish accent. I couldn't understand a word he was saying so I just said 'yes' to get rid of him. He then turned a key on the wall, which lifted the stage curtain, and turned off the house lights as the audience stood up in their seats and started cheering and applauding half an hour before the show was scheduled to start!

At another show, the front row of mic stands got caught up in the stage curtain and ended up dangling 40 feet above the audience.

One night, sitting backstage, the Blockheads told me the story of when they were hired to be Roger Daltrey's backing band. All of them were looking forward to ripping into some Who classics but were disappointed when he told them he only wanted to play Leo Sayer songs and ballads like 'Send In The Clowns'. They recorded an album with him called 'Parting Should Be Painless', but the live work mostly consisted of TV shows, miming, and sitting around backstage drinking. Mickey told me that while they were doing an awards show in Switzerland, everything was provided, gratefully received, and consumed. Watching from home, his wife and kids burst out laughing as the camera zoomed in for a close-up on his crossed eyes. An incident that prompted this piece of advice...

"Always wear sunglasses when miming."

The band had also been lined up to perform at the Hay-on-Wye Festival of Literature & Arts, which welcomes 80,000 visitors each day every May. A few days prior to the show, Mickey Gallagher had booked ex-Flesh for Lulu drummer Hans Perrson and myself into The Swan at Hay, with the band scheduled to make their way down on the day of the show. The hotel was in a superb location, close to Hay-on-Wye's multitude of bookshops, restaurants, bars and cafés, while there was also a bustling pub downstairs.

It was a lovely sunny day so, after we had set up and tested all the equipment, we went to chill on the grass in front of the stage. As we were sitting there in our shades enjoying the sunshine, we noticed two elderly ladies in straw hats approaching. They made their way over to where we were sitting and asked us if we needed anything? I jokingly replied…

"Strawberries and champagne please."

They both chuckled and wandered away. About 20 minutes later, the silhouettes of the two elderly ladies reappeared on the horizon, but this time they were clutching the handles of a large picnic hamper. They placed it on the grass in front of us and opened the lid.
To our astonishment, it contained several bottles of Moët & Chandon champagne, punnets of fresh strawberries and a set of crystal champagne flutes. As that old adage goes… if you don't ask, you don't get.

I was soon 'poshly pished' in our new picnic area, drunkenly directing the band to the dressing rooms as they arrived in their cars from London. During that evening, every time I saw one of the straw-hatted, elderly ladies, I shouted:

"MORE MOET!" Which they swiftly supplied.

It was the easiest changeover of all time because the opening 'band' was English fitness expert Diana Moran, aka 'The Green Goddess', reading extracts from her new book. Hans and I tossed a coin to see who would move her stool. During Ian's show, drummer Dylan Howe's hi-hat cymbal clutch mechanism broke. I walked across the stage to try to fix it but, as I approached the drum kit, I realised that my hands were full, as I was still holding a Champagne flute and a bottle of Moët. Dylan fixed it by himself, so I wandered away.

Even though the audience were seated the show was great as always, after which Ian and the band immediately headed back to London.
Of course, it would have been rude not to raid Ian and the band's dressing rooms to fill our bags with more Moët for the hotel and the trip home back to London.

It was Hans who drove back, and a great weekend was had by me… Hic!

Sadly, Ian passed away on 27th March 2000, aged just 57. I think Suggs from Madness summed him up best when he described Dury as:

"Possibly the finest lyricist we've seen."

I attended the wake and Trapper set the band up to perform at the funeral…

"I actually did the funeral and, in the church, they performed a song they'd written with Ian as the casket was going into the furnace. Norman didn't want to bring his bass, so I lent him my Precision. Unfortunately, the input jack was dodgy so there was a massive crackling that sounded like burning fire coming through the amp. I had to rush over and hold the jack. I just remember thinking... Please no, not at a bloody funeral."

Ian's passing was subsequently commemorated at the Brixton Academy with a cancer benefit show.

For that special event, we booked a few days' rehearsal at John Henry's in North London to prepare the guest artists. I was playing the backing tracks through the mixing desk so that each guest could have a sing-along before the band played the song live. A lot of artists showed up unprepared, trying to learn the song on the spot, but I have to say, Robbie Williams was a class act. He only needed one run through and performed 'Sweet Gene Vincent' word-perfect, as well as having his dance routine worked out. At the end of the song, the Blockheads all gave him a deserved round of applause. The show was suitably fantastic. Madness performed 'My Old Man'. Kirsty McCall sang 'Hit Me With Your Rhythm Stick' and Tom Robinson performed 'I Wanna Be Straight'.

It was a fitting farewell to such a one-off genius, and I feel privileged to have been a part of it.

Mickey Gallagher had previously toured with The Clash as well as adding keyboards to their album, 'London Calling'. His children, Ben and Luke Gallagher, had also sung with The Clash on the re-recording of 'Career Opportunities', released on their 'Sandinista' LP. Ben and Luke now had a band called 'Little Mothers', who'd just signed with Island Records and been invited along as special guests on the Joe Strummer and the Mescaleros' UK tour. Mickey asked Hans and me to take care of his kids on tour, so we shared the driving and looked after the equipment while legendary 'Blockheads' and 'Madness' sound engineer Ian 'Dad' Horne handled front of house.

On my 39th birthday, Joe Strummer and the Mescaleros played at the Astoria on Charing Cross Road in London. By the time I had finished packing away the gear at the end of the night, everybody had left. The stage was empty, and the venue seemed deserted. Once I had loaded the last case into the back of the truck, I locked the doors and returned to the venue. One of the security guys walked over and told me I was needed upstairs. Pushing open the dressing room door I was stunned to discover a packed party in full swing. In the middle of the room, Joe Strummer, Bez from Manchester ravers the Happy Mondays and Cerys Matthews from Welsh alternative rockers Catatonia were all standing on chairs and proceeded to sing 'Happy Birthday' to me. What a moment. Naturally, I fell to my knees in disbelief, bowed and proclaimed...

"I'm not worthy."

We arrived at Glasgow Barrowlands one afternoon and found Joe, his crew, and the Mescaleros sitting on the front of the stage with their suitcases piled up behind them. They had been thrown off their tour bus. The previous night, Bez and his crew had been partying in the back lounge when the driver walked in and saw a gun on the table. That was it, he refused to go any further and told everyone to leave.

A few years after that tour, I was sitting backstage in the catering area at Glastonbury when Joe Strummer walked in. Joe was immediately beckoned by half of the room to join them at their tables. I continued eating, thinking he wouldn't remember me. To my delight, he walked over, sat down, and said:

"Alright Del, how's it going? Who are you here with?"

R.I.P. Joe. A legend, an icon and a role model.
He certainly left a lasting impression on me.

The next Little Mothers tour was with Semisonic, a Minneapolis-based pop band. Every night, as Hans and I were putting the equipment away, they would start their set with an annoying piano riff for a song called 'Closing Time'.

Plink plonk, plink plonk, plink plonk, plink plonk...

Within a week that piano riff had started to grate heavily so, we'd race to pack and load out to escape the building before we had to suffer one more annoying...

...plink plonk, plink plonk, plink plonk, plink plonk...

We never quite made it but were getting closer and, by the time we got to The Garage in Glasgow we managed to pack and load the bus in record time. They still hadn't started the song as we drove away cheering. When we got back to our room at McCreary's Bed and Breakfast, we high-fived each other and punched the air in triumph. Still sweating from the fastest load-out of the tour, I opened the window to let in some fresh air only to notice the venue's rear loading bay was only a couple of yards from our room and the stage door was wide open...

One, two, three, four... plink plonk, plink plonk, plink plonk, plink plonk.

Aaaaarrrgh!

By the time the Little Mothers' tour rolled into the Wedgewood Rooms in Portsmouth, Hans had somehow managed to manoeuvre himself into the position of tour manager, collecting the money each night while having a leisurely cup of coffee with the promoter in his warm office while I frantically loaded out alone in the pouring rain. This was no doubt one of the reasons why I was starting to get run-down, and soon developed a severe case of the flu. After loading in, I felt terrible, so I tried to sleep underneath the monitor desk for an hour before the show. I struggled throughout the set and was nearly home and dry when Ben's guitar stopped working as he introduced the last song.
The lead from the guitar to the amplifier was checked. No problems. I also checked the amplifier. Working fine. I checked every lead on the pedalboard. All were working fine. Pedalboard to guitar. Amp to speaker. Guitar to pedalboard and still nothing.
I knelt there at the front of the stage, dripping in ice-cold influenza sweat as Ben showed little mercy, shouting…

"For fuck's sake man! Hurry up, it's the last song."

At that moment, I slipped into a dream-like state of delirium and was struck by a moment of realisation…

What the fuck am I doing this for?
I've sold more records than these cunts.

I was about to stand up and walk off the tour when I thought I'd just try one last thing. I reached up and twisted his guitar volume switch from '0' to '10'. The silly bugger had forgotten to turn his guitar up.

The sound engineer Ian Horne later dubbed it 'Pilot error'.

On the way to another show a heated debate broke out in the back of the bus when someone let slip that singer/songwriter Ben Gallagher had received a publishing advance. The standard band writing/publishing argument then ensued.

"So we all have to get the bus to rehearsal while Ben turns up in a Porsche?"

"Why shouldn't we all have an equal slice of the cake?"

As the argument escalated and tempers flared, I was told to stop on the hard shoulder of the motorway so they could 'sort this out'. Once the handbags were over and everyone had calmed down, the stony silence aboard the bus was broken when drummer Casper piped up with a classic thick skin beater quote:

"Well, I write my drums."

Island Records dropped them after one album.

Alan Price and The Animals had a similar dispute over the royalties from 'House Of The Rising Sun'. The song is an old traditional American folk song, but the original writer is unknown. Price put his own name on it as an 'arranger' and was therefore credited with the royalties from The Animals' classic version.
Singer Eric Burdon was willing to forget about the past and asked him if he was ready to start sharing future royalties for it.

"When he refused, that was the last time I ever spoke to him," said Burdon.

Nick Marsh from Flesh for Lulu used to employ this argument:

"If Rembrandt paints a picture, he doesn't put the names of the people who mixed the paint and provided the canvas in the corner."

I did a short run of Alan Price's solo shows with his touring band. I knew it was going to be a high-octane rock 'n' roll tour when Alan asked me in a quiet voice:

"Hey Del, can you tell the driver not to go around any roundabouts too fast as we've all got bad backs."

In addition to Price's shows, I also started working for trip-pop pioneers Sneaker Pimps, who were touring to promote their new album Bloodsport. Kelli Dayton the original singer had already left so founder member Chris Corner had taken over lead vocals.

Songwriter Liam Howe had decided he didn't want to tour any more so drummer and chief peace negotiator Dave Westlake was trying desperately to hold the whole thing together. Liam showed up at a few shows and, after one late-night party on the tour bus, he decided to colour his face in with a black sharpie pen. Cosmic.

As part of a summer festival tour the Sneakers played at the historic Monza Grand Prix track near Milan, Italy. Monitor engineer Dan Bartley was a huge Formula One fan so he arranged with the promoter to take a lap around the track. From the front room of the VIP restaurant we had a good view of the starting grid so we crowded around the window to watch for his car. To our astonishment, he was standing on the track pretending to have a steering wheel and making engine noises with his lips.

Since he couldn't find a car, he'd decided to run around the circuit instead!

Earlier on that tour, guitarist and bass player Joe Wilson had walked out of the band. His bass parts were added to the hard drive recorder, but it didn't sound quite right, so Chris and Dave asked if I would stand in on bass guitar for a couple of songs. I was now stage managing, doing quick guitar changes, then picking up the bass and playing 'Kiro TV' and 'The Fuel' as the Sneakers Pimps' band and crew started to rapidly diminish.

The band were invited to play in Moscow so original keyboardist and writer Liam Howe decided that he was going to come along for 'this one'. When we arrived at Heathrow Terminal 5, the booking agent had booked 10 seats on British Airways, but Caroline, the band manager, had also reserved 10 seats, so we now had 20 seats for the 10 of us.

As usual for this band, we were bringing everything except the speaker cabinets and the studio sink so, on check-in, we got presented with an astronomical excess luggage bill. We argued we'd paid for two seats each so why couldn't we have twice the luggage allowance, which sort of made sense. This led to a huge standoff, so BA's check-in manager was summoned. The plane was about to leave so we caved in, paid the excess, and managed to make the flight in the nick of time.

Once we arrived in Moscow, we were booked to play the Sixteen Tons Club, named after a song by Tennessee Ernie Ford. The local promoter visited us backstage carrying a silver tray containing a large selection of local vodka shots of which it would have been rude not to partake in and, inevitably, the rest of the evening became a blur. I vaguely remember playing the bass guitar on stage while an unrehearsed Liam hammered away at the keyboards. We both stopped for a second, looked up, stared quizzically at each other and then dropped our heads simultaneously as we continued to perform the song in two completely different keys. At least the hard drive recorder was sober!

Different band - Different continent - Same incompetence!

CHAPTER 28 – DRUM AND DRUMMER

What's got three legs and a cunt?

A drum stool.

That's my favourite drummer joke. The Test Tubes have had a long line of temporary and stand-in drummers over the years. Once, we even tried out Stomp's co-creator, Luke Creswell. Luke told me a few years ago in the Dragon pub in Kemp Town in Brighton that he was glad I hadn't invited him to join the band, as he now had sold-out shows running simultaneously across the world and Stomp even has a street named after the show in New York City.

Young Dave Kent, at just 15 years old, was one of our first temporary skin beaters. We'd been booked to play a Rock Against Racism benefit at Brighton Art College, opening the show for Misty in Roots, a British roots reggae band. Dave turned up in the afternoon wearing a Nazi uniform thinking it was a Rock For Racism benefit, the bright red dinner jacket type. Misty were sitting around and jamming on a piano and smoking spliffs when a bemused Dave walked into the bar. As soon as they clapped eyes on him, they all fell about laughing and began giving him high-fives. I met Dave Kent again recently, at Glastonwick Festival in Lancing, and he swore to me that he'd written 'Fuck Off' in Biro above the swastikas!

Another brief drum riser dribbler was Gary Bacon. For some unknown reasons, he made his debut at a jazz festival in Munich. Jazz was invented in the late 19th century when someone went to the wrong note and declared 'Hey man. I meant to do that!'

We hadn't bothered to rehearse so I told Gary that I'd count him in and when my eyebrows went up to stop drumming and to start playing again when they went down. Unfortunately, I got pissed at the free bar and my eyebrows were all over the place.

That day, I'm sure we out-jazzed some of the jazzers.

A couple of tours followed but Gary continually complained about how much he hated it and how much he would have preferred to be at home reading the newspaper and watching Neighbours.

"I don't mind being helicoptered in and out for festivals but all this sitting around in a van for hours is doing my nut in."

He eventually stopped playing for us due to a custody battle with

Trapper over a fully grown woman.

The French city of Avignon is situated on the banks of the river Rhône and enclosed by mediaeval walls. Of more historical significance, it is also known as the Test Tube drummers' graveyard. This is where Ogs played his last ever show and Gary Bacon resigned. Ogs had been reluctant to commit to Trapper's French tour from the start because, immediately after the Avignon show, he was due to fly to Japan with the British acid jazz band, Incognito. After the show we were heading to the airport to drop him off when the ancient drummer's curse struck again...

Not for the first time on the tour, Trapper's VW camper van started to make strange noises before it ground to a halt on a small road in the middle of some marshland near the banks of the Rhône. The sky was pitch black, but we could see the airport lights on the horizon. Ogs was panic-stricken and convinced he was now going to miss his plane and, with it, his connection to Japan and the Incognito tour. Manically grabbing his bag and passport, he started running across the marshes toward the distant lights of the airport. Once he had vanished into the reeds, I started to imagine that he may never be heard of again and could end up living out his days in the swampy marshes as some sort of humanoid pile of vegetable matter, a half-slime, half-drummer hybrid. Later we learned that he got a ride to the airport from the support band... but I much preferred my fantastical version of events.

The cursed city was the site of many other disastrous Test Tube affairs, such as when our roadie Rik Smith had to fight off the whole audience with a beer garden table, or when Trapper lost his jacket containing his passport. Ogs, not wanting to drive back to look for it, preposterously declared...

"It was a shit passport anyway!" To which Trapper replied...

"Got me in and out countries, didn't it!"

"Only just!" concluded Ogs...

...bringing the ridiculous point-scoring drivel to an end.

After another show in Avignon, I was on my way to a party when I realised that the girl driving the car was completely out of it, driving on the wrong side of the road and going straight across roundabouts instead of around them. Would I be the next victim of the walled city? Eventually she lost control of the car and, as we skidded into a ditch, I saw every shit tour I'd ever done flash before my eyes.

Meanwhile… back at the hotel. Walnut was also being shat on by the universe, as the giant skinhead promoter burst into his room and confronted him…

"He stormed into my room and started demanding the keys to our van because his girlfriend had lost her handbag. They were accusing us of stealing it. Andi, our driver, and I are the only two people with a key and we both refused to give it to him. This was winding me right up so we had a big row, before they finally left. We thought it best to follow them down to the street in case they tried to damage or break into the van. At that point in the evening, Del had gone off to a party and no one knew where Peter was. Andi and I followed them out of my room and saw them talking to AD, who said we should open the van because the bloke was threatening Sam the French tour manager in another room saying if he couldn't have a look in the van, he was going to phone all his mates to come over to beat us up. He also mentioned one of them had a gun and would shoot Sam. This pissed me off even more so I reluctantly opened the back and told his girlfriend to 'go on then, have a good look.' I also shouted at her… 'YOU'RE GOING TO FEEL FUCKING STUPID WHEN YOU DON'T FIND ANYTHING. I PACKED THIS VAN PERSONALLY AND YOUR FUCKING BAG AIN'T IN THERE.' She started to look around, taking bags and guitars out, so I shouted at her again… 'YOU BETTER PUT EVERYTHING BACK EXACTLY HOW YOU FOUND IT.' Eventually, she was happy it wasn't there so I pushed her out of the way and started reloading. They then started becoming all friendly and calling us mates. Cheeky bastards. This place is called La Poistroquet in Avignon, France. If you're in a band, never play this place, it is a pile of shit. Do me a favour… torch the place! Just when I thought things couldn't get any worse, Del returned and said he'd been in a car crash. Luckily he was shaken, not stirred!"

There was one joyous occasion, on the way to Avignon, when Ogs stood up in the bus and farted in my face while trying to piss into a crisp packet! Ah – memories are made of this!

We'd hilariously started calling AD 'Beans'… But why?

The English breakfast drummers; Bacon, Ogs, and Beans.

So when Beans became toast (sorry), the question now presented itself…

Who was going to have the unfortunate pleasure of becoming the next Test Tubes drummer? Surely a Parisian harpist from the Scottish Symphony Orchestra would make a perfect punk rock drummer?

The artist formerly known as Christophe Saunière (no breakfast-related name?... shame... don't worry, I'm sure I'll think of something) told us he was a multi-instrumentalist like Prince so obviously, could also play the drums.

Croissant, I mean Christophe (stop now) was already a fan of the band and couldn't have looked anything less like Prince, so we gave him a shot. Christophe recalled the moment when he first became aware of Peter and the Test Tube Babies...

"The first time I saw the band, they were playing their very first gig in Paris in the early Eighties. I was half-sitting on stage, watching Del's fingers closely, my ears inches from the PA, resulting in me being deaf for an entire week!

I have been a fan ever since I heard the band on a local radio station and bought the 'Run Like Hell' single. This band was definitely something else for me: a combination of punk rock energy with great musicality (the funny lyrics were lost on me at the time since I couldn't understand a word...) When Del asked me to play the harp on 'The Final Nail' album (a compilation of rarities and singles,) I drove straight to Brighton from Paris.

After that, I became friends with the band, and Peter and I would see each other often because Peter had a girlfriend in Paris.

One evening in a pub, he asked me how well I knew the Test Tubes songs and began to quiz me by 'singing' only the drum parts. I got all the songs right and Peter bought me a pint. I didn't realise at that moment I'd just auditioned for the job as their drummer.

Next thing I know I'm playing Rostock Force Attack Festival for the first time: we were headlining in front of 10,000 East German punks and skinheads and when we played 'Elvis Is Dead', Colin from GBH climbed behind the drumkit and joined me in the chorus while Wattie from the Exploited was also on stage filming us with his brand-new video camera. So there I was: playing in a foreign country with my favourite band in front of a huge crowd, singing and sharing a mic with Colin, whilst being filmed by Wattie! Later on that night, I shared a taxi with Charlie Harper... it was a punk rock dream come true.

There's another great punk band I'm involved with, the Toy Dolls, and that's also partly thanks to Del as well. One day I was staying at Del's place and there was a gig that night at the Concorde with two American bands, The Dickies supported by US Bombs. The young guy at the door refused us entry and, as the gig was sold out, there was no way we could get in.

We walked back around the side of the venue where one of the players from US Bombs, with whom I had a chat earlier on the Calais-Dover ferry, recognised me and opened the backstage door to let us in.

So ironically I got in for free to a gig in Brighton, not because I was with the songwriter of the most famous band in the town but because an American dude recognised a French bloke from the channel crossing!

Once inside we were drinking and eating the band's catering when I noticed Olga, frontman of the Toy Dolls, who was playing bass with the Dickies at the time, alone in the corner.

Olga has said in many interviews that, for him, Del is the best guitar player ever.

So I went to speak to him and we had a fun evening! Later, I became friends with the Toy Dolls and did a few recordings for them but that's another story..."

I had begun working for a band called 'South' who were based in a studio in Camden Town. Joel Cadbury, Brett Shaw, and Jamie McDonald were three young, pot-smoking multi-instrumentalists from North London who made a huge sound. Initially mentored by ex-Stone Roses frontman Ian Brown, the band later worked with UNKLE's James Lavelle, who signed the band to his label Mo Wax. In 2000, they composed the soundtrack for 'Sexy Beast,' a film directed by Jonathan Glazer, starring Ray Winstone, Ben Kingsley and Ian McShane.

On 11th September 2001, just after 1:46pm BST, I got a call from Trapper.

"You're going to New York with South on Thursday, aren't you?"

"Yes, I am."

"I don't think you are, turn on the TV."

I ran downstairs and grabbed the remote just in time to see the second plane crash into the World Trade Center.

CHAPTER 29 – SHEEP WORRYING

In the year 2000, I turned 40.

London had become congested and overcrowded and was bursting at the seams. Parking was impossible, the traffic was always gridlocked and there were times on the Underground when you had to wait for two overcrowded trains to pass before you could squeeze on to a third. One sunny afternoon I took Liam, now two years old, to the children's play area in Queen's Park, only to discover that the sandpit was full and that we would have to wait in a line behind 10 other people to take a turn on the swings.

In Hanover Road, Walnut, who lived with us at the time, and I rarely ventured far, and would often end up around the corner in Maggie's Irish Bar in Kensal Rise for the free six o'clock Irish stew. You could live like that anywhere... but with the added bonus of breathable fresh air.

Taking all this into consideration we decided to sell up and move back to Brighton where I'd partied away my teenage years. The then town of Brighton – it became Brighton & Hove city in 2001 - was always full of fun and diversity with a thriving gig culture and many Irish and punk rock pubs such as The Windsor, The Buccaneer and the Green Dragon in Sydney Street. As the years rolled by, the smaller sleepier venues could no longer afford the new mega rents of the greedy corporate landlords so they got pushed away from the town centre and into the suburbs to make way for homogenised crappy pre-club pubs, after work drinkeries, and commercial coffee shops.

It's the same everywhere in the UK, towns and cities have become shells of their former character, you could be helicopter-dropped into any city centre, be it Leeds, Sheffield, Portsmouth, Belfast, Glasgow... Remove your blindfold, take a 360-degree scan and you wouldn't know which location you were in. Among the boarded-up family businesses, you'll now find big-name conglomerate clones. McDonald's, Burger King, Boots, WH Smith, Barclays, Subway, Starbucks, Costa... all the same corporate shit, generic and gentrified.

We chose a Victorian terraced house in the Hanover area, also known as Muesli Mountain because of all the hippies and alternative people who lived in the neighbourhood. 38 Hendon Street was located in Bakers Bottom below the famous Brighton Racecourse and was built in the mid-1800s to accommodate railway workers constructing the new London to Brighton line.

During our time in Alhaurin, Rachael enjoyed horse-riding and had even won a few races, much to the annoyance of the macho, chauvinistic locals. As soon as she arrived in her new hometown, she took a job at Brighton Racecourse. One night, while chatting with Phil Bell, the racecourse manager, he asked her what her husband did for a living. He was impressed to learn that I was a member of Peter and the Test Tube Babies because his favourite album of all time was 'The Mating Sounds Of South American Frogs'. Phil gave me a VIP membership badge so I could get in for free and use the exclusive members' lounge on race days. He also suggested I enter a 'Test Tube Babies Sweepstakes' into the racing programme and gave me the complimentary use of the racecourse for my 40th birthday party.

I set up a stage, invited everyone I knew, and did what I had to do - not in a shy way – I sang 'My Way' with tribute act the Sussex Pistols!

Back at work, the 'South' shows had been rescheduled for November, two months after the 9/11 attacks so, as soon as we arrived in New York we hurried down to Lower Manhattan to do some rubbernecking at the World Trade Center. The smell of burnt rubber and plastic permeated the air with the tables and chairs in the local bars still covered in fine concrete dust. Unsurprisingly, Ground Zero was completely sealed off, so we went on a pub crawl instead, ending up in Hell's Kitchen at Al Capone, Frank Sinatra, and my own favourite local dive bar, Rudy's Bar and Grill. (Hic!)

From the city that never sleeps to the city that annoyingly closes at 2am. On February 2nd, 2002, Tony Hawk's 20th anniversary surprise party was held in Long Beach, California. Organised by Birdhouse Skateboards, a company that makes decks and wheels, a marquee had been erected and decked out in style for a celebrity party on the grounds of the Hyatt Hotel. When Tony was a young lad, he had attended his first punk concert when The Adicts and the Test Tubes both performed at The Grand Olympic Auditorium venue in southern downtown Los Angeles. Birdhouse had therefore booked both bands to perform at the party.

We were treated like kings by the Birdhouse team, with a sushi chef and a bottle of Jack Daniel's the size of a small child adorning our huge rider. At the end of the show, Tony Hawk and the Test Tubes joined forces with The Adicts to perform a rousing rendition of 'Leader Of The Gang'. Ground-breaking then, but now painfully dated!

The morning after the show, Peter planned to fly to South America and was looking forward to receiving some US dollars to spend in Brazil. This was the point when what had been a fantastic evening took a nasty turn. At the after-party, the guy from Birdhouse came to the dressing room and gave Peter a cheque for $5,000. Peter went ballistic and flew into a rage shouting that a cheque was no fucking good to him. (I mean, did he really expect someone to be walking around an LA party with $5,000 in cash in a suitcase?) One of his idiot American hangers-on then threatened to get a gun from his car unless they paid Peter in cash. It was all too embarrassing, especially after how well they had treated us. I pulled Rachael away as she tried to get involved as the dispute escalated and we went off to enjoy the party somewhere else. Returning to the dressing room a while later, the stand-off was still going strong. Rachael got sucked into the argument again, as various people volunteered to visit a number of nearby ATMs to get Peter's precious holiday money. A friend of mine who works in the computer gaming industry once told me:

"Computer games are now outselling music CDs. If you got one of your songs on a Tony Hawk's video game soundtrack, you'll never have to work again."

Back to work on Monday it is then.

Christophe returned to Paris and Peter flew to Sao Paulo with his partner Corrine as planned. We spent the remainder of our trip in Los Angeles with some friends, Craig and Lori Kapner, along with their two sons Clay and Curtis. The first few days were spent going into Birdhouse Skateboards with our tails between our legs, trying to get the cheque reissued in Lori's name so we could put it through her US Wells Fargo checking account. Lori worked for Walt Disney so she kindly arranged some free tickets to Disneyland for us where Rachael got Minnie Mouse's autograph. Score!

After a wonderful week as guests of the Kapners, we said goodbye to LA and the California sunshine and headed to the northernmost part of Scotland, the Shetland Islands. Brrrr!
We flew British Airways, changing to a smaller plane in Aberdeen, during which H noticed comedian Ronnie Corbett collecting his golf clubs from the carousel.

"Hey, Ronnie, coming to see the Test Tubes in the Shetlands this weekend?"

"Certainly not!" came his short sharp reply.

With an aerial view of the dramatic cliffs, rolling seas and tumbling hills, it was an awe-inspiring approach to the islands. Jeff Ampleforth, the promoter and local taxi driver, picked us up at Sumburgh Airport and explained how gigs used to be impossible in Lerwick because they had to hire a sound system from the mainland and have it shipped over to the island at great expense. However, a few organised individuals, including Jeff, had got together with the Shetland Arts Council to put in a lottery bid. They were now the proud owners of a £32,000 P.A. system.

Dr Nigel Hindley, who ran our first website, decided to join us on the islands and reviewed the trip on the website blog:

"What the hell was I doing going to the Shetland Islands at my own expense to see Peter and the Test Tube Babies play just two dates? Perhaps it's because I love the band. I located Del, Walnut and Christophe in the nearest local pub, it had been called 'The Martlet' I think but had since changed its name. Due to a severe case of over-generosity on the part of the British Airways' trolley dollies, it wouldn't have been pushing it too far to say that the lads were well oiled by the time I saw them. Needless to say, the conversation wasn't one of the most intellectual of all time, but I enjoyed the evening anyway. The conversation with the barmaid (Jackie) was rather amusing:

Del: 'Where are we?'

Jackie: 'Here.'

Del: 'Where's here?'

Jackie: 'Well if you don't know where 'here' is, you're obviously too drunk to be served.'

We then went on to another pub, Captain Flint's, where we spent the remainder of the evening. On Friday we played at the Norscot Angling Club in Lerwick and on Saturday at Lunnasting Hall in Vidlin. Both shows were well attended even though I was sure it was mostly the same people at both shows. While 90% of the Norscot audience quite obviously had a whale of a time, there were one or two whose motivation for attending seemed a little questionable. In particular, there were some people on a table in front of me who seemed to grimace all the way through the show and were quite obviously offended by some of Peter's comments. Now those who know the Test Tubes' shows would hardly be surprised at the banter, but I really did wonder why these people had actually turned up? It wasn't the kind of venue that you could have accidentally arrived at and stranger still, the gig had been advertised all over the islands (shops helpfully obliging everywhere, thanks), with full-size 'Final Nail' posters (Peter nailed to a cross). Now I can't speak for other people, but you might have thought perhaps that any band advertising gigs with pictures of a mock crucifixion on Brighton Beach were hardly going to extol the virtues of good Christian living at one of their shows? During the Lunnasting Hall concert, I was aware of a couple sitting next to the merch table virtually from the start of the gig. They seemed to be enjoying themselves quietly and I wouldn't have given them a second glance but for the fact I noticed the guy was very heavily built. During the encore, the band launched into 'Elvis Is Dead' at which point our muscular friend went ballistic, hammering on the table to get my attention, bellowing something along the lines of the following in my face. 'Elvis was the King of rock 'n' roll, fuck you, you fucking cunts' and other such choice words. Needless to say, as the nearest (and unfortunately only accessible) 'representative' of the band, I copped for the lot. The last I saw of him; he was being led off by his wife, still uttering 'Fuck off back to England you fucking English twats.' Who said freedom of speech was dead?"

Jeff, the promoter's brother, told me he was determined to prove to the world that Shetland Islanders were the first people to discover America. To demonstrate this fact he was building a boat to sail the Atlantic. He explained his theory that if the vessel was constructed from a very rare type of wood from a special tree, the ship would be able to propel itself across the ocean without the need for energy or manpower.
On the Saturday afternoon before the show, he gave me a guided tour. It was a pretty impressive vessel and when he opened the door to the galley it was packed to the brim with provisions for the expedition… crates of Tennent's Super lager and multiple packets of curry-flavour Super Noodles. He also proclaimed that each year, after the sheep had eaten the first batch of freshly sprouted magic mushrooms, they would develop the ability to speak both English and Old Norse!
Jeff's house had an attic where H, Walnut, and I were staying. We went to bed as the all-night party raged on downstairs, but a giant hairy Viking kept climbing up the loft ladder, trying to get into the attic. He was impervious to our barrage of shoes and boots and at one point H put his foot on the ascending hairball advising the would-be intruder:

"Fuck off! You can't come up here, we're trying to sleep."

The growling Viking zombie continued to try to force its head through the hatch like a scene from cult horror classic 'The Evil Dead'.

The blonde lady who drove the only bus in Lerwick (the No.1) was at the all-night party and at both shows. In the morning, Walnut, H and I decided to hit a few pubs in town, so we walked up to the bus stop. As the No.1 pulled up, there she was again, smiling behind the wheel after no sleep.

Travelling through Scotland we stopped at a pub for lunch, where Peter ordered burger and chips. While Peter was in the toilet his burger and chips arrived so Christophe thought it would be a hilarious wizard jape to hide Peter's burger. On returning from the bathroom, he was (inevitably) furious. Christophe sensed his rage and quickly put the burger back on his plate, but it was too late, he had stepped on a landmine. Peter had a Chernobyl-style nuclear meltdown, yelling that he wasn't eating the meal now because Christophe's filthy French hands had been all over it. Rather than let it go to waste, Walnut quickly stuffed down the burger, while the rest of us steamed into the chips. Christophe, eager to make amends, went to the bar and queued up to buy our hungry and harassed lead singer another burger and chips, only to find out they had stopped serving food.

This incident later came to be known as 'Burgergate' and Christophe quickly learned that no man, especially a drummer, should ever come between Peter and his food. That heralded the beginning of the end for the French maestro, and he was subsequently moved 'upstairs' (a term meaning to give someone a job or position that appears to have a higher status but instead has less power and influence). While 'upstairs', Christophe would help with song arrangements on the next record if we ever got round to making one.

Christophe later reflected on his fall from grace:

"Drumming with the band came to an end for various reasons. Of course there was the infamous 'Burgergate' incident but I think the main reason was that I was living in Paris and the extra cost of flying me over each time there was a British club show wasn't worth it. Del once told me I 'played the songs exactly like the recordings' so I took that as a compliment at the time but now I realise, with hindsight, it might have been one of his sarcastic time bombs. Anyway, I was moved upstairs, whatever that meant? I actually wrote several songs with Peter (which were never used!) and a few years later Del asked me to contribute to arranging more songs, so my story with the band continues…"

Future Test Tubes drummer Dave O'Brien recalled seeing this line-up live in Brighton:

"I saw an advert for an upcoming gig in Brighton... the Dead Kennedys with support from Peter and the Test Tube Babies. Crikey, it was 20 years since that teenage experience of excitement, this would be very interesting. That night a very different Test Tubes took to the stage than the band I had witnessed 20 years previously. New bass player H stared at his shoes and, like a Shakin' Stevens tribute called 'Stationary Stevens', he barely moved a muscle, giving a showcase performance in his stagecraft specialty of making the most exciting event appear mundane. His solid playing, however, gave the band its only musical anchor that night, even if that anchor was being dragged across featureless sand, unable to find anything solid on which to gain a grip. In 1981, drummer Ogs had filled my teenage self with inspiration, lurching from fast and powerful punk rock to even faster and tight as fuck disco-funk grooves, how were the band going to top that? They weren't. New guy Christophe Saunière, despite being head and shoulders above the rest of the band in terms of technical musicianship and being a fine and respected orchestral harp player, put in a lacklustre performance as a drummer in a once exciting punk band. He played in perfect time although his 'feel' was always a little behind the beat, never pushing or changing the dynamics. The drummer is supposed to be 'driving the bus', poor old Christophe was being run over by it. Zut Alors!... nil points!

Strangefish was a total mess, his eyes swivelling drunkenly in his head as he invoked the spirit of Les Dawson and, like Eric Morecambe in that hilarious, famous André Previn comedy sketch, played all the right notes in all the wrong places. Del's arms seemed to hang loosely from his shoulders, the clumsy, cauliflower-like growths that had once been his hands twitching over the strings in a hopeless effort to reveal his deeply concealed talent. This was a man giving his best ever performance... if he had been performing in a drinking competition.

Overseeing the whole sorry affair was a furious looking Mr Bywaters, the skinny and cheeky young man with a hilarious quip to cover every mistake of his old band had now been 'replaced' by a corpulent schoolmaster jaded by the years, his sense of humour a thing of the past. Like a confused ringmaster whose circus animals were floundering and misbehaving, he failed to keep the show together. Instead of covering the disaster with jokey remarks and acid wit as he once might have, he said barely a word between numbers and betrayed the whole debacle to the audience by overtly staring daggers at his hapless guitar player.

At the end of the evening, Peter asked me what I thought, and I replied that the Dead Kennedys were still absolutely brilliant after all these years but you lot were shit. I explained to Peter that Christophe just didn't seem to fit the bill as a punk rock drummer... 'He's got no oomph' I said. Peter must have cogitated upon that.

A couple of weeks later I got a call from him:

'You fancy a weekend in Rimini?'
(You fancy a weekend rimming me?)
'What do you mean?'
'Rimini in Italy.'
'Doing what?'
'I'd like to try you out as our drummer.'
'I don't think Tracy would be thrilled if I fuck off to Italy.'
'Bring her along.'"

Dave continues...

"*I'd been a founding member of a dodgy heavy metal band called the Masked Raiders. After that, Del was playing the drums for Walnut and the Wankers. Peter and Walnut wanted to do more Wankers gigs, but Del was too busy. So I played drums for them for a while. Now I was being pulled into an ever-closer orbit to all things Test Tube. Given the size of Peter's constantly expanding stomach and the gravity field it generated, it was a pretty hard orbit to resist.*
I was now about to be sucked past that orbit and screaming towards the centre of the black hole known as Peter and the Test Tube Babies."

Your mission, Dave, should you choose to accept it, is to stay sober enough during the day to be able to play the drums at night.
As always, should you be caught or killed, we will disavow any knowledge of your actions.
This chapter will self-destruct in 10 seconds.
Good luck, Dave.

CHAPTER 30 – A FOOT FULL OF BULLETS

Incoming!

My mother-in-law, Greta, was staying overnight at our house as Rachael was about to give birth. In the middle of the night, her waters broke (Rachael's not Greta's) so I phoned the hospital in Brighton to let them know we were on our way. Alarmingly, I was informed that they were now closed and that they had no midwives or staff on hand.
Greta grabbed the phone and yelled:

"You had better open up and find some staff because my daughter is coming in... NOW!"

On the day before Bonfire Night, we were the only couple on the 13th-floor, Labour Ward of the Royal Sussex County Hospital. The evening sky was alight with fireworks as Sean Lawrence Greening entered the world. I always wanted two boys, so I could have one on each end of the stretcher as I'm carried out of the pub at closing time!

The Test Tubes' rags to even fewer rags story continued as Paul 'H' Henrickson (bass) and 'Caveman' Dave O'Brien (drums) received sentences of 17 and 12 years respectively, to be served consecutively in HMP Peter and the Test Tube Babies - some of the great train robbers got less!
Dave came as a package deal with the saintly Tracy - or 'Mother Theracy' as I used to call her - who became our driver, merchandiser and carer for the next 12 years. Dave had previously sung and played drums in an anarcho-punk band called Flatpig whereas H was an old regular Brighton drinking buddy, who had played in a host of lost failed local bands, including Bone Orchard and Killer Gorilla. Once, Danny Bell and I almost formed a band with H called 'We Disagree', but we could never agree on when or where to rehearse.

H recalled one of the first tours with Dave in the band.

"I remember our van was off the road so Austin, the guitarist from Dave's other band, Flatpig, had very kindly lent us his for the weekend. 'Little' Mark, or 'One Way' Mark was driving and had been newly nicknamed due to his inability to drive home the next day, still being too inebriated from the night before. The journey from Brighton to Bristol isn't supposed to be a long one but, due to some superb map-reading skills by Peter, we took an exciting new route via Glastonbury, which took hours.

He was supposed to be navigating but had fallen asleep. When he woke up, he made us do a complete U-turn and head for Honiton, completely the wrong way. Of course, this wasn't his fault as we 'never had a sniff of the M4', he moaned. We eventually found the venue in time for soundcheck."

Dave described that first 'professional' soundcheck…

"Once we'd set up the gear, it was immediately obvious that the sound engineer was some kind of a cunt. He had emptied out every lead in his array of equipment on the floor and, despite his panic-stricken rummaging, was getting nowhere near setting up the sound system. Over an hour later, the bumbling incompetent fool still didn't have so much as one mic stand ready on stage. This must be the sort of thing that drives a band to serious drinking, as they try to blot out the monotony of hanging around. When the 'set up' was finally complete he actually managed to get us a good sound on stage and I began to think he might not be such a twat after all, but I was soon to revert to my earlier opinion.

Back at the guest house, we were given a warm welcome by the 'Carry On' comedy-style landlady who said that she was learning to play the organ and needed some musical tutoring. Del showed her a few chords but I'm sure she was more interested in other types of organs of a non-musical nature. A few pints were sunk in the tiny bar and then it was off to do the show. Our worst fears about the soundman were confirmed as we were immediately deafened by the onslaught of feedback, the onstage sound bearing no resemblance to the levels that were set in the so-called 'soundcheck'. How can people make a living from being so fucking hopeless at their chosen task? The audience was appreciative but I pitied them for having to put up with such a bad sound after parting with their cash."

H continues...

"The next show was at Panama Joe's in Barnsley where Del laughingly described the city centre as 'a boxing ring with a Christmas tree in the middle.' Our mate Scoffa turned up at the gig with his kids, so we had extra backing vocals and more kids on stage than a McBusted concert. The next day we declined breakfast and went to Wetherspoons for a hair of the dog, where Del spotted my doppelgänger. This bloke had the same coat, baseball cap and features as me except he was about 100 years old. Del had even shouted 'H' at him in the street, thinking it was me. Plenty of 'old H' jokes ensued then it was off to London. After several liveners, sharpeners and some pharmaceuticals, we pulled a good show out of the hat. We played at 10pm as we had to race across London for our second show of the night at our mate Mark Belkin's 40th birthday party at a *studio in Islington. We had soundchecked earlier in the afternoon, which contributed to the 'crew's revolt'. Little Mark and Walnut had been led to believe that, as they were working two gigs, they would receive two days' wages. Del and I thought a day's work gets a day's pay. There was a 12-kilowatt P.A. rig so it was mega-loud! Great party, and only one punch-up! As Mark is a paramedic, there were plenty of hospital bods about. Very convenient in case I had a heart attack, would have been defibrillated in no time! Mark, the birthday boy, sang on 'The Jinx' (didn't know when to come in) and 'Banned From The Pubs' (bit out of time) and I think he really enjoyed himself.*

After the overpaid crew loaded up, we headed to Northampton for some kip. We had two rooms booked at a Travelodge where a classic urine-related disaster took place. I had wisely shared a room with Del, Walnut and Lil' Mark. Dave and his new wife Tracy, Dan and Peter were in the other room. During the night, Peter awoke to see a shadowy figure looming over him, knob in hand! Pete thought Dave was fucking about until the stream of piss hit him in the chest!! Chin isn't keen on watersports at the best of times, but he didn't even get the chance to squat in the shower! I do feel sorry for Dave, 'cos we'd all had a skinful and it wasn't deliberate. Much 'piss taking' went on from that point. Chin took it very well, but all conversations were kind of wee related and Dave looked rather sheepish, but hey, it's so punk rock and what's a bit of piss between mates. Ogs' crown as the Prince of Pissers was now Dave's.

At the show, Damp Dave played a blinder - Pete had asked him earlier 'are you going to sober up today?' - while our fancy-dress stalker chick invaded the stage. She was wearing a schoolgirl outfit this time and, for some reason, likes to pour mineral water down her knickers while frantically dancing, all very embarrassing."

During the soundcheck at the Night Owl Rock Club in Cheltenham, the owner told us that The Jimi Hendrix Experience had once played there. Chinese punk band 'The Noname' were opening for us on that tour and their guitarist was so moved he burst into tears. Instead of kissing the sky he fell to his knees and kissed the dirty dusty old stage after hearing Jimi had once trod those boards.

Later that night, Caveman Dave and I got extremely hammered at the after-show disco, dancing like idiots and hurling each other into other clubbers who were trying their best to enjoy their evening. At the end of the night, the two of us had a few more 'topshelfers' at the bar and then decided to try and find the hotel. No such luck. We wandered around aimlessly, not knowing where it was or what it was called. Eventually, we wound up back at the club after going round in a circle. After much fumbling and bumbling, Dave discovered that he had Tracy's spare key to the back of the van, so we decided to sleep in there with the equipment.

In the early hours of the morning, I dreamt condensation was dripping on me – or was it raining and the van was leaking? I eventually awoke to droplets of what I thought was water, splashing against my face. I was horrified to discover it was, in fact, Dave, still completely out of it having a piss over the equipment. So that was Peter and myself, Dave now just needed H to complete his rack of urinated-upon Test Tubes.

At another soundcheck I couldn't hear H's bass parts so I went over to check out his set-up. The bass guitar and amplifier were working fine so we restarted the song but again still no bass? I looked across again and soon determined that he was strumming away in mid-air without making any contact with the strings. American jazz trumpeter Miles Davis once famously declared...

"It's not the notes you play, it's the notes you don't play."

But not playing any? Genius perhaps?

As a result, H earned the new nickname 'None of Four' (strings) after Star Trek's Borg character 'Seven of Nine'.

A new Test Tubes record was long overdue so, back on the golf course in Germany, Henry was striking up another earth-moving, money-losing record deal, this time with Chris Boltendahl from Locomotive Records. Chris also sang with Eighties German metal band Grave Digger. His keyboard player, Hans Peter 'HP' Katzenburg, also worked as a filmmaker and helped produce 'Paralitico', our follow-up movie to 'Cattle And Bum'. You can read more about our trip to the Oscars in the next book!

In contrast to the glitter of Hollywood, the sleepy village of Ford in West Sussex is most famously known for its men's open prison. In the summer of 2005, we began recording 'A Foot Full Of Bullets' at Ford Lane Studios on a farm. The engineer on this project was the always helpful and enthusiastic Rob Quickenden. 'Bullets' was an arduous record to make as Rob and I would have to start early in the morning and work long hours. Peter's marriage was breaking down so it was difficult to get him enthusiastic about the project and there were lots of heavy sighs and cries of *"What's the point?"* to deal with. Each night, as I drove home from the studio, I dropped CDs of the latest mixes through his letterbox, hoping for some kind of positive feedback or opinion. They never came – I doubt he even listened to them. Dave was a builder, and H a painter and decorator so they managed to wangle just enough time off work to come in to do their parts. One day I ended up getting drunk and missed the last train home. Rob wouldn't let me sleep in the studio, so I had to drive the van along the A27 pissed out of my head while squinting out of one eye.

Don't do it kids. (Make a punk record that is!)

Back in the studio, I was recording some guitar when the owner walked in with a potential customer, a young guitarist and his father. I was fiddling around with a wah-wah pedal when the kid offered to show me how to get the best sound out of it. He started playing and I secretly recorded him, then just used his parts on the track. I have no idea who he was and I guess he'll never know he ended up featuring on the album.

We had started working on a new track called 'Distorted View' in which Dave, H and I were each going to sing a verse, with Peter taking the choruses later. In the evening, Walnut and Little Mark popped in, and, after downing two flagons of cider, were cajoled into shouting at the beginning and end of the song. Walnut sang:

"I resign. Fuck off!" (Soon after, he did just that.)

Little Mark, mistakenly shouted:

"Get the train or get the fucking train."

He probably meant to sing 'Get in the van or get the fucking train', but as the former brilliantly made no sense, I refused to let him do a retake.

We hadn't seen or heard from Peter since he came in to lay down some guide vocals, so he was yet to hear 'Distorted View' and remained unaware of its existence. Later we snuck it into the live set without telling him and, as the beat kicked in, he grabbed the mic without knowing any of the lyrics and shouted along anyway, confidently putting his foot on the monitor while giving us all a confused side-eye. Textbook!

Here's how 'All Music' rated that album:

"These perennial UK punk rockers are still resolutely ploughing the same furrow they began in the early 1980s, which says much both for their stamina and their loyal following. Though their sound has tightened considerably since the days of their first single, 1982's 'Banned From The Pubs', their preoccupation with drinking and drinking establishments has

continued, as witnessed by the raucous 'Driven To Beers', the lachrymose 'Ye Olde Pub Rocker' and the joyful 'Still Love The Pub', proof they haven't forgotten their punk roots supplied by the scathing 'Haves And Have Nots'."

Since the addition of Dave and H, the band dynamics had changed with the drinking and partying getting ramped up to the max. We could play the songs with intense power and dynamism, but resisting a drink during those tedious early hours of poorly arranged travel, produced some outrageously bad shows as Dave recounts here:

"Alcohol has played a constant role both for good and bad in this band, titles such as 'Soberphobia' and 'Pissed And Proud' are forever etched in punk's history (or perhaps on its tombstone), but some of the most awful performances have been alcohol-related. Del and I became drinking partners and were often the 'naughty boys' of the band, rolling onstage too drunk to play properly and leaving poor old Peter to play the role of an angry schoolmaster, a role for which I am sure he would have never willingly auditioned. However awful and embarrassing those times were, I treasure hundreds of bleary memories, including being naked at the front of the stage in Kiel while Peter smeared my genitals in mustard, and of laying underneath Del while he dropped his trousers in Paris and I played his bollocks with my drumsticks. I guess I should have been playing the drums but I think the audience was just as entertained."

One show at the Corner Flag pub in Rushden was particularly poor, as reflected in Dave's journal on the band's webpage:

"Instead of doing the decent thing and maintaining my commitment to playing music reasonably sober, I continued to imbibe throughout the day with consequences that were tragic indeed. We arrived at the venue in the pouring rain and loaded in the equipment hastily before settling down to a few more pints. After the soundcheck we made haste to a different pub, lest we were subjected to having to listen to the support band and I began to realise that I was very, very drunk indeed. In order to clear my head back at the venue, I had a few more pints and sensibly smoked a pipe of crack - big mistake!

With my musical ability suitably enhanced, I took to the stage and played like a cunt, my only memory is being unable to hold down the simplest of rhythms. Amazingly, the crowd wanted more of this inept rubbish, the rest of the band must have been great 'cos I was most certainly shite, so the encore was performed to a welcoming audience. If only I had left it at that. Instead of doing the decent thing and fucking right off I went back on stage alone, the rest of them sensibly deciding not to join me. There isn't much you can do as a drummer without any other musicians, especially when the treasured and expensive drum kit is lying all around the stage where I trashed it like a silly wanker, so I told some crap jokes (my wasps got no nose). I then put the kit back together (ish) and performed a tragically incompetent drum solo. If only I had left it at that. Having run out of material for this pitiful one-man show I decided to get my knob out, the organ in question was horribly shrivelled as I was so out of it, therefore, out of embarrassment I shall not include that incident in this journal. This performance guaranteed that I was awarded the coveted 'Toffee Legs' award for the worst cringe of the weekend. Little Mark then kindly drove me home where I unloaded the drums before being reminded that I was still on tour so they had to be loaded back on the van. Further proof of my intellectual sophistication."

At the end of the night, as Dave and Walnut tried to piece together what was left of the drum kit, I attempted to escape from the gig, navigating my way through the crowd towards the exit with my hood up to avoid being recognised and associated with the embarrassing debacle that had just taken place. As I passed the merchandise stand, a hand shot out from the crowd and tightly gripped my arm. Expecting an angry request for a refund, I was surprised to hear a voice exclaim...

"Del, that was FUCKING amazing!"

While we're all in a confessional mood, my worst show fuck-up, or finest hour, depending on your capacity to maintain a sense of humour, occurred in the Test Tubes' calamity capital of Europe, Paris. We'd played the previous night's gig at the Mondo Bizarro club in Rennes, Brittany, a lovely little rock 'n' roll venue once owned and run by a dear friend of ours, Bruno. Following a solid performance to a sold-out crowd, we took full advantage of Bruno's generosity at the bar. We were knocking back traffic lights, red, yellow and green shots of God knows what well into the early hours before we somehow managed to stumble back to the hotel and crash out. About an hour later, I was rudely awoken by the maid wanting to clean my room…

"Allez, allez, le temps d'aller, il est huit heures, nous devons la chambre." Roughly translated… *"Get Out!"*

Nevertheless, still completely out of my mind, I managed to navigate my way out of the hotel and into the sunshine of a pretty square dotted with small cafés. For the next few hours, I sat outside a bar and continued drinking. That night we were headlining La Pena Festayre in Porte de la Villette so we needed to catch a train to Paris. Mother Theracy wasn't with us this time so Dave's replacement carer, Steve Potts, dashed off to get a few bottles to pass the time on the journey. After guzzling a few pints of wine on the train, we arrived at the indoor festival in Paris and entered a dark dingy dressing room behind the stage. In an even darker corner, a couple of shady-looking characters were doing drugs. I thought to myself, there's absolutely no way I can play in this state, so as any self-loathing human wreck would do… I indulged, eventually badgering a line from them. We then hit the stage to begin our 'performance'. The effects of the drugs were swift and brutal. I started to feel strange, not the usual coke buzz I was expecting, but more like I had been hit square on the jaw by Mike Tyson. About three songs into the set, my brain shut down leaving my body to fend for itself. Both my arms went numb and my legs turned to jelly before I finally lost consciousness and in true Looney Tunes-style, stumbled ass-backwards into the drum kit, rolling down the stairs back into the dressing room with my guitar still around my neck.

Walnut found a wooden chair and tried to get me to play sitting down, but I continued to drift in and out of consciousness. As a result of the language differences, the darkness, and my drunkenness, I had failed to realise that the line I had snorted before the show was grade A heroin and not cocaine at all.

Allez Oops!

CHAPTER 31 – TOMBOLA TIME

During another particularly bleak midwinter shit British tour, the Test Tubes arrived at the Leicester Charlotte, a pub and concert venue on the edge of the city centre, opposite De Montfort University. While we were waiting for the soundman to come and unlock the mixing desk, (a pastime that became known as 'padlock staring' by those of us in the band who hated getting to venues early) I started flicking through a discarded newspaper and came across an article reporting that George Michael had been taken into custody for 'engaging in a lewd sexual act' in a public restroom. It went on to mention that since the news of his arrest, his record sales had increased dramatically. As Peter emerged from the dressing room toilet, I offered up a suggestion…

"Why don't YOU go and have a wank in a public toilet, then we might be able to shift some more albums?"

"Just had one," came the reply.

Finally we can move on as a species.

The non-stop-out-of-control freak show rolled on with the 'Foot Full Of Bullets European Tour'. Traditionally, at the end of each Christmas tour, we would have what came to be known as 'The Tombola'. A competition where all the leftover bottles of spirits from the rider would be raffled off between Henry, the band and the crew. In an effort to add some much-needed interest to the tour, I suggested getting rid of 'The Tombola' and having everyone take turns creating their own cocktail of choice as 'guest bartenders' for the evening. Peter brought a book of cocktail recipes and Tracy packed her shaker set. Strap in.

On the opening night, I announced that my cocktail for the evening was going to be a Woo Woo, a drink made from vodka, peach schnapps and cranberry juice. I foolishly imagined an evening of sophistication and articulation while sipping and savouring delicious home-made cocktails. However, I was rapidly reminded to steer clear of my own ideas, as the plan blew up in my face.

Filled with dread and fear of missing out on their share, everyone greedily guzzled as much as they could. Between songs, Dave sat behind the drumkit gulping it straight down from the mixing jug.

That night he woke up covered in his own piss after wetting the bed on the tour bus and, in an attempt to cover his embarrassment, he hatched a cunningless plan to swap his bedding with the spare bunk. Due to his delirium, he hadn't noticed Walnut, H and I were storing our bags there and, on waking, we discovered that all our clothes and belongings had been emptied out on to his stinking, piss-soaked mattress.

After the horrendous soul-destroying 'Alien Pubduction US Tour' of '98, we decided to try a new way of touring America – by flying to every gig. What could possibly go right? The first problem was, to get to the airport on time we had to be up at 7am every day (about an hour before we planned to go to bed). I remember H getting lost at one of the multi terminals. I eventually found him, frozen like a rabbit in the headlights, amongst hundreds of zigzagging commuters rushing to make their connections.

When we arrived in New England we were picked up by a uniformed driver in a limousine. Fantastic we thought, finally the recognition we didn't deserve. When we got in, we found all the bar optics were empty, there was no alcohol on board at all, and the sunroof was leaking water on Dave's head. I viewed this as a microcosm of the rest of the United States in general. Shiny on the outside but dark and decrepit on the inside. I also find this to be true when you check into a hotel. You have an over-friendly, top-hatted concierge, a $50,000 antique chandelier hanging in the lobby and a guy in a tuxedo playing a grand piano in the corner. On entering your room, you discover you can't open the window and the wallpaper is hanging off.

The limo driver dropped us off at the hotel, where we dragged our bags up the steps ourselves, to avoid having to pay a tip. When we tried to check in, the receptionist had never heard of us so we dashed back outside, but the limo driver had driven off and no one had taken his number. After much blame-throwing, moaning, and phoning, we tracked down the promoter only to find (thankfully) that we had been dropped off at the wrong hotel. Tracy looked out of the lobby window and spotted a large neon sign for the correct hotel on the other side of the freeway. Dave, Tracy, H and I waited for a gap in the traffic and legged it across but Peter, who always brings a massively oversized bag on tour, refused to carry it all that way and flagged down a cab. Unfortunately, in the US some of the freeways go one way around the major cities so to get to the other side of the interstate, the cab driver had to take him out of the local area and around the city loop. He arrived back an hour later with a long face and an $80 cab receipt! After 'Bullets', Dave, H and I were keen to do another record. Locomotive Records had gone bankrupt (labels often stopped trading after our releases), so Diana Schuler from Randale Records had kindly offered to cover our recording costs for the next album. This collection of songs would eventually go on to become 'That Shallot' but at the time the working title was 'Grandad's House'. This was due to the fact that

Peter had inherited some money from the sale of his recently departed grandfather's property. He, himself, had suggested investing some of his windfall to help out with the recording costs. However, that turned out to be all fur coat and no knickers, as zero dinero materialised.

Diana's offer was more than generous but it wasn't enough to produce the great-sounding record we all wanted to make. I came up with an idea to do an interim covers album entitled 'Piss Ups' (A play on words from Bowie's covers album; 'Pin Ups') utilising songs by other artists that we had recorded over the years, along with a selection of new recordings of ridiculous cover songs we had played live during encores. Diana would then provide enough free copies to sell online and on tour, which could then be used to subsidise the recording in addition to Diana's initial offer. (Note to self: Stop thinking, you know how this usually ends!)

We played a show at the Fermain Tavern in Guernsey and the next morning over a few beers in the garden of the hotel, I explained the idea to Peter, and he seemed well up for it.

I'd been working on more new songs, 'Trampkiller', '17 Red' and 'Silicone Beer Gut', which I'd originally written for The pUKEs, who are a brilliant ukulele punk band who at that time mainly consisted of about 20 punk ladies. Caveman Dave and I drunkenly composed a song after a gig at 'The Thatched House' in Stockport, entitled 'Youth of Today', a track written from an older adult's perspective. After the show, pub landlord and promoter, Banjo, had given up and gone to bed leaving the bar at the mercy of Caveman Dave and myself. At about 4am we ripped down an already defaced poster of Manchester punk rock band 'Goldblade'.

The poster read…

'Music is our weapon - The lyrics are our bullets'.

To which Peter had added underneath - *'Slogans are our downfall!'*

We turned the poster over and scribbled the new lyrics on the back with a large black marker pen. In the morning when we woke up on the floor of the pub, I folded up the now ripped, beer-sodden poster/lyric sheet and slipped it into my rucksack, adding the music later when I got home.

'Youth of today
Keep outside my hedge
I won a rosette for growing that veg

Youth of today
Stop throwing those stones
Osteoporosis in my bones'

Dave and I were particularly proud to have managed to get the word 'osteoporosis' into the lyrics of a two-minute punk song!

To prepare for the new record, Dave, H and I rehearsed all winter in Dave's home-built rehearsal studio in Worthing, and in the summer, along with Peter, we recorded some tracks at the 'Edge Recording Studios' in Cheshire. After the release of 'Piss Ups' a recording date was set, so I reserved the hotels, booked the studio, made the travel arrangements and those of us with jobs arranged time off work.

In a new surprising negative twist, I received a late-night phone call from Dave telling me that Peter had changed his mind and didn't want to do the new record. I really couldn't fathom why? I could only assume it was either sheer laziness or just a lack of self-confidence. He was certainly at ease in his comfort zone, barking out the classics but, sailing into uncharted waters, he soon lost his sea legs. Of course, later the usual one-dimensional excuses were reeled out… 'No good songs'… 'Look what happened with Cringe'… 'No need to rush stuff out'. In fact, our previous studio album 'A Foot Full Of Bullets' had been released in 2005, 10 years earlier! (Note to self: Give up). With the new record deal now dead in the water, the stakes could not have been lower. 'That Shallot' was put on hold as we spluttered along at the back of the pack behind our prolific contemporaries… and that's where we stayed, robotically reeling out the same set every night, opening with 'Moped Lads' and closing with 'Blown Out Again'. Even regular attendees to our shows were getting fed up. Spotting me in the bar beforehand, they would eagerly ask whether there were to be any new songs in the set?

The reply would always be a disappointing 'NO'.

After that unhappy conclusion, Caveman Dave and Mother Theracy decided to leave the band and who can blame them? After 10 years without a record, a never-changing set, and Peter insisting that the band perform at an endless list of horrendous shitholes, they had reached the end of their life on the road. Lucky Bastards! The long distances that Tracy was being asked to drive were also a large factor, sometimes with the first gig being in Doncaster or Darlington, with the following show somewhere like Dundee. Peter was oblivious and unfazed by the long drives as he would roll out of his house, sleep the whole way, play the gig, and then force Tracy to drive around looking for late-night kebab shops well into the early hours. That's when we came up with a new name for the band – 'John o' Groats and the Kebbabybodies'.

Dave then wrote to me…

"Dear Mr Strangefish,

I still feel a bit weird about stuff, although the sense of freedom is almost all-consuming, I thought I'd better let Henry know so I sent him this… always a bit worrying when very drunk at the computer……love you. X

Dear Mr Hitler,

Tonight, the Test Tube Babies performed a storming show to a Brighton crowd who were almost all known to us as personal friends. Attractive ladies gyrated provocatively on the stage and old pals congratulated us on our wonderful performance. After the show, I found myself, as I had hoped, alone in the dressing room with Peter and, after taking one last look at his horrifically unpleasant penis, I told him I would no longer be performing with Peter and the Test Tube Babies. I had come to this decision myself this very morning but I did not want to sour his mood any further by announcing my thoughts until after the show.

My relationship with Peter goes back over 3 decades and I can still remember saying, after my split with the "Masked Raiders", that I would continue to love him as a friend but could no longer tolerate life as a fellow band member.

We clearly see things from vastly different perspectives and, from my own point of view, there remains little animosity in our relationship. In my opinion, the last tour of Germany was a fabulous success… the band threw themselves into their various (ridiculous) roles in a way that appeared to me to go down very well with the audience at every venue. I thought your choice of support band, The Riots, were perfect for the situation. I thank you for your professionalism, for Mia as our representative and for the excellent organisation throughout.

I thought that any other band who were received on stage with such love and delight from a clearly adoring audience would have come away from each performance deeply satisfied with the reaction of an ecstatic crowd and would be happy to spend a little time together in a self-congratulatory mood, even if this may seem a little too smug or conceited. However, after every show, Peter was little short of furious.

Despite my lowly status of an ignorant simpleton, I am not unaware of the drink and drug dependencies from which I suffer and which have frequently caused difficulties for the band. I am a weak and foolish character and aware of my own fallibility. However, I felt the Wizard of Oz tour was a resounding success given the level of the band and was shocked at the utterly miserable attitude of Peter after repeatedly successful (by our standards) shows.

It was therefore with some reluctance tonight that I said to Peter that I would no longer be prepared to perform for the band. He sees me as a drugged-up alcoholic, and I see him as a man who will never be able to find happiness or even contentment no matter how successful the performances may be.

I want fun in rock and roll and Peter seems to want perfection with which I can never provide him. Please forgive me for this rambling dialogue but I wanted you to understand my point of view. I have said my musical farewells to H, Del and Chin tonight and, as the 5th Beatle, I wanted you to know and hopefully understand.

Thank you for the years of help and support you have shown me personally and to the Test Tubes. I hope the next drummer will be able to give the sober and professional performances I clearly failed to achieve. Most of all I hope Peter and Del will one day be able to accept their differences and work together in order to continue to make the fine music of which we know they are capable. I sincerely thank you Henry for your support (miso soup) and friendship over the years.

Cheers INDEED old Armenian chum.
Caveman Dave. XXX"

As the quest to get a new Test Tubes record out had been stopped dead in its tracks by Peter, I put myself back in the shop window for some more invigorating touring work. Ah!

The New York-based music management group called Hornblow Inc. had approached me to look after the Grammy award-winning band, OK Go on their forthcoming UK tour. OK Go were Damian, Andy, Dan and Tim, a four-piece mediocre rock band whose use of performance art allowed them to stand apart from their contemporaries.

I ended up sharing a room on that tour with American sound engineer Mike Kent. He excitedly rambled on and on about how much he was looking forward to arriving in Scotland and sampling some of 'those fine Scottish whiskies'. He was pale, ginger and 1/200th Scottish on his grandmother's side or something like that. He was nervous about driving on the left-hand side of the road so I volunteered to drive up to Glasgow and on arrival, felt tired and went to bed early. Mike went off on his Scotch whisky hunt… stumbling back into our room just after midnight. After a couple of hours lying in bed groaning, he got up, stumbled about a bit more and then proceeded to throw up all over my bed. Before the first wave hit, I had managed to pull the blanket over my head. I was not a happy puke-covered bunny but took pity on him, turning on the light and helping him find his way to the bathroom. I changed my bedding, turned off the light and went back to sleep. He was in the toilet for ages, so I guessed he'd passed out. In the morning he had vanished…

The next morning, there was still no sign of Mike. As I came out of the shower there was a loud knock on the hotel room door and when I opened it there he was, naked and wrapped in a carpet. It transpired he had gone back to bed but felt sick again and, while attempting to return to the bathroom, hadn't been able to find the light switch. Mistaking the door to our hotel room for the one to the bathroom he had walked out of the room.

He'd also forgotten the room number so rather than disturb me again, he decided to wrap himself in the stair carpet to stay warm and sleep in the hallway.

Oh! Those fine Scottish whiskies!

The support on that tour was a band called 'The Bright Space'. That's where I first met sound engineer and tour manager John Delf, who later went on to become a close friend of mine. In addition to taking care of my own acts, I always made it my business to look after the other bands on the bill as well. I would make sure towels and water were provided for the stage, move equipment, and share drum kits and speakers.

Additionally, I would make sure they got decent dressing rooms and I donated a fair share of the headliner's rider whenever possible. I managed to therefore impress John sufficiently that he offered me a position looking after a young female artist while he was in Sweden mixing the sound for American singer Rickie Lee Jones. One of my own rules is that I only work for artists that I like, so after the tour I went home and listened to a few tracks by that then-unknown artist on her MySpace page. Her name was Lily Allen.

I liked what I heard and said yes.

CHAPTER 32 – THE SHITE-INERY

I already knew Dave and Tracy 'selfishly' wanted to have a life of their own outside the band so, if anyone asked, I always summed up Dave's departure with this little anecdote.

Once upon a time we were on board a sailing ship encountering a severe storm. As the tempest worsened, we cowered below the creaking decks fearing for our lives. On the upper deck, shipmate Unable Semen David O'Brien clung to the mast, drunkenly clutching a bottle and howling at the driving rain. As he stumbled closer to the edge of the deck, I tiptoed upstairs unnoticed, and with the slightest of nudges, delivered the guidance he had been desperately seeking as he disappeared over the side and below the waves.

A blessed release from the shackles of Test Tube purgatory.

More recently, Dave reflected upon his reason for leaving...

"I know that my drinking became too much and the time to leave the band had come. Looking back at my letter of resignation to Henry it is interesting to see the person I was then, full of drink and drugs and full of blame for others when only I was in charge of my own conduct and habits. That was a very different person to who I am now. I served longer than any other drummer in that band and I still want my long service medal (I don't think I will get the 'distinguished service' medal, that has got to go to Ogs) and as I always say I am fucking glad I did it but I am fucking glad I am not doing it now. I knew at the time that Chin, Del and Henry must have been laying plans for a replacement drummer and they made a very wise choice in Sam. He and Nick make a fine rhythm section and they certainly have the 'oomph' that was missing at one point.
I still remain good friends with Peter and Del. The man who drank too much to be in the Test Tube Babies? I'll take that.
Better to be pissed and proud than sober and ashamed.
Oi!... Strangefish... Where's my fucking long service medal?"

H hobbled off in Dave's footstep a year later, claiming he had to resign to get his life 'back together'. Within a year he had split up with his wife, become homeless and ended up in hospital having his leg amputated. Should've stayed in the pickle jar with us.

With the Test Tubes now rhythmsectionless again and my diary as empty as Paul H's sock drawer, I decided to return to my role of tour manager and revisit the good old US of A, with the band 'South'. I asked my old mate Marcus Mystery if he would be interested in helping out with the driving and equipment.

Marcus and I had been through more than a few scrapes over the years. Back when he was playing rhythm guitar for the Test Tubes, we were attempting a soundcheck in the basement of Freiburg's Crash in AZ in Germany. A full-scale riot was taking place upstairs involving the local police, punks and skinheads. Marcus and I decided to check out some possible escape routes just in case it all kicked off during the show. We discovered a small metal ladder attached to the wall behind the stage. We climbed up it and found a submarine-style hatch at the top. As we turned the wheel and slowly lifted the lid, we noticed two guys sitting on the wall at the top with their backs to us. We leaned over their shoulders to see what they were up to and spied one of them loading some bullets into the chambers of a revolver. As catapult stones whizzed past our heads, we silently closed the hatch and retreated slowly back down the metal ladder to the relative safety of the soundcheck.

South's US tour would see us opening for Japanese producer and musician Keigo Oyamada, better known as Cornelius. As well as Joel, Jamie and Brett, we had Will as touring keyboard player who later went on to animate and design the puppets in Lily Allen's 'Alfie' video.
   My usual touring partner, Hans Perrson, had handed me the tour at the last minute, so I had no time to prepare the shows or check any details, but he assured me that he had taken care of all the pre-production arrangements. A copy of the itinerary was forwarded to me and I was told, rather unconventionally, that if the tour ran over budget, the excess costs would be deducted from my wages, which was both unusual and worrying. Checking the itinerary on the flight, it was akin to one of his Swedish countrymen's IKEA flatpack furniture manuals, half of it was missing!
   Due to a delay in our departure at Heathrow, we arrived at Newark Airport in New Jersey in the early hours of the morning with no-one there to meet us. I struck up a conversation with a couple of Latino guys sitting in a pickup truck in the airport car park, and for an extortionate fee, they agreed to take all the equipment, suitcases and myself to New Jersey, while I put the band in a cab.
   On the first page of the shite-inary, 'Hotel New Jersey' was listed as our first stop after arriving in the country, which of course, didn't exist. It must have meant to read 'Hotel in New Jersey' (find one yourself!) Everyone was in desperate need of rest so after giving up on trying to find the mythical 'Hotel New Jersey', I phoned around and found a

dodgy cheap motel downtown, which had vacancies. On arrival, singer Joel was hungry so he went to get something to eat. He couldn't find anything, so upon returning to the hotel, he turned to the vending machine. He placed his wallet on top while he fumbled around for some change, got his snack, and walked away forgetting about the wallet. There were a couple of shady looking characters hanging around outside, so of course, when he returned, unsurprisingly, his wallet wasn't there. Joel was really upset, especially since his wallet contained a picture of his girlfriend. Not a stellar start to the tour.

Before heading out on the actual tour 'South' were booked to play the SummerStage Festival. This is a free, outdoor arts event that takes place every year in New York's Central Park. When I arrived at the stage, I thought I was seeing double, there were two of everything lined up in front of each other. Two drum kits, two Fender Rhodes keyboards, two guitar amplifiers, etc. Hans had ordered everything from one rental company but the festival production team had ordered it all again from another. Deja Deux!

It was a beautiful sunny day so after soundcheck, Marcus and I went exploring around Central Park, identifying all the famous movie murders and fight scene locations at the various bridges and tunnels.

After the show, I went to get the $2,000 settlement fee but the promoter told me our New York-based booking agency, Frontier Booking International (FBI), had retained it as their commission for the rest of the tour - we hadn't even played it yet!

Cornelius' trucks had offered to transport our equipment, so I had booked a nine-seat luxury van but now we didn't have the vehicle deposit or any gas money to start the tour.

"Nice one Hans."
(This became the tour chant every time something went wrong!)

The next morning, Marcus and I took a taxi to New York and sat in FBI's office, refusing to leave until they had returned some of our performance fee in cash. After they'd crumbled and coughed, we picked up the van, filled it with gas, and set sail into the American unknown.

Setting up South's equipment on Cornelius' stage was like bringing a grandfather clock into an Apple Store. Our stuff was held together with gaffer tape, whereas all the Japanese equipment was, of course, brand new and top of the range with all the latest software. You could set your Apple watch to their set, and the whole evening was one continuous visual computer-synced track in which every sound matched the video projections, never a millisecond off. Their musicians switched between guitars, drum pads, chimes, and theremins without missing a single note, each playing three or four instruments. Every night, they wore the same clothes, stood in the same position, and said the same thing. Like spontaneity never 'appened.

At least they didn't drink, so every night we filled up our van with their leftover rider… Score!

In the United States, there really is no such thing as a short drive. After one particularly long and stressful one, we stopped over and spent the night in Buffalo. Marcus was desperate for a drink as we needed to relieve ourselves of the aches and pains, so we dropped the band off at the motel (tee hee!), then drove off into the countryside and found a dive bar. Fat arsed regulars lined the bar, sat on their stools watching Sunday night football, eating pizza, chowing down on chicken wings and loudly expressing their opinions. In order to avoid any unwanted attention, we ordered a couple of beers and sat in the farthest corner. I told Marcus to keep his English accent down, but it wasn't long before one of the local beer monsters spotted us out of the corner of his eye, pulled his britches up over his huge belly and wandered across to start a typical one-way conversation.

"Where y'all from? In-ger-land, I'm a-guessing. Y'all know that Queen? Ha Ha! Y'all got that Euro over there now. Huh? Got two hundred different flavours of buffalo wings goin', over there at the bar. If chicken's yer thing? I'm guessin' it ain't? If I were you…"

Blah, blah, blah, and so on…

We drank up quickly and left.

On our way to Detroit, we came off the freeway on the wrong exit ramp and arrived in a rundown neighbourhood. While we read the map, the locals stopped what they were doing and walked slowly toward us, as if in a scene from the Walking Dead. Others started leaving their houses while a few kids approached on push-bikes. Travelling in a brand-new rental van with NYC plates, we began to fear the worst, thinking we might lose more than just our spare tyre. Just then however, an air horn sounded behind us as a police patrol car pulled up alongside and signalled for us to roll down the window.

"We're guessing you boys ain't from around here? I suggest for your own safety that you follow us, like, now."

We followed them through the ghetto, past a couple of burned-out cars and back up onto the safety of the interstate.

Our next 'mission impossible' was to complete the 1,800-mile drive between Minneapolis and Seattle, so we decided to try and attempt 600 miles a day, stopping at cheap motels along the way. Kenetic, South's record label based in New York City, then called me whilst we were halfway across the country asking whether we could do an in-store appearance via Portland, Oregon. That was 200 miles in the opposite direction. We voted, and the answer was a resounding *"FUCK OFF!"*

As we hit the West Coast, we got invited for a morale-boosting tour of the Nike World Headquarters in Beaverton, Oregon, where we picked up some lovely free trainers. This cheered the boys up no end as the PD's had run out and I was on the verge of going over on that dreaded wage reducing budget. In search of the cheapest motels, Marcus and I started to play a driving game where we'd check out the advertising billboards at the side of the freeway. You'd have to 'stick or twist', pull in or drive on and gamble on there being an even cheaper one further down the road. I spotted an unbelievable offer of $19 each for a double room. We pulled in and were about to check in when we discovered that the rooms were in fact, Native American teepees. The band had reservations...

"Come on Del, you're taking the piss now, haven't we suffered enough."

After a quick pow-wow the idea was abandoned.

In a final blow to the tour the drummer, Brett, announced he had lost his passport. Earlier on he had met a girl and, against my better advice, decided to travel with her to a few shows. Later, after a band laundry run, he couldn't locate it, so I suggested he call her just in case he'd left the passport in her car. As soon as he made the call, she found it in her glovebox. Therefore, at the end of the tour, we had to change his ticket to allow him to fly home via New York in order to pick up his passport and return to the UK.

A few months later, one Thursday afternoon in Brighton, I received an unexpected phone call from Hans.

"South are playing tomorrow night and we've forgotten some of the equipment. Could you pick it up and bring it along to the show?"

"OK, where is the show?"

"Coachella Festival, Colorado desert, California! Could you also bring John Brice the manager - come on Del, I know you can pull this off."

Sound engineer to the stars John Delf always used to say my one superpower was my ability to get things done whatever the circumstances…

"I don't have to worry about calling you up every five minutes to ask where you are, I know you'll be there with everything prepared."

Hans booked the flights so I picked up the missing equipment and John Brice before driving to Heathrow Airport. I then called my old friend Craig Kapner in LA who had looked after us at the Tony Hawk anniversary party. He picked us up at LAX in his pickup truck and drove us out into the desert. We eventually arrived at the Empire Polo Club in Indio, with all the software and the bits needed for the show on board. South were due on stage Saturday lunchtime so when I entered the hotel reception late on Friday night, Hans nearly dropped his phone.

"Hooray. Del! I knew you could handle this."

I was so exhausted after the festival I went to bed while the others went to the celebrity after-show party. A few minutes later, I awoke to the sound of voices coming from the other room. When I opened the bathroom door, I found Craig and a fat crack whore doing lines on a tile they had de-grouted and removed from the bathroom floor. I closed the door and went back to bed. Later, band manager Johnny Brice returned from the party and started getting ready for bed. As he entered the bathroom to brush his teeth, he got the shock of his life. I pretended to be asleep and heard him fidgeting around in the dark and muttering *"very weird"*.

The next morning, I was expecting a breakfast bollocking, but John saw the humour in the previous night's events and laughed, saying it was like walking into a scene from 'Pulp Fiction'.

Another lengthy 'South' US tour saw us opening for the English rock band 'Elbow'. The crew were all desperate to get home as we finally reached the last show in New York City. As we were about to leave for the airport, the management called to inform me that I would have to stay an extra week in New York as the record company needed the band to shoot a video for their next single. To me, this felt like having your appeal reconsidered and then rejected by the Parole Board.

As soon as I returned to the UK, I went straight back out on the road again with 'OK Go' again. With their Michigan drawl, they had now started pronouncing my name 'Dale'.

I'd become good friends with their guitar player, Andy Ross, who showed an interest in British culture and, in particular, soccer.

One day he asked me:

"Hey Dale, maybe you could take us to go see an English soccer game if we manage to get some time off during the tour?"

I checked the itinerary and saw there would be a Saturday off in London – on April Fool's Day. My fears deepened when I read the fixtures and saw Brighton were due to play Millwall at the New Den in East London. Millwall fans are notoriously violent so I hoped Andy would forget the idea, even though I was a lifelong Brighton and Hove Albion fan.

When the day arrived, we were staying at the Kensington Close Hotel. After breakfast I was starting to look forward to spending the rest of my day off in West London, catching up with some old friends when my hotel room phone rang and it was Andy…

"Hey Dale, l have some great news, I've seen your team Brighton are playing in London. I've bought us some tickets, so we'll meet you in the lobby at midday."

Yikes!

I subsequently met up with all the guys but was alarmed to see that Damien, the singer, had decided to wear his new pink suit. A pink suit to the New Den!

Double Yikes!

During the ride over, we passed the huge 'warning sign' that reads WE ARE MILLWALL, YOU WILL DIE! graffitied on a nearby railway tunnel. The taxi driver dropped us off by the away end and we made our way into the ground to find there was already a great atmosphere.
The bar was heaving with everyone singing at the top of their voices.
The match hadn't even kicked off when Mike Kent, their American sound engineer, felt he was about to have a panic attack and returned to the hotel.

We subsequently took our seats in the stand and then Brighton took the lead. The tension in the stadium was now boiling over as the home fans took an instant dislike to our area. The young Phil Mitchells were giving us 'wanker' signs on one side of the pitch while the older Grant Mitchells were simultaneously giving us the finger on the other. A large tattooed, overweight gentleman, resembling a rottweiler, then spotted Damien in his pink suit and took a particular dislike to him, mimicking throat-slitting gestures and then turning his back, bending over and pretending to widen the cheeks of his arse. Damien leaned over and spoke to me out the corner of his mouth.

"Hey Dale. I don't think that guy likes me. What have I done to upset him?"

Brighton centre back Paul McShane scored again to make the final score 2-0 to the Seagulls. At 40/1, I'd had a tenner on him to score last, so I was absolutely ecstatic with my £400 win. The Millwall fans, though, were not so ecstatic and waited for us outside the ground while more of them made their way to Victoria to attack the Brighton fans there. We were kept inside the stadium for an hour following the match for our 'own safety' before being funnelled toward the station between two large fences erected to keep the rival fans apart. The escort was going to take us to Victoria Station and then on to Brighton, even though we were staying in West London. I had to get the band out of there. So, as we were being forcefully ushered along past barking police dogs and snarling middle-aged men, I noticed a young policewoman up ahead, smiling and joking with some of the other Brighton fans. In order to get her attention, I quickly showed her my hotel key and explained that I was with an American rock band and we were being escorted back to Brighton even though our hotel was in Kensington.

"Is there any chance we could slip through the fence and jump in a cab pleeeeaaaase?"

Minor disaster averted, on the way back to the hotel, Tim Nordwind turned to me in the cab and said:

"Hey Dale, never take us to a British soccer game ever again."

CHAPTER 33 – ALRIGHT 'LIL

"Who do you think they will get to play me, if they ever make a movie about my life?"

"Dawn French?"

Lily Allen and I shared a similar sense of humour and mischief so the fact I wasn't fired on the spot meant we were going to get along just fine.

"What's she like?" is a question I am frequently asked once people discover that I worked for her.

I first met Lily Allen, the budding pop star, when she was just 21 years old. As a young female solo performer, she still had more 'sex, drugs and rock 'n' roll' about her than most of the bloated old rock bands I'd previously worked for. She was generous, kind, and didn't give a shit about money, often declining lucrative offers because she couldn't be bothered or found the idea 'boring'. Lily would often openly express her unfiltered opinions when she saw fit, causing many to take offence. Her short attention span would lead her to act difficult or disinterested just for the fun of gauging a person's reaction or adding some tension to a situation. If you ever attempted to compliment her after a show, she would yell over you or tell you to *"fuck off"* mid-sentence. I admired the fact she didn't give a shit, that made her punk rock in my book and we soon became good friends.

She certainly had a fine punk rock heritage. Joe Strummer was her Godfather and, on her Myspace profile page, she listed The Clash, X-Ray Spex and the Specials as her musical influences.

I managed Lily's first show as her acting tour manager on Sunday, 18th June 2006 on Channel 4's 'T4 on the Beach', featuring the Pet Shop Boys and The Pussycat Dolls. We hired two luxury estate cars to travel from London to Weston-Super-Mare, one for Lily, her manager and the record company, and another for the band and me. I met her for the first time at a petrol station on the M4.

We set out at 6:30am in order to arrive in time to rehearse the camera run-throughs for Lily's performances of 'Smile' and 'LDN'. We'd hired a session drummer who I picked up in West London. Since he hadn't slept after his last show, he asked the driver whether he could rearrange the bags and guitars in order to make a makeshift bed in the back of the estate car. After we arrived at the 'T4 on the Beach' site, the cars went back to London instead of waiting around all day. I showed everyone to their dressing rooms but, as the crew were setting up the stage, I noticed there was no one arranging the drum kit. That was when I realised the drummer was still asleep in the back of the car and on his way back to London!

Our first club shows were in nightclubs around the UK with producers Tunde Babalola operating a laptop, Darren Lewis on a keyboard and the newly acquired canny South Shields lad Merrick Adams on bass.

At that point Lily had only performed live a couple of times before at the Notting Hill Arts Club. The first show of the tour was at The Rescue Rooms, an annex of Nottingham Rock City. Shortly after soundcheck the doors opened and, as I was tidying up the stage, I looked around and noticed Lily sitting on her own in the venue seats being jostled by fans.

"Would you like to go to the dressing room?"

"Oh! Do I get a dressing room?"

"Of course…"

As we entered the dressing room, the first thing to catch her eye was the lavish spread of food on the table and the heavily stocked fridge.

"I'm hungry."

"Well, why don't you help yourself to some catering?"

"Oh! Is this all for me?"

Lily later reflected on those days in her 'My Thoughts Exactly' autobiography:

"We got on well. We were on the level. We were on the road together living out of a splitter van with a table in it and nine seats.
Our rider consisted of Strongbow and Monster Munch crisps and we would sit, eat and chat. It wasn't starry or crazy and no one was paranoid or behaved badly. It was a right laugh. It was the best of times. I long for those kinds of times now."

Despite being signed to Regal Recordings, Lily wasn't being given the support that she deserved because the label was predictably preoccupied with their more established artists, Coldplay and Gorillaz. Fed up with waiting for them to act, she started posting her unreleased tracks up on her MySpace page. These began to attract thousands of listeners. After that I started to notice a change in public perception. As she was getting out of the van at The Faversham in Leeds, a mob of fans surrounded her, jostling for position to take selfies and ask for autographs. As the situation started to spiral out of control, Lily had to step back to avoid being knocked over so I had to jump in and guide her to the safety of the dressing room.

The track 'Smile' was released in the spring of 2006, eventually spending two consecutive weeks at number one on the UK singles chart. As a result of this chart success, the rest of the UK tour was immediately cancelled and we drove straight to the Key West Hotel in West London to prepare for her performance on BBC TV's 'Top of the Pops'.

John Delf, however, had just finished touring with Rickie Lee Jones in Scandinavia so he was due to come back to reclaim his job.

Lily piped up from the back of the van…

"I'm not going to lose you am I, Del?"

"You are number one in the bloody charts - you can have as many people working for you as you want," I replied.

While playing the smaller clubs, it was hard enough trying to squeeze an extra pizza out of the promoter but soon after the release of her debut album 'Alright, Still', everything changed. Lily was now selling a lot of records and subsequently being written about in the national press so, after scraping along on a limited budget, she was now being gifted clothes, flown first class and getting picked up in courtesy limousines.

We had some of the best adventures touring the world with the crew - sound engineer John Delf, monitor engineers Shabby and Dan, and of course Lily and her assistant Emily. For the first time I was working with an artist who had gone from being completely unrecognisable, having a pint with you in the pub, to a celebrity with a number one record now hunted and hounded by the paparazzi.

The night before Lily's promotional tour of the East Coast of America and Canada, I received a late-night call from Empire Artist Management, freaking out and telling me that bassist Merrick had lost his passport in an East London nightclub. The flights to New York City were scheduled for 7am the following morning so it was impossible to retrieve it as the venue was now closed. I was then asked if I could learn the album before tomorrow morning. Why does fate keep forcing me to learn the bass guitar? So, I stayed up all night working out all the songs and playing along to the record. I shoved all my notes into my suitcase, packed my bass guitar and ordered a taxi to the airport. About five minutes before my cab arrived, Merrick called again to say he had found his passport. He had stashed it in his apartment before going out so that he wouldn't lose it and, absent-mindedly forgot. The panic was over and going that extra mile was put on hold for another day.

Of course, as soon as success arrives, the chiefs start outnumbering the Indians. From six of us in a Mercedes sprinter it went to a full band with brass section, tour manager, production manager, lighting director, musical director, personal assistant, stylist, two sleeper buses and an articulated truck.

We then began Lily's first full production UK tour at the Manchester Academy on Saturday, 21st October 2016 where Lily's father, Keith Allen, the famous actor, comedian and broadcaster showed up backstage.

Lily's strict instructions to me were:

"Please don't let my Dad on stage during the show."

Inevitably, Keith was champing at the bit to get on, so I had my arm placed firmly across the narrow entrance to the stage. Despite my best attempt at being a human barrier, there was absolutely no stopping him. Getting down on all fours, he crawled between my legs and ran on to the stage where he 'performed' a strange monkey dance, pulled his trousers down, showed his arse and then left. As Lily came down the stage steps after her set she stared across towards the backstage area at Keith and yelled…

"Dad, you're a fucking wanker" while giving him the finger.

Lily introduced the two of us later on that tour.

"This is Del, he looks after me. He's in a punk band called Peter and the Test Tube Babies."

"Ah yes, I got your first single 'Warm Leatherette'."

"No, I think that was by a band called The Normal."

"No, it wasn't. It was by you!"

Erm. OK then.

I tended to have this effect on women (2)
Lily Allen & Del, US Tour 2007.
(Photo: John Delf)

Pinheads
Lily Allen & Del, Tokyo, Japan 2007.
(Photo: John Delf)

Laugh
MTV, Los Angeles, USA 2007.
(Photo: John Delf)

Blowjobs at MTV
Lily, Merrick Adams & Del, Los Angeles, USA 2007.
(Photo: John Delf)

Thwack!
Our long-suffering manager, Henry Klaere.
Berlin, Germany 2012.

Abba Abba Hey!
How can I resist you? L-R: Caveman Dave, Peter, Paul & Del.
PTTB Xmas Tour, Berlin, Germany 2012.
(Photo: Tracy O'Brien)

Turn on, Tune in, Fuck off!
Rebellion Radio with Jimmy Skurvi.
Winter Gardens, Blackpool 2022.

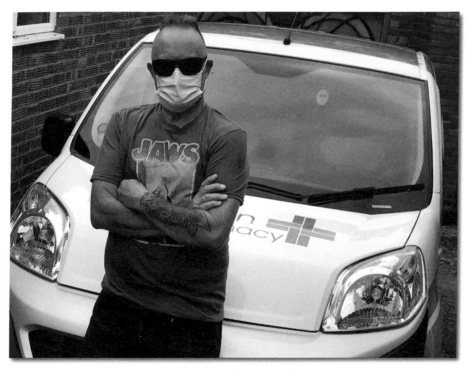

Losing out to Lionel
'NHS' - The new rock 'n' roll stars?
Punk Rock survivor Del, Brighton 2022.

Keith turned up again on a later date at the Bataclan in Paris as he was on his way to Budapest, where he was filming the second season of BBC TV's Robin Hood. In exchange for the reimbursement of his travel costs, he had convinced the BBC he didn't want to use their trailer as a dressing room and was going to buy a camper van instead. After pulling up in his new van and blocking the sidewalk in front of the venue, he went off with Lily to find a restaurant. As they were leaving, Keith borrowed €40 from me to pay for the dinner. After they returned, he was unable to stay for the performance because he had to move his van and couldn't find a place to park. Later that evening, Lily told me how she had explained to him over dinner how I had been her rock, helping her through her initial year of touring. Keith responded:

"Na' roadies are ten a penny, luv."

Cheers.

We continued to tour the world non-stop, like a gang of naughty school children, hiding our partying from the management whilst new tour managers came and went as Lily ruthlessly sacked them. Burning the candle at all three ends was inevitably starting to take its toll, especially on Lily, being the centre of attention. After one particularly long flight to Los Angeles, Lily believed she was about to have a day off and was looking forward to going shopping and catching up with some friends. It wasn't to be. Some US record company exec had the bright idea of having her perform at the MTV headquarters to a team of accountants. Some kind of slave trade for exposure. She was only informed of this as we arrived at LAX and became so pissed off she took a swing at Adrian, one of her managers. The crew and I stayed a healthy distance behind... slowly rolling those luggage trolleys.

On arrival at MTV, she put her handbag down and started to strip off in the middle of a packed office floor. After being told she couldn't get changed there, she shouted:

"WHY NOT? I'M JUST A PIECE OF MEAT PRODUCT!"

They then found us a room, where we set up the equipment.

I became slightly alarmed when Lily wanted me to teach her the notes to 'The Queen Gives Good Blowjobs' on the bass guitar. Keyboard player Shannon quickly learnt it, and I was ordered to sing. She insisted we were going to perform the song in front of the executives at MTV. When he returned from his meeting, Adrian the manager's hair started to turn grey and he began to shake with fear as the idea was agonisingly explained to him. Luckily for all concerned he managed to persuade her that this might not be the best marketing strategy to try to conquer the US.

As Lily's success and workload increased, she spent a lot of her time hanging around in makeup and green rooms. In order to relieve the boredom, she would sometimes pick a fight with someone just to see how far she could push them. Eventually, it became my turn:

"What am I actually paying you for, all I see you do is sit around doing nothing and drinking my rider."

I managed to scramble together a thin line of defence…

"Actually Lily, I don't have to do anything because I've sorted it all out in advance, it's called pre-production. If you ever see me in a mad panic, sweatily running around backstage with bits of paper flying out of my pockets… that's when you'll know I'm not doing my job properly."

I don't think she bought it for a minute.

Once Lily had completed her TV or radio performances, she'd soon get bored again having to hang around and would want to get something to eat, go to a party or go back to the hotel. One consequence of this was that I'd have to hang around instead to fake her signature on the performance release papers. Pretty soon I was the official autograph forger. We would sit on the tour bus and the driver would pass back piles of CDs, magazines, photos and set lists and I'd sign them, pass them to Lily, and she would hand them out the bus window…

'To all my girlies from Lily.'

In Switzerland, Lily took all the crew out to a traditional fondue restaurant where you can enjoy various melted cheese dishes served in a communal pot. You enjoy it by dipping bread into the cheese using long-stemmed forks. There was a delicious cheddary sauce everybody took a liking to, leaving the smelly sock ones more or less untouched. Lily insisted the delicious cheddary melt was for her alone and told everyone else they should eat the stinky sock ones. However, everyone kept taking sneaky dips into the nice cheddary one so, to ensure we stopped trying to dunk our bread in 'hers', she had a meltdown (pun intended!), put her hand down her knickers, pulled out a handful of pubes and sprinkled them on the most popular sauce – Cheese-us!

While on tour in the US, I began teaching Lily how to play the guitar. One morning she decided to go and buy her first one at the Hollywood Guitar Center on Sunset Boulevard. We jumped into a taxi and on arrival headed straight downstairs to the vintage guitar room, where guitars start at around $1,500. We'd been up all night and must have looked pretty dishevelled because, when I went to remove one from the wall, we heard a concerned voice behind us say:

"Um. Excuse me. Can I help you guys?"

The failed musician/shop assistant was nervously looking over his shoulder at us as he attended to an overweight businessman in his lunch hour, struggling to play 'Smoke On The Water' or 'Stairlift To Bedroom'. I don't remember which.

"Don't worry, we're not going to steal anything mate, can we try this one please?"

"Humph."

Following that grunt of disapproval, I pointed out a $1,900 mustard Fender Telecaster single-cutaway semi-acoustic. Moments later his look of impatience turned to one of shock as Lily's assistant, Emily, brought out the Coutts credit card as Lily announced she was taking it. The overweight businessman was instantly ditched before we marched out of the store with a vintage Telecaster and a Fender Blues Junior amplifier.

In your face 'Stairway'.

I also got along well with Lily's band. A strange mix of characters but all good guys and great musicians. The brass section was made up of three young, corruptible music students: Jack, Nick and Steve. Lily didn't like hanging around with session musicians so banished them to the boring musos' bus where they would sit around listening to jazz or reading books with their glasses on the ends of their noses. Lily wanted to be in the sensitive free crew zone where everyone would be constantly partying and taking the piss out of each other. At one point someone suggested mixing up the personnel on the two buses to make a nice change.

I joked:

"What do you get if you mix up the musicians and the crew?"

Answer:

"A ball of gaffer tape that doesn't know what day it is."

Lily was always trying to trick the rest of the crew. One morning, in the early hours, while we were still partying away in the back lounge, she decided to punish the sleeping tour personnel by running up and down the corridor of the bus shouting…

"LOAD IN, LOAD IN... WE'RE AT THE VENUE..."

Disoriented crew members slowly emerged from their bunks half asleep, banging their heads together while searching for their pants in the dark.

The time was 5am.

Lily's song 'Smile' became a hit in the US so we jetted over to New York to perform it on 'Saturday Night Live' – a 90-minute sketch show filmed at 30 Rockefeller Plaza featuring a weekly guest celebrity host, with Lily being the guest musical act. Presenting that week was Emmy award-winning actress Drew Barrymore, who was a fan and had requested Lily for the show.
A few tours previously, when the band 'South' had finished their slot at The Coachella Valley Music in the Colorado Desert, I'd returned to the dressing room and squeezed into the only available seat between two scruffily dressed plain-looking girls wearing Coachella festival hats.
We chatted for a while before they left to catch another band.

Once they'd vacated the dressing room, singer Joel turned to me and said:

"Del. Do you have any idea who you were just talking to?"

"No. Who?"

"Cameron Diaz and Drew Barrymore."

At Tony Hawk's 20th-anniversary party Barrymore's then-husband,

Canadian comedian Tom Green, had got up and played drums for the Test Tubes during our encore while she watched on from the side of the stage.

When Lily played the Coachella Festival herself, I had the once-in-a-lifetime opportunity to drop another name. Quite literally. The chance to kill American media personality, socialite, businesswoman, model, singer, actress, and DJ?... Paris Hilton.

The stage crew had started unloading the trucks and rolling the equipment up the stage ramp on to the stage when we noticed a huddle of photographers busily making their way across the field toward the backstage area. As they drew closer, we saw they were surrounding Paris Hilton as she posed for the cameras. They suggested she stand halfway up the ramp to get the back of the stage and equipment into the shot. It was a lovely sunny day so to get some exercise I was giving the local crew a hand to set up. I'd just got the 165lb Ampeg SVT bass rig to the top of the stage ramp and was standing there with it tilted on two wheels waiting for a stagehand. Andy, our tour manager at the time, came over and whispered in my ear:

"Go on, do it."

She was about a third of the way up the stage ramp, posing away with her back to us, when the stage crew around me started chanting…

"DO IT, DO IT, DO IT…"

A dicey proposition indeed. All I had to do was let go and that would have been Miss Hilton's final photocall…

CHAPTER 34 – TOURING'S BORING

Lily frequently changed tour managers, with legendary promoter John Curd's former 'hitman' Craig Duffy filling this role for a spell. I knew Craig from his time managing the stage at the old Lyceum on the Strand. Nick, my old manager, had told me Curd preferred to employ him, rather than constantly trying to prevent him from causing trouble, bunking in and starting fights.

Curd use to complain:

"He was so annoying; he was always up to something."

At the time, Curd was managing the Tunbridge Wells punk band the Anti-Nowhere League and the rockabilly group The Meteors, so to kick-start Craig's career he nudged him to get a driver's licence so he could road manage their European tours.

Craig was on a fitness kick during Lily's US tour. One morning in New York, monitor guy Shabby, backline tech Jamie Grime and I stumbled into the hotel after an all-nighter. The elevator door slipped open and there was Craig standing there in his shorts on his way across to Central Park for an early morning run.

"Where have you lot been?"

"Just finished in the gym" (Hic!) we chuckled.

For the first time, Lily Allen's new stylist had started making her wear false eyelashes. After a few drinks, the extra weight would cause her eyelids to enter into a spasm, earning her the new nickname 'Mrs Blinky'. Mrs Blinky's next choice as tour manager was ex-Prodigy production manager Andy James. As we climbed aboard the new tour bus Lily told Andy:

"I'd like Del to sleep in the bunk underneath mine as he likes to come up in the middle of the night and have a fiddle about."

Not guilty M'Lud!

However, I would often be woken in the middle of the night by Lily shouting:

"EMILY, TOOTHBRUSH!"

Emily would then have to get up, locate Lily's bathroom bag containing her electric toothbrush and deliver it to Blinky's bunk for the groaning to commence.

In March 2007, Lily played at Seattle's Showbox. She always insisted we shun the local catering and go out to find somewhere more interesting to eat. The show was completely sold out and, as we left the venue, there was a large queue of fans stretching around the block. I told Lily to go and get in the line and queue up for her own show to see if anyone noticed. There were a few confused faces but most of the onlookers settled on her being a super fan and lookalike.

That night we hooked up with Lynval Golding, the rhythm guitarist of English 2 Tone and ska revival band The Specials. In 1979, six years before Lily was born, I skanked the night away at Brighton Top Rank to The Specials, Madness and The Selecter. I loved the new ska when it first started, it was like a breath of fresh air, not unlike punk's influence of a few years earlier.

I'd previously got to see The Specials when they first started - in a tiny club, during that infamous boating holiday on the Norfolk Broads. Trapper told me recently he remembered hearing the opening chords to 'Gangsters' but then passed out in the toilet before eventually getting pulled out by security at about 3am after the club had closed. He then attempted to walk back to the boat, which took him about three hours. When he eventually arrived, he missed his footing on the bank and fell into the broads, which was a blessing in disguise as he was covered in piss, toilet paper and god knows what else.

That has to be up there with one of the best gigs I've ever been to, but for Trapper, not so Special!

Later, I became friends with keyboard player and lyricist Jerry Dammers, who founded their label 2 Tone Records. He was going out with a friend of mine, Tracy, who followed The Clash around but hailed from Brighton. One night I took him to a local punk pub, The Buccaneer, opposite the pier on Brighton seafront.

Jerry was happily playing Space Invaders in the corner when a bunch of skinheads drinking at the bar recognised him. The Specials had recently stopped a concert to chase out some right-wingers who were trying to disrupt their show and cause trouble. Jerry then went to the toilet but, as he left, I glanced over my shoulder and spotted the skins following him downstairs. There was an altercation and, when I arrived, they had him surrounded. It looked like he was going to get a serious kicking. My old mate and Space Invaders king Simon Gaul vaguely knew a few of the skins so we eventually managed to convince them all to stand down.

After that, Jerry said he was going to make the Test Tubes the first punk band to sign to 2 Tone Records. Needless to say, that never happened.

Brighton punk stalwart, Smelly, recently reminded me of that night...

"After the near kicking, Jerry took us all out for a curry, and then we all went back to Peter's flat where he played us The Specials' new unreleased, never heard before single, 'Stereotype'. He was singing along explaining the lyrics - 'he drinks his age in pints'. Showing our gratitude after he'd just picked up the tab for 14 curries and 28 bottles of wine, everyone in the room turned around and told him – THIS IS SHIT!"

Later on, when I moved to London, Jerry popped around my flat a couple of times while house-hunting in Brixton and would always thank me for saving him that night.

The Specials' guitarist Lynval was now living in Gig Harbor in Washington State near Seattle. Lily Allen had been performing the Specials song 'Blank Expression' in her set so I set up the spare amp and Lynval brought along his beloved cream Telecaster guitar.
After the show, he was sitting on the tour bus when I pressed him about the possibility of The Specials getting back together. He told me he would love that to happen but sadly, Jerry would never go for it as there was too much water under the bridge. Later that year, Lily was booked to play the main stage at Glastonbury and for that performance she wanted to do something special. She asked me to get in contact with the Blockheads and maybe do something with them. I suggested getting back in contact with Lynval, who also managed to convince The Specials' lead singer Terry Hall to take part. They both came along to rehearsal and 'Gangsters' was duly added to the set alongside 'Blank Expression'.
I arrived at the Glastonbury Pyramid stage and was introduced to my old mate, loveable Jock from Brummie punk rock buddies GBH, who would be head of my local crew of assistants. I had Lynval's amp set up and their microphones on stands at each side of the stage, but worryingly, there was no sign of Terry Hall. It was only 10 minutes to show time and the Pyramid stage area was packed and buzzing with whispers of a possible historic performance. As it was going out live, the irate BBC director, sound and film crew were all starting to panic:

"Where's the set list? Are we doing The Specials songs or not? If not, which tracks will you perform instead?"

Lynval didn't want to go on unless Terry was doing it as well, so we frantically ran around the backstage area asking if anyone had seen him. We eventually found him sitting in the Dub Pistols' caravan, with the infamous drug smuggler and author Howard Marks. I rushed Terry through security and we made it by the skin of our teeth as I dashed across the stage during the first song to bring on their mic stands.

Lynval still says to this day, the Glastonbury show with Lily played a *"massive part"* in the group's 2009 reunion.

I'm not one to blow my own brass section but you could say my efforts had a hand in the re-formation of The Specials. Sorry, Jerry.

Our theme tune on Lily's Australian tour was 'Cocaine Banana', sung to the tune of Barry Manilow's 'Copacabana'. When we landed, Lily asked the limo driver whether he could get any cocaine bananas? He turned around and replied in a broad Aussie accent:

"Sorry luv. I don't think they're in season at the moment."

The annual music festival, Big Day Out (or Big Day Off as we called it) is held in five Australian cities: Sydney, Melbourne, Gold Coast, Adelaide and Perth, as well as Auckland, New Zealand. English punk poet John Cooper Clarke and Leicestershire rockers Kasabian were also on the bill, so we went to watch them every night. Lily wanted John to open the show on her upcoming UK tour but her management said her audience would have no idea who he was. She replied...

"Well, they need to be educated then."

At the start of the next US Tour, Lily took me to one side and told me to be particularly nice to the opening act, the LA indie-pop musical duo 'The Bird and the Bee' composed of Inara George (the bird) and Greg Kurstin (the bee). She was hoping that Kurstin would work on her next record, which he did, producing her next number one single 'The Fear'. He also went on to win seven Grammy Awards working with Paul McCartney, Pink, and the Foo Fighters. At the end of the tour, Greg came up to me, shook my hand and told me that when he was a kid, he had played the Test Tubes' debut LP 'Pissed And Proud' until the grooves had worn out.

Also on that tour, we faced a particularly challenging situation when we played in an arena where there was nowhere to hide from the gaze of the audience, since the balcony seating wrapped right around and behind the stage. The dressing rooms were too far away, making privacy impossible. Lily used to like me to sort her out a cheeky livener after the set and before the encore, so for this show, I had to explain:

"Lily. No line tonight as there is nowhere private to do it. The crowd can see us from all angles."

"YOU WILL FIND A WAY!" she replied in a commanding voice, just as she stepped onstage to start the show.

During the concert I got the lighting guy to drop an extra curtain, which I twisted into a large funnel shape. I then wheeled an empty flight case across the backstage area to use as a table as I duct taped the edges of the curtain to the sides of the table/flight case and made a tent flap. As the last song of the set finished, Lily dashed across and slipped inside. All the audience could see was the backs of my work boots and her pink stilettos sticking out. After the job was done, we both emerged from my makeshift teepee to a round of applause from the local crew.

At another festival, we wandered over to watch Ziggy Marley from the side of the stage. His material was getting a mild reaction from the crowd until at the end of the set he threw in his old man's 'Is This Love' and 'Jamming'. The crowd went crazy, so I suggested to Lily she should try some of her Dad's material at the end of her set to get the crowd going. Maybe 'Vindaloo'? Her eyes lit up, but once again when it was suggested to her management team, the idea fell on deaf ears.

On Sunday 1st July 2007 it would have been Diana, Princess of Wales' 46th birthday. In her honour, Lily performed at the benefit 'Concert for Diana', along with Elton John, Rod Stewart, Status Quo and Take That, held at the newly rebuilt Wembley Stadium in London. Diana's sons, princes William and Harry, hosted the concert, coming around to shake everyone's hand as we were setting up. I came up with the idea of Lily taking to the stage in a smashed-up Mercedes, covered in blood.
Lily loved the idea but, once again, the management (who must have been sick to the back teeth of 'my ideas' by now) weren't so keen. Still can't think why?

After the performance John Delf told me there was an after-show party upstairs and we could go and grab selfies with Posh and Becks, Kayne West and Donny Osmond among others. I blew it out and went back to the hotel to get drunk on my own.

It was the 2007 London Fashion Week, and Lily was performing for Fashion Rocks at the Royal Albert Hall. Samuel L Jackson, along with Uma Thurman, played hosts in the evening and the afternoon. Backstage, skeletal naked models stood around vacantly staring into space waiting to be dressed. After soundcheck, we cleared off to The Goat in Kensington High Street, where I noticed a bloke in the corner having a drink with a stepladder. Odd I thought. As he left, I noticed he had a camera bag, which explained it. There was £20,000 worth of goody bags to be had, but they were all locked in one of the backstage dressing rooms. There was a small gap between the top of the dressing room wall and the ceiling, so the crew and I contemplated going out to buy a fishing rod.

The Moët was flowing in Lily's dressing room, which was full of models wearing expensive six-figure designer gowns, while I was sitting in the corner in my trainers and skateboarder shorts, which I'd managed to blag on the 'South' US tour. After a few glasses, I thought I had better shout something stupid:

"HANDS UP WHO'S BEEN PREGNANT BY ME?"

The room fell silent as everyone turned to stare in my direction until British supermodel Kate Moss put her hand up and started giggling.

We were then hanging around in the wings watching Dame Edna Everage when Shirley Bassey's personal security started shoving us out of the way shouting…

"DAME SHIRLEY COMING THROUGH… DAME SHIRLEY COMING THROUGH."

I shoved them back and shouted…

"DAME LILY LEAVING!"

The last show I ever did with Lily was the Christmas of 2007 at the Nokia executives' Christmas party in the West End of London.
She was getting something like 120 grand to perform four songs. Nokia were covering all the expenses so I rented a car and booked a hotel and a rehearsal room for three days before telling the band to show up if they so wished. She'd recently been complaining that she never saw enough of her Dad so I bought her a Christmas present - the Sheriff of Nottingham Keith Allen action figure from the BBC online shop. She was chuffed when I presented it to her in the dressing room, where she then invited me along to the Groucho Club for some pre-show drinks. First things first, though, I had to go back to the stage to put out the towels, water and the four-song setlists. When I returned to the dressing room, they'd all left without me. I had to go to find the crew in the local Irish pub instead. Know your place, Greening!

In the end, the novelty of being a pop star started to wear off once Lily realised being on tour was mainly hanging around all day and the rock 'n' roll thrills were few and far between… She didn't give a fuck about the music 'biz' anyway, illustrated perfectly by her production company being aptly named 'Touring's Boring'. One Sunday afternoon in Santiago, Chile, towards the end of her South American tour, I was sitting backstage in Lily's dressing room when she suddenly burst into tears.

"What's the matter?" I asked, before adding…

"This is it, Lily. This is what all the hard work has been for. A number one single and a sold-out tour in South America."

"I hate it," she cried.

"I just want to be home with my Mum and family having a Sunday roast."

A year later she had changed management, which meant that they'd brought in their own crew. We heard through the grapevine that they wanted to 'clean up the act', which was something that pissed off John Delf as he hardly ever drank.

Sometime after that, I was sitting in the Prince Albert in Brighton with my mate Paul H when my phone rang and an unrecognised number flashed up:

"Hello Del."

"Who's this?"

"Lily."

"Lily who?"

"Lily fucking Allen, you fucking wanker."

"Alright 'Lil."

"I'm playing at the Brighton Centre tonight."

"That's great."

"Why aren't you here at the soundcheck?"

"I didn't even know you were playing."

"How many do you want on the guest list?"

"Well, I'm in the pub at the moment... there's about thirty of us."

"OK. I'll put you all on the list. Del plus thirty then..."

X

CHAPTER 35 – THE DEL STRANGEFISH SHOW

Having crawled out of the stagnant Test Tube gene pool, I quickly evolved and leapt like a lice-infested farmed salmon into the world of radio.

I was invited to appear on 'Shouty' Dan's Community Payback Show on Brighton and Hove Community Radio (BHCR) with Paul H. After the interview and before leaving the studio, we were invited to write in the guest book, so I signed it:

Del 'When do I get my own show?' Strangefish.

The next day I got a call from the station asking me whether I was serious? This piqued my interest and, after successfully completing my first pilot show, I joined BHCR, going live every Wednesday at 6pm. 'The Del Strangefish Radio Show' was born.

My initial aim was to create a light-hearted punk rock comedy show with classic punk tracks, new releases and regular guests. Unfortunately, there were some problems with the station premises and it was looking likely BHCR might fold so I sent one of my shows to Radio Reverb, which had a broadcast licence on 97.2 FM. Soon after, BBC Sussex presenter and director Melita Dennett responded, saying she liked what she heard and, with a few tweaks, I could get a regular spot there instead. My new hourly radio show on Radio Reverb went out every Wednesday at 8pm and was repeated throughout the week.

'Shouty' Dan's occasional co-host was Jimmy Skurvi, singer of young, 'up and coming but never quite arriving' punk band Skurvi. I could see poor Jimmy struggling to say anything between tracks so I invited him on to my show to become co-presenter. He later revealed how the Test Tube Babies had left him mentally scarred as a child…

"I had been a Test Tubes fan since I was a little kid. I got into punk at an early age. I loved the Pistols and the Clash but the politics of those bands' songs were a bit too grown-up for me, whereas the Test Tubes were shouting "Up Yer Bum"! London wasn't calling for me but Brighton was! An A3 poster of the Test Tubes adorned my bedroom wall, the famous picture of them standing on Brighton beach from the 'Pissed And Proud' album cover. It hung there from when I was a young kid until I left home in my late teens, so Del's eyes were staring at me over the many formative moments of my life, including when I had my first hand-shandy.

Often, whilst listening to the Test Tubes in my bedroom as a child, looking at that poster, I would think to myself they only live down the road in Brighton, I wonder if one day I might get to meet them. Let me tell you now, it's true what they say... NEVER meet your heroes!

Skipping forward to my late 20s, I now had my own band, Skurvi. The Test Tubes and their brand of humour were a huge influence on us and my songwriting. Many times, people compared our two bands, with phrases like, 'you're like the Test Tubes, but good' or 'you're nearly as ugly as Peter from the Test Tubes!' As Skurvi improved and we played more gigs I hoped that one day we would get to play a gig alongside my heroes.

Then in 2012, Skurvi were invited to play the Rebellion Festival in Blackpool on the 'introducing stage'. We were sent the details of who was stage managing that day and there was the name, Derek Greening. I recognised the name but couldn't quite place it. It kept rolling around in my head, where do I know that name from? Anyway, I arrived at the festival and there I was, outside this amazing huge building, The Blackpool Winter Gardens. As I queued on the steps before the doors opened, Peter from the Test Tubes was stood next to me, talking on his phone. When he hung up his call, I excitedly said 'Hi' and nodded. He looked at me like a piece of shit and walked off, without so much as a hello back. What a massive bellend I thought, an opinion that was both correct and remains unchanged to this day.

After collecting our wristbands from the box office, we got to the stage where we were playing and, after the utter disappointment of meeting Peter, it finally twigged, Derek Greening, Del Greening, DEL STRANGEFISH! I was excited again but worried he would also turn out to be a massive twat.

While checking out the stage, we were introduced to the stage manager, 'Hi I'm Paul H, I'm covering for Del today.' Brilliant, another disappointment, no Del. Still, at least I had met another one of the Test Tubes, even if it was only the bass player.

The next day, through a series of fortunate events we were asked to fill in for a band that had cancelled at the last minute, so we headed across to another stage. In the distance I saw a figure, it was him! He was older than he looked in the pictures, sure that was inevitable, but somehow with age he was even more handsome than he was before. How was this even possible? Then finally he introduced himself. 'Hello, I'm Walnut, the stage manager.' It was Del's brother, who I have since christened 'the better Greening' for many, many reasons.

So, after all my excitement, I never did meet Del at Rebellion that year, but I did meet a few of the Test Tubes' wider circle who I would later come to call... wankers I had met.

Later on in 2012, Skurvi were interviewed on a punk show for Brighton and Hove community radio by a strange bizarre northern man I would later go on to christen 'Mad Dan', mainly because his name was Dan, *and he was fucking mental. A few weeks after the initial interview, Dan called me up to ask if I would like to bring my oozing charm and natural charisma to his show as a full-time co-presenter. The weeks rolled by, and I had fun doing the punk show with Mad Dan and, after a while, Del had got his own show that was on directly after ours.*

One day, as we were wrapping up our show, a withered old man shuffled in who had the looks of a person who would find it acceptable to wear his carpet slippers out of the house. I thought bollocks, Del's show must be later after the 'Golden Oldies Hour'. Then Paul H, who I had met at Rebellion, rounded the corner, 'alright H, what are you doing here?' 'I'm doing Del's show with him' he said, gesturing towards the sad pathetic heap that had sat down at the mic. It was him, in all his rejected-from-the-halfway-house glory, the one and only...
DEL STRANGEFISH!

Eventually he asked me if I wanted to stick around and be on his show. He was probably desperate for not only the help, but also for some company. We had a riot on that first show and afterwards Del asked me, while trying to conceal his enthusiasm, if I would like to be on the show again the following week. I jumped at the chance.

Every Wednesday, I kept staying late so I could join Del on his show and from there we built a brilliant show, with the young lairy pillock winding up the old man until the coffin dodger took the whippersnapper down a peg or two... and that's how I ended up on the awfully titled 'Del Strangefish Show' - my suggestion of the 'Jimmy Skurvi Show' was vetoed on a weekly basis."

Over the course of the series, we had some great guests including, Jean-Jacques Burnel from The Stranglers, Shaun Ryder from the Happy Mondays and Clem Burke from Blondie among others. I was more than happy to help support new talent and local bands.

Martin Fish, the lead singer of vaudeville punk legends The Fish Brothers, remembers appearing on the show in what became known as the 'Chubby Sessions'.

Martin takes up the fishy tale:

"Obviously I'd heard of Peter and the Test Tube Babies before I moved to Brighton in about 1985 but I was more into Derek & Clive, Bonzo Dog Doo Dah Band and The Clash. Semi-serious attempts at becoming famous with my acid punk band 'Salad from Atlantis' (eek) had failed and myself and best mate Dave 'Chunky' Edelsten decided to form a music hall/punk crossover that mostly involved getting pissed and annoying people.
When I first met Del at Blackpool Rebellion Festival, he said: 'You're

a fucking Test Tubes rip-off.' I think he was a bit pissed off when I said I'd only ever heard one track of theirs. I tried to explain it was a mere coincidence that I looked like Peter's twin brother (we both weigh 20 stone and are fat, ugly bastards, wear shorts onstage, and sing about rude and amusing things). Regardless, Del forgave me and we hit it off to the extent he kindly invited The Fish Brothers on the Strangefish show. Fish Brothers? Strangefish? How many coincidences can you get?

Myself and then-guitarist – but now up in heaven with original Fish brother Chunky – Dan Woods, rocked up with an acoustic, while drummer Mass Murderer McGhee brought a box of shaky things. Of course, we met Del ahead of the show in the nearest pub, the Lord Nelson, got it all down live in one take accompanied by numerous tinnies and then back to the Nelson for more lethal cider. Del's show was brilliant and I hope it returns someday soon."

Back out on the road with the Test Tubes, I would bring my microphones so I could record and write sketches for the show. Dave, H and I would take on the roles of various characters. Sketch titles included 'Traffic Island Discs', 'Tramp Of The Year Show', 'Ready Steady Burn', 'Hate Island' and the weekly magazine 'Agony H', where listeners would call in with their personal problems. We also came up with an idea for a radio soap opera called 'The Karchers', an everyday story of a family of pressure washers.

When we played the Punk Rock Bowling Festival in Las Vegas, I hooked up with an old schoolmate, Paul Mingham, who invited us to stay at his house in Torrance in California, not far from LAX airport. This would be a great way to save money on hotels and, of course, catch up with Paul, but Dave and H didn't know him and weren't so keen, expecting some sort of hideous punk rock squat. As soon as I told them he had a bar with draught beer in the back garden, the deal was promptly sealed. We even had our own rooms. Paul Mingham had a 13-year-old son named Harrison so while we were hanging around in the garden bar, I wrote a sketch entitled 'American Boy' for the Agony H section of the radio show:

AMERICAN BOY

Agony H: *Hello and welcome to Agony H. This week I'm coming to you Stateside. I'm here, as usual, to deal with your problems and this week we have a troubled young man.*
Hello Harrison and welcome to the show. How can I help you today?

Harrison: *I'm a typical young American boy. I love to play baseball,* basketball and I also love to go surfing at the weekends. My problem is I'm not happy and my dream is to become an ageing 50-plus punk rocker with a huge beer belly and diminishing health. Have you any tips to help me achieve this and live out the American dream?

Agony H: *Indeed I have. How old are you now?*

Harrison: *I'm 13.*

Agony H: *You must immediately stop all dental care and looking after your complexion. Fall out with your parents by setting up a drum kit in the front room. Start hanging out with smelly deadbeats, people normal society would reject. These will be the first steps towards alienation from your Mum and Dad. Then you must drink heavily and sedate yourself with any designer or off the shelf drugs you can find. Make yourself unavailable for work at all times and don't get up until after the sun goes down.*

Del: *How do you feel about this advice?*

Harrison: *I'm overwhelmed. I'm going to try it.*

Agony H: *When you're down on your luck, pawn your guitar and then bend for a friend on Sunset Boulevard to buy some crack cocaine.*

(The studio door bursts open and Harrison's father storms in...)

Harrison's Dad: *Hey man, that's my son you're talking to. What are you trying to get him into, you're sick? I'm this kid's father. This is what I got for you.*

(Agony H is punched hard in the face...)

Agony H: *Get out of the studio or I'll call security.*

(H is punched again, several times...)

Harrison's Dad: *This is what you deserve you sick weirdo.*

(H is punched unconscious...)

While we're still awaiting our radio Grammy, here's another sketch transcript...

TROUBLE AT HOME

Agony H: *Hello and welcome to Agony H and another call has flooded in. Caller, please identify yourself and tell me your problem.*

Caller: *Hello H. I'd rather not identify myself, it's a bit of a personal issue really.*

Agony H: *Anonymity is assured.*

Caller: *I was going to work the other day and after I got up, the wife seemed very keen to get me out of the house. She was helping me to get dressed and virtually pushed me out the front door. I didn't even have time to get breakfast. So I got in the van and drove off down the road to work. After a couple of hundred metres the van broke down, so I walked home to call for breakdown assistance, where I found my wife in bed with another woman. What am I going to do? I love her. What am I going to do, H?*

Agony H: *Well, when was the last time you had it serviced? Have you had it up on blocks lately and looked underneath? Have you checked your points? Maybe you were just out of petrol?*

Caller: *I've been quite neglectful of the servicing to be honest.*

Agony H: *What about your big end? Maybe it's gone? I think really you need a full service and overhaul.*

Caller: *If you see the state of my service history, I've not really done a lot. I've been useless to be honest.*

Agony H: *So you've had a blinking warning light on your dash for some time and you haven't done anything about it. Typical. It's this sort of shilly-shallying that has put this nation on its knees. Now back to Del.*

Del: *All sounds rather ex-hausting.*

Groan!

On New Year's Day 2016, fellow southern Saxon and British astronaut Tim Peake was circling above the earth on the International Space Station, so I wrote a sketch to celebrate that momentous occasion...

TWIN PEAKS

Del: *It's time to check in on the International Space Station and find out how captain Twin Peaks is getting along orbiting the Earth today on New Year's Day.*

Captain Twin Peaks: *Hello, they won't let me in. They made me do this spacewalk and I'm still out here. I keep tapping on the window, but they keep sticking their fingers up and they've drawn all sorts of stuff like 'kick me' on the back of my spacesuit. It's horrible out, I think I'm going to run out of oxygen.*

Cosmonaut Yuri Gogetim: *Hey. Listen here to me. I am Yuri Gogetim Russian cosmonaut. We're not letting your stupid friend back in the spaceship. Ha ha ha. We laugh at him, watch him outside until he shrivels and dies while we drink all the vodka for New Year's Day. Ha ha ha.*

Del: *Captain Peaks, are you still there?*

Captain Twin Peaks: *You haven't been talking to those horrible Russians, have you? I can't believe what they're doing to me. I think I'm going to die. Help me.*

Del: *Yuri, could you let Captain Peaks back into the spaceship, please?*

Cosmonaut Gogetim: *What is point? He annoys us all. He is rubbish at chess. Ha ha ha. We are all grandmasters, we laugh at him, pointless Twin Peaks.*

Del: *Later on in the show we'll be going back up to the ISS to find out whether they've allowed Captain Peaks safely back on board the space station. We'll keep you up to date with what's happening up there.*

Captain Twin Peaks: *Help me.*

International recording artist Adele had recently headlined Glastonbury with an epic display of swearing, letting four-letter words rip 33 times in a 90-minute set, achieving a new world record. This inspired unstoppable good-idea-machine Jimmy Skurvi to come up with a plan to pre-record a comedy sketch to see if we could break another record by swearing 33 times in 90 seconds. The idea was to bleep them all out so that the punchline to the sketch would be just one long continuous censorship bleep. As we began the pre-record, the station received an irate phone call from one of the Radio Reverb directors. The previous DJ had left the live button on, so we ended up swearing for 90 seconds during the old-age pensioners' retirement show 'At Home This Morning'.

Now that I had my own radio show, I thought I could make some easy money by DJing live. I played at a couple of parties at the Hotel Pelirocco on Brighton seafront before Jimmy and I started a residency downstairs at the Hope and Ruin live music venue on Queens Road near Brighton Station. I also got booked to DJ between bands on a couple of German Test Tubes tours, but I think that was just Henry and Peter's way of trying to stop me from drinking.

During my DJ shows, I would spin two white-label vinyl 12-inch records on the turntables, with both master volumes turned down. Under the table, my laptop would pump out the jams from a previously worked out set that I'd prepared at home the night before. I'd pretend to fiddle with the knobs and faders but if anyone came up to me and asked for a request, I'd flick through the box of records, shake my head and say…

"Nah mate, I don't have that, sorry."

As the evening dragged on, I would get bored, find a chair and sit there with my arms folded. I guess I'm just not a giant foam rubber hands type of guy.

Not content with failing at punk rock and live DJing, I decided to try my hand at writing a musical. Paul H and I came up with the idea of a play based on the lives of serial killers Fred and Rose West. Initially entitled 'The Fred West Side Story', I wrote a couple of scenes:

The kitchen occupies the upper half of a horizontally split stage. Rose is at the cooker as Fred enters stage right, munching on a raw onion. During their conversation, the bottom half of the stage lights up and splits horizontally beneath their feet as the buried skeletons of their victims break into a dance routine. Harold Shipman, another notorious British serial killer, also appears in the play and bursts into song…

One Friday afternoon, after a few pints, H and myself pitched the idea to Chris Stewart, the landlord of Brighton's premiere music venue 'The Prince Albert', who had been kindly sponsoring 'The Del Strangefish Radio Show' over the years. Jimmy used to broadcast an 'Albert Rundown' every week with tickets, times and prices for the shows upstairs.

Initially, Chris and Will Moore, the venue manager, loved the idea of the serial killer musical and decided to finance it but, on sober reflection, Chris pulled out with concerns it might negatively affect the victims' families. Nevertheless, I still believe it would have been a killer West End smash.

CHAPTER 36 – PRIMA DONNA BERMUDA TRIANGLE

I've spent many a late night sitting on a tour bus waiting for the band to emerge from the venue after a show and… surprise, surprise, more often than not, the singer would be the last. One by one, the other band members would return to the club to look for him and then infuriatingly not return themselves. The singer would finally show up and then go back inside to find the others, and so forth, like some kind of prima donna Bermuda triangle.

I once toyed with the idea of bringing an old English sheepdog on tour, waving a pair of the band's leather trousers under its nose and sending it off into the club to round everyone up, growling, sniffing and nipping at their arses until everyone was back on the bus.

"Come-bye… Fetch…"

For one weekend every year in August, punk rockers of all types and ages, from all over the world, flock to Blackpool Winter Gardens in England for the Rebellion Punk Music Festival where more than 300 artists perform on seven stages. Previously known as Holidays in the Sun and Wasted, it was first held in 1996 and is run by lovable promoters Jennie and Daz Russell-Smith. The event also features an acoustic stage, an introducing stage, and a punk art gallery, as well as workshops and merchandise stalls. There is never any violence or trouble at the festival, and Blackpool Council has commended its involvement with local charities. The Test Tubes have worked and played at the festival since its inception in 1996.

During the 2008 festival, I managed the Bizarre Bazaar stage upstairs in the Spanish Hall. On the eclectic bill that year were Seventies glam rockers The Glitter Band, Peckham punks Splodgenessabounds and erstwhile chart-toppers Doctor and the Medics.

Only two dressing rooms were available, one on each side of the stage. Doctor and the Medics were already in one so I had to put Splodgenessabounds and The Glitter Band together in the other. It had been more than a decade since the arrest and deserved downfall of their ex-lead singer Gary Glitter after pornographic images of children were discovered on his laptop. The past hovered around the proceedings like an unshakeable spectre as The Glitter Band crowded around the small dressing-room mirror to put on makeup and squeeze into their leotards. I spotted Max Splodge sitting in the corner looking like he'd had one too many. I feared the worst as I saw his cheeky grin begin to widen from ear to ear. He was bursting to say something, so I desperately whispered…

"Please no Gary Glitter jokes, Max…"

I was still shaking my head from side to side as he sputtered out the inevitable…

"Any of you boys own a computer?"

At the end of the night, Doctor and the Medics were having a party and refused to vacate their dressing room. After several attempts, the crew and I gave up, cleared off to the pub and left security to deal with it. Promoter Daz got a phone call at three in the morning informing him that Doctor and the Medics were trapped in the Winter Gardens. Security had given up as well, gone home and locked them in the dressing room!

Another memorable year, the powers that be decided to have some stand-up comedy on our stage. An overweight, bespectacled, bearded young man from Manchester with all his jokes written down his arms, was the first on in the afternoon. We assured him everything would be fine as he sweated and trembled with nerves. Peering around the stage curtain I could see just one person. He was sitting at a table in the middle of the dance floor, reading a newspaper. The comic ran onto the stage grabbed the mic and delivered his opening line with all the power of a soggy piece of bread:

"HELLO BLACKPOOL, HOW YOU ALL DOING?"

The solitary audience member slowly lowered his newspaper and shouted back:

"FUCK OFF!"

On another occasion one of the artists asked if I could get him an ironing board, so I had one swiftly delivered to his dressing room. A short time later he came marching towards me, hilariously furious…

"Where's the fucking iron?"

"You never asked for an iron, just the board!"

We had the great honour of having boogie-woogie piano and bass legends Chas & Dave grace our stage one year. There had been a rumour circulating the festival that it wasn't the original Dave. Daz the promoter stated if it was not the original Dave then they would only get half the money. Don't panic, it was the real Dave. In the audience, towards the front I noticed Andy Aggro so I beckoned him over and asked him to follow me. He thought I was going to offer him some drugs, but the reality soon became clear, we just needed a fourth person to get Chas Hodge's piano up in the lift. Mustn't grumble Aggro.

Chas and the real Dave were both a little apprehensive about playing to a ballroom packed to the rafters with punk rockers, but they needn't have worried. After a few piano tinkles and some one-twos to test the monitors, they launched straight into their top 10 smash hit 'Rabbit'. Quite wonderfully, the whole place erupted into a pogoing frenzy.

Chas said later that their set was one of the best three gigs they'd ever done. After the show, I took an inebriated Chas to the taxi rank and as he drove off, he leant out the window, raised his beer can in the air and jokingly shouted:

"Oi Del, if you see any of those blue-haired mohican birds with ripped fishnets, I'm in room twelve at The Sea View."

English singer-songwriter and arguably rock and roll's greatest failure, John Otway, came into the production office to discuss the stage set up. Peter asked him if he wanted any coke and John replied:

"I haven't done drugs in sixty-five years, I'm not gonna start now."

Organiser and 'Rebellion Introducing Stage' manager Johnny Wah Wah remembers being impressed by my stage-managing skills…

"I first met Del when I sort of joined the Rebellion crew. I became one of promoter Daz Russell's drinking gang which is the sure-fire way of infiltrating the inner circle of what has become the best and craziest Punk festival in the entire known world. I presume this is how Del got in. Anyway, I was booked into the same hotel in Morecambe (this was when Rebellion was called 'Wasted' and it goes without saying, the name had many meanings. I was popping pills like sweets and high on ecstasy when I got back to the hotel bar. There, alongside Lars from Rancid was Del with an acoustic guitar in his and…What the fuck …?
'Alright mate,' I said.
Del casually responded…
'What do you think of this tune…?'
I barged my way past the now irrelevant geezer from that annoying American band and squeezed in next to Del. I was more excited than a child who'd accidentally found his dad's coke stash on Christmas Eve.

Del proceeded to play me a new song he'd just written, 'My Unlucky Day'. I probably would have been impressed anyway but this was truly a great song and is now a stalwart in the Test Tubes' set. I feel kind of honoured to have heard the song in its infancy and for it to have been played to me personally. Obviously, Del was drunk and I could have been anyone but I don't care because to me, I was the only one he ever played it to like that… so sod off!

After I started working for Rebellion in an official capacity, I like to think that I have become friends with Del. I have his number on my phone!

He runs the radio show at Rebellion now but I will never forget the time before that, when he was stage managing Welsh hip hop group, Goldie Lookin Chain. I was hoping to eventually elevate myself from Darren Russell drinking duties to a respected stage manager so I popped along to the Pavilion stage to see Del the professional in action...

I couldn't believe my eyes when I arrived, the 8-piece band were all on stage with about 15-20 members of the audience dancing with them. Cool, I thought, so I looked around to see how Del was managing this impromptu performance and the audience invasion. That's when I noticed that he was in the middle of it all, a can of cider in each hand and leading the chorus cries to 'Your Mother's Got A Penis'!

To this day I feel privileged that I not only know the guy who wrote some of the best songs of my youth, but I also know the person who taught me how to be the best stage manager in the world and how to control a situation by being more pissed than any of the bands!"

To celebrate all of those wonderful experiences at the festival, I wrote an 'Ode to the Rebellion Crew' for the festival's 20th anniversary annual.

WAKING UP WITH BEERS AND YAWNS
LOADING IN AT CRACK OF DAWN
SOUNDCHECKS NOW ALL DONE AND DUSTED
IT'S TIME TO GET INEBRIATED
BINGO WINS AT LUNCH WITH MAX
MAGIC SHOWS, ACOUSTIC TRACKS
TEACHING ALL THE SONGS TO BEANO
FINISHING OFF THE LUNCHTIME VINO
ANOTHER BAND, ANOTHER JOB
HELP WITH OILING UP JOHN ROBB
BLANKING MOANING PRIMA DONNAS
JUST GET READY AND GET ON. YEAH!
ONE MORE CHARLIE PHOTO OP
DAZ, "CAN YOU SEND PLOP WITH MOP?"
DON'T ASK ME - JUST READ THE POSTER

PEDRO BRINGS THE CLOCK AND TOASTER
ARRIVING ARTISTS UNPREPARED
LITTLE FRANK MUST BE REPAIRED
TRYING TO FIND THE POOING DRUID
TOPPING UP WITH YET MORE FLUID
SEMI NAKED BURLESQUE VOGUEING
PARALYTIC DRUNKEN POGOING
TESTING PATIENCE TO THE LIMITS
MAKE THIS YOUR LAST – YOU'VE GOT 5 MINUTES
OFF TO A&E WITH KEITH
STILL CAN'T FIND MY B&B
BLINDING LIGHTS AND BLEEDING EARS
ANOTHER ROUND OF SHOTS AND BEERS
TRYING TO STAY OUT OF TROUBLE
BUYING DAZ ANOTHER DOUBLE
DEALING WITH THE ARTISTS' STRESS
SWEEPING UP THE ADICTS' MESS
FEELING BETTER, FEELING ILL
REALLY MISSING SHARKY STILL
CATCHING UP WITH LONG LOST FRIENDS
NOW WE'RE FEELING GREAT AGAIN
COOKING SHAM'S LASAGNE PIE
ALMOST TIME TO SAY GOODNIGHT
UP THE STAIRS AND THEN BACK DOWN
TRYING TO SHUT THE DJ'S DOWN
SWITCHING OFF THE LIGHTS AND AMPS
ANOTHER SWEATY NIGHT OF CRAMPS
IT'S TIME TO MAKE THAT WALK OF SHAME
20 YEARS OF ACHES AND PAINS
BUT... YES !!!... WE'LL DO IT ALL AGAIN!
NEXT YEAR. XXX

...and what else did the greatest punk festival in the world deserve?

That's right. A punk rock festival radio station.

I got together with festival organiser Jennie and her friend Tara on their drunken visit to Brighton in 2013. Since I already had my own show in Brighton our night out led to the idea of creating a festival radio station. I offered to record the highlights of each day's action and mix in music and interviews with announcements to keep festival goers informed of all the latest additions and changes.

At first, I didn't think many performers would be interested in appearing on the show and, if I was lucky, I might get a handful of listeners. Despite all my misgivings, the recording sessions turned into action-packed full-on parties, as I grabbed hold of drunken performers as they stumbled around backstage. Once they'd got involved, people were keen to stick around and join in the fun. I edited it all up in the evenings and around midnight I would publish a podcast of that day's highlights – Boom!

The first year's set-up was a rather low-tech affair, with just a laptop and a hand-held recorder in a requisitioned dressing room but, the following year I was given my own area. A swanky little private boardroom upstairs, wittily dubbed 'The Headmaster's Office' by TV Smith from The Adverts.

Hastings' punk rock four-sister band Maid of Ace took part in one of our earliest sketches, a punk version of the British dating game show 'Blind Date', with Jonny Wah Wah taking on the Cilla Black role. I also wrote a sketch with TV Smith and Gaye Advert from the Adverts in mind, in which they were to appear in a Rebellion version of another TV game show 'Mrs & Mrs', with couples trying to match each other's answers regarding their love lives. Fortunately for Tim and Gaye, they had recently split up.

Bands came in and played acoustically, The pUKEs performed one of my songs 'Silicone Beergut', and Charlie Harper popped in to say hello and gave us an exclusive first listen to 'Rebellion Song' from the U.K. Subs' latest album 'Yellow Leader' before he proceeded to leave the master CD behind. We also collaborated with the literary stage crew to transmit some of the interviews from the guests appearing on that stage, including Wattie from the Exploited, Captain Sensible from the Damned and filmmaker Don Letts. We even broadcast a wedding live from the festival.

The overall response was incredible with thousands tuning in, and on one particular weekend we surpassed 15,000 listeners/downloads.

Every gifted broadcaster needs a disfigured hunch-backed assistant to help breathe life into his new creation so Jimmy 'Igor' Skurvi joined the Rebellion Radio team…

"During the early days of outstaying my welcome on Del's radio show at BHCR in Brighton, Rebellion Festival time had rolled around again. It was August 2013 and Del had decided to start a new festival radio station named 'Rebellion Radio'. He was set up in some backroom high above the Blackpool Winter Gardens surrounded by booze and drugs, most of which I consumed. Of course, I made it my mission to try and muscle in on this show too. That first year was incredibly fun, running around dragging whoever we could to be interviewed… normally so pissed you *couldn't understand a word that was being said… and the guests we were interviewing were no better!*

In 2016, Del's oldest son Liam came to work at Rebellion. He was young, fresh-faced and, for some reason, stayed completely away from booze and drugs. However, he is also a technical whizz so, with the aid of the sound guys, he was able to record many of the literary stage interviews which we could then use on the radio. It took me a while to twig but this was an absolute stroke of genius on Del's part because it meant he didn't have to bother with any of the difficult stuff like asking people questions."

One morning I walked out of the Rebellion Radio office and was amazed to see that a large geodesic dome had been erected opposite the studio door. Out stepped the tall handsome figure of tribal warrior, a long-time friend and lead singer of Blackpool punk rock band The Fits, Mick Crudge. Back in the early 80s, I had played and toured with Mick and the band, and the Test Tube Babies had released a split 12" single entitled 'Blown Out Again' featuring The Fits' song 'Peace And Quiet' on the flip side. Mick later became a spiritual healer while continuing to play, perform and write songs. Always keen to help and get involved he agreed to play a song on the radio with fellow legend Buck, from Belfast punk rock band The Defects, while Mick's lovely wife Orsi filled the airwaves reading tarot cards live.

It was in late August 2021 when I received the devastating news that Mick had sadly passed away in a tragic accident while out walking with Orsi in the Devon countryside. Mick had climbed to the top of a Lover's Leap landmark but had slipped and fallen 40 feet into the river below. I was gutted and Peter wrote a heartfelt eulogy on the band's Facebook page…

"There are tears in our eyes and they are tears of frustration. Punk rock, and life in general, have been dealt a devastating blow by the untimely and very sad death of our good friend Mick Crudge of The Fits. Mick was an extraordinary person whose love of life and optimism couldn't help but put a smile on your face. We knew Mick well. We toured together, shared the same management, shared a 12" single, and Ogs and Del even played in The Fits on the odd occasion. It's hard to believe Mick has gone. We are devastated. Mick was a deeply spiritual man and wherever his spirit is now, that place has been profoundly enriched. Our thoughts and condolences go out to his partner Orsi and his family. Rest in peace Mick and enjoy the Peace and Quiet."

A glorious, erudite nugget of festival radio wisdom was proposed by Arthur from 999 and The Lurkers, and I quote:

"I don't have to be pissed out of my head to talk fucking bollocks."

This almost became the station's tagline.

Arthur remembered our first ever encounter:

*"When I first met Del, he was completely naked, gagged and trussed up with baler twine in a stable at an equestrian centre near Brighton.
I'd gone there to meet my Uncle Lester who was a well-known knob jockey and always on the lookout for young men to abuse.*
Poor Del, being pissed out of his mind as usual, had been easy prey for 'Lester the Pester' and had unfortunately been right royally rogered by the dirty diminutive devil and was now in agony with riding crop welts all over his arse.
Feeling sorry for Derek, I kicked my uncle square in his now empty ballbag, called him a cunt and wrapped a pony blanket around the terrified Test Tuber. I took Del to his gaff, which was above Brighton's gayest bar – 'Bar Bum Hug' – and put him to bed with a hot toddy of whisky and his favourite teddy bear called Tarquin.
To this day, he has never forgotten what I did for him and we have now been acquainted for decades via our punk rock-playing shenanigans. Last week he told me in confidence that being buggered in that stable had not psychologically damaged him in the least compared with having to put up with Peter as his singer for the last 43 years."

Another classic Arthurism came about while we were live on air discussing the age-old problem of being 'too old to dance'. I confessed to Arthur that the last time I tried, I emerged from the mosh pit with a broken arm and no trousers. To which Arthur replied:

"I usually take my trousers off before entering the mosh pit."

CHAPTER 37 – COMMENTS OF MASS DESTRUCTION

Retreat!

After spending a long day filming a TV show in Los Angeles, Lily Allen decided to celebrate by having a party in her room at The Château Marmont on Sunset Boulevard. Actress Lindsay Lohan and Sean Lennon, John Lennon's son, were in attendance. Lily was sat at the end of the bed, chatting with Sean about possible first baby names. There are times when I'm a bit too quick-witted for my own good, often already regretting what I'm saying as I'm saying it. The next morning I was having breakfast with Craig Duffy when, with a furrowed brow and a deep breath, he proceeded to remind me that I had suggested Mark Chapman for Sean Lennon's first-born baby's name. As you'll no doubt know, it was Mark Chapman who had murdered his father, John. Excellent? No. Cringeworthy? Yes.

I was still totally hungover from the night before and started to grimace with embarrassment at my latest wince-inducing social faux pas, until Craig cracked one of his knowing smiles, and that was the moment I realised it was one of his little wind-ups. Sometimes my sense of humour can teeter just a little too close to the acceptable line, but I rarely ever stumble over it.

Chaaaarge!

I was enlisted to look after the stage for English singer and King of the Wild Frontier Adam Ant, while Trapper was pretending to be having a toenail removed but in reality had gone AWOL to do a Skunk Anansie tour. Neither the rest of the crew nor I were permitted into Adam's rehearsal room in King's Cross so we had to wait outside for the band to finish rehearsing before we were allowed to go in and mark up any of the equipment for the upcoming tour. I was warned by the management not to look at Adam and to stay outside his 10-metre bubble.

The first show on our tour of duty was at the Villa Marina Entertainment Venue on the Isle of Man, the home of TT Racing, white police helmets and very little else. It takes approximately three and a half hours on the notoriously rough Isle of Man's Steam Packet ferry crossing from Liverpool to Douglas. The only flight that day was fully booked, so Adam had to travel with the band and crew on the boat. He wore sunglasses, a bandana, and a baseball cap so no one would recognise him. After I had queued up in the crowded canteen and selected a plate of lukewarm fish and chips and an apple, I turned away from the cash register and you can guess who was standing right in front of me, nose to nose. Correct. Adam Ant. Now what?

Although I was already way inside his 10-metre bubble, I couldn't just walk away and ignore him. So I just said, *"alright mate"* and went to find a space to sit down. Next thing I know he was sitting next to me chatting away.

"Bit choppy out there. Anyone been sick yet?"

"I've seen a couple of people rushing to the toilet and that girl over there looks like she's about to go." I replied.

After exchanging a few seafaring stories, he went off to find somewhere to lie down. Soon after, one of the other members of the crew came scuttling over to complain:

"I can't believe it; I've worked for Adam for ten years, and he's never spoken to me once. You've only been on the bloody crew for ten minutes."

On the Isle, we stayed at the four-star Empress Hotel on the central promenade overlooking Douglas Bay. The morning before the show, I was waiting by the elevator to go down to breakfast when the lift door slid open and a few nervous-looking members of the band emerged. They told me not to go down because Adam was *"still down there."* I thought, bollocks, I'm hungry. On arrival, the maitre d' welcomed me into the huge empty breakfast area and, pointing in the direction of Adam Ant said:

"I have a place all ready for you sir, over here with your friend."

I felt bad for him; he cut a lonely figure sitting there on his own in the corner. I'm sure he just wanted to be treated like a normal bloke and join in the fun with the band and crew but, like many artists, he was overly protected by the management and their unnecessary rules.

Regardless, I wasn't presumptuous enough to join him for an awkward breakfast, so I just replied to the head waiter:

"I'm a little claustrophobic, do you mind if I sit by the window?"

Before the show one of the crew explained that on a previous tour, Adam had gone ballistic and started yelling at Trapper when feedback started screaming at him through his monitor. Since this would have been a sound engineer's problem and nothing to do with the stage manager, I asked the house manager to drop an extra black stage drape in front of my workstation. Then, with a pair of scissors, I cut two eye holes so that I could watch the show without fear of being reprimanded!

Boots on the Ground

Since the early Eighties, the Test Tube Babies have always clicked with Colin, Jock, Ross, and Scott from fellow punk rock foot soldiers GBH. It's hard to explain, because we're a bunch of good for nothing beach bums from the sunny Costa del Brighton, while they live between two giant carbon dioxide-spewing chimney stacks in Birmingham, just off the M6.

One day we were headed out to Spain to do a festival together and singer Colin was seated next to me on the plane. As the cabin crew were preparing for landing, the stewardess began making her way down the aisle holding out a bin liner…

"Anyone got any rubbish?"

"Colin's got some lyrics."

Colin, being a diamond geezer, chuckled and took my comment of mass destruction in his stride.

Air Strike!

Senser, a UK rap-rock band, were about to embark on an American tour when I picked them up to take them to Heathrow Airport. The last person I collected was DJ Andy Clinton, who bounded out of his house with his skateboard under his arm and jumped into the front seat next to me.

As we headed down the M4, he asked me whether we would be using this van for the entire US tour. I replied...

"Sure. They are going to strap it to the wheels of a Boeing 747."

Friendly Fire

In April 2008, I landed what I thought would be an easy gig when I was asked to tour-manage a couple of DJs. How hard can carrying a couple of record boxes into a venue be? My assumption was wrong.

The Audio Bullys were Tom Dinsdale and Simon Franks who had recently reached number 3 on the UK singles chart with their song 'Shot You Down' which sampled Nancy Sinatra's original recording.

They were nice lads, strangely intense (probably due to substance abuse), but also up for a laugh as long as it didn't interfere with their music. They were also their own worst enemies, as they simply wouldn't get out of bed in the morning. En route to UK shows, the crew and I would have to wait outside their flats in Richmond Park while they had breakfast at their leisure before deciding what to wear for the show. They would frequently arrive late at the airport and miss their flights after Tom had sent my cabs away for 'five more minutes' in bed.

Usually, musicians spend years practising together and become accustomed to some sort of timekeeping routine to avoid spending more time than they have to in a dark, dingy rehearsal room. These two just didn't comprehend the touring-band mentality and felt that they could just drift onto the red carpet whenever it suited them. One illustrative occurrence, typical of their 'ethic', was when we played at the Pohoda Festival at Trenčín Airport, Letisko in Slovakia, at which DJ legend Fatboy Slim was the headline act. As a bonus, the promoter had rented Norman Cook and his then partner Zoe Ball a castle for the weekend. My travel agent set us up with a traditional laid-back riverfront hotel on the Váh River, a tributary of the Danube. I thought the band would love it but in the morning over breakfast, Tom raised the question:

"Norman and Zoe have got a castle; how come we haven't got one?"

"I tried really hard to get one but all the castles had already been taken," I lied.

Missing in Action

Tom hated the hotel again when the Bullys flew in to play Bucharest in Romania. I got a call from him saying that he felt like he was suffocating and wanted to stay at the brand-new Hyatt which he'd spotted on the way in from the airport. The promoter reluctantly agreed to move the band and pay the additional fees. Tom also insisted he should upgrade the crew as well, even though we were all happy where we were. After more wrangling with the now irritable promoter, I managed to arrange for the crew to change hotels as well, but Mac, our Scottish lighting designer, refused to move because he'd already unpacked his bag and set up his computer. Sigh!

Once we were all settled, we were invited out for a traditional Romanian meal by our accommodating but now not-so-friendly promoter. Sadly, the guys weren't interested in that either, wanting to have tapas instead. Dejectedly, the promoter said:

"Sorry, we are a poor eastern European country, not Barcelona."

The morning after the show singer Simon's brother, Jim, wasn't downstairs for the lobby call to be taken back to the airport. When I rang his room there was no answer, so I went upstairs and found that his bed hadn't been slept in. (Well worth the upgrade!) I frantically searched the hotel without success before having to contact the promoter again, who in turn contacted the venue. Nothing. This was getting serious as our flight time was fast approaching, so I decided to leave without him because replacing one flight ticket would be cheaper than having to buy eight new ones. On the way to the airport, rumours of kidnapping, murder, and white slavery began to circulate on the bus. Simon was beginning to worry about his brother, suggesting I should stay behind, call the local police and track him down by putting up posters, and handing out pictures.

"I'm your tour manager, not Lieutenant fuckin' Columbo."

Later, after telling Caveman Dave the missing person story, he designed a poster that I could have used if I had decided to take the case:

'Have You Seen This Idiot?' it stated, with a distorted picture of Jimmy with bulging eyes and a load of comedic abuse in the small print. I got drunk one night and showed it to them. It didn't go down well at all, being received with a mixture of confusion and anger. Jim eventually showed up at the airport in a taxi a few minutes before the check-in closed, explaining that he'd fallen asleep in a bar.

Tom then turned to me in the queue and said he didn't want to go home now; would it be too late to change his ticket to fly to Barbados as he fancied a holiday?

The irony was so thick you could have choked on it.

On My First Whistle… Run Toward the Bullets!

The Audio Bullys' trip to Kazakhstan, the home of Borat, was a geographical nightmare. The Labatt Brewing Company had paid the band a ridiculous six-figure sum to perform at the national football stadium but, due to the aircraft's late departure from Heathrow, we missed our connecting flight in Frankfurt. Therefore, I had to reroute the whole trip through various eastern European countries.

During this hideous extra journey, we were detained at multiple immigration checkpoints for not having the proper paperwork or visas and finally arrived in the capital, Almaty, after travelling for 26 hours to play for just an hour. As a show, it was awful, with insufficient lighting and sound systems and more armed security and police than actual audience members. As Borat might say: *"It's a very nice."*

On Saturday, 28th June 2008, the Audio Bullys were booked to play at Glastonbury Festival Dance Arena. The guys wanted to make a weekend of it, so everyone agreed to make their own way down to Somerset. At the last minute, and after an infinite amount of mind-changing, Simon and Tom decided they now wanted to arrive on a tour bus. Of course, there were none available because every other artist performing at Glastonbury had booked their buses nearly a year in advance. Simon pointed out that Van Morrison once arrived by helicopter, so why couldn't we do the same?

Cue yet another sarcastic comment from yours truly:

"If a chopper was circling your house waiting for you to get ready, it would eventually run out of fuel and crash in your back garden."

We ended up taking a London double-decker route finder bus, 'Summer Holiday' style. The old London bus was a 'hanger-on' magnet so Tom and Simon decided they wanted to stay for the whole weekend in order to DJ on the bus with their celebrity mates. Mac, their lighting engineer, had a rigging course in Brighton the next day so I approached Max, the Audio Bullys' manager, and told him Mac and I had to go home as we had commitments the following day.

"It's nearly two-hundred miles back to Brighton, so if you can find a cab in the middle of Glastonbury at three in the morning, I'll cover it," Max told us as he laughed and walked away.

Mac and I didn't let that deter us and accepted his challenge. We left the chaos of the crowded DJ bus and went for a wander around the festival eventually ending up hanging around outside the VIP area. Out of the dark, and as if by magic, a London black cab appeared and Heavenly Pixilated Peaches N Cream Geldolf (or someone similar) jumped out... We couldn't believe our luck!

"How much to Brighton mate?"

"Three-hundred quid."

"Okay, let's go."

We bought a flagon of cider, did half an E and got the cab driver to take us on the scenic coastal route so we could watch the sunrise over the English Channel. Over and out. Mission accomplished.

No Man's Land

My next tour of duty was with blonde, Illinois-born, singer-songwriter Elisabeth Maurus, better known as Lissie. At the age of nine she had been cast as Annie in the musical of the same name. Coming from a theatrical background rather than a battle-hardened rock 'n' roll one, she tended to burst into tears at the slightest inconvenience, like the time when she opened the fridge on the tour bus and a small tub of margarine fell out, landing on her toe.

We got along great and I must say she had one of the most powerful female singing voices I've ever heard, booming across the largest of arenas and commanding the smallest of stages. She was signed to Columbia Records in the UK, who were trying to turn her into a pop star. They were hoping to achieve this with endless remixes by waste of money 'name producers'. I believed these shortcuts to success were unnecessary since she already had the voice and talent to establish herself as a long-term international artist. But hey, what do I know, now shut up and go and get the money...

Lissie's album, 'Catching A Tiger', had reached number one in Norway, so we spent the best part of 2010 travelling back and forth via Oslo Gardermoen airport doing TV and radio shows as well as appearing at various summer festivals. Eric Sullivan and Lewis Keller, guitarist and bass player respectively, were Buddhists and did not drink alcohol. One night on the stationary tour bus, I assumed I was the only one on board so started clearing up. When I turned on the light in the back lounge, they were sitting there, meditating in the dark.

Among the band flight cases lived a horrible, hippie knitted handbag that had been with them since the start of the group. The bag contained various personal items, including three gold-coloured capos that I was told not to lose under any circumstance. Capos are clamps for the neck of a guitar, used to raise the pitch of the instrument, allowing you to play songs in different keys. Lissie, Eric and Lewis were obsessive, as if the whole show depended on them.

During one of the Norwegian festivals, the band performing before us also happened to be using the same gold-coloured capos, which were clipped to the microphone stands ready for use. As I was clearing the stage and setting up for our performance, I noticed their capos were still on stage clamped to the festival's microphone stands and sparkling in the sun. All the rest of their gear had already been packed away and they were about to leave. An evil thought occurred to me: maybe if I could claim these capos for ourselves, we would have three extra back-ups in case we lost any of our own. The previous band's three gold-coloured capos were still there, glistening and whispering to me to come and claim them. Suddenly I was slapped awake by my conscience as I ran over to the previous band's bus and handed them their capos through the window as they drove away into the sunset.

While setting up the next day, Eric and I unbuttoned that horrible hippie knitted handbag and lo and behold, there were now six 'lucky' gold-coloured capos nestling in there, smiling up at us. Strange indeed. Don't ask me how they got there? After I told Eric what had previously happened at yesterday's festival and how I had done the honourable thing, he replied:

"Karma. That's how it works."

The Final Push

Using the same management at that time were The Pierces, a Los Angeles-based band, consisting of two sisters Allison and Catherine Pierce. On October 23, 2010, they appeared on BBC TV's 'Later... with Jools Holland'. I had worked on that show before with Lily Allen, including the annual Hogmanay special, when everyone has to pretend it is New Year's Eve when it's actually filmed in early December. Jools Holland pretends to slur, while the performers, crew and audience count in the New Year. Among that year's performers were Adrian Edmondson doing a version of 'Anarchy In The UK' plus Amy Winehouse and Paul Weller dueting on 'Don't Go To Strangers'.

'Cu' is one of the oldest word sounds in recorded language, although the earliest usage of 'cunt' has been in the English language since the Middle Ages. Paul Weller and Lily argued with the director and the BBC producers as to whether the word should be included or changed in Lily's song 'Friday Night'. Weller insisted it should be allowed as it was a legitimate Anglo-Saxon word. While this kerfuffle was going on I googled the BBC bar times, saw it was about to open and sneaked off to get a drink. Amy Winehouse had beaten me to it, however, already ordering two large G&Ts before heading out to the balcony for a smoke. Ex-Test Tubes drummer Ogs was also there working on the show for English indie rock band The Zutons so, during the after-show party, a couple of The Zutons, Ogs and myself took the lift up to the Director-General of the BBC's office, where we all did a line of coke on his desk.

Happy New Year! (Early December!)

This time, The Pierces were to perform one song 'You'll Be Mine', in the middle of the 'Later' set. We were to be rolled on and rolled off again on a small riser while Jools was introducing another act. The BBC stage crew gave me the schedule which read 'The Pierces, set up: 52 seconds.' I called the floor manager back.

"Surely this should read five minutes and twenty seconds?"

"No, you've got fifty-two seconds to roll on all the equipment, plug it in, test it and get it off before Jools walks into shot... and don't make any noise."

An hour-long show is pre-recorded for Saturday night but, before then, a half-hour version airs live on BBC Two at 9pm on a Tuesday. Of course, it went horribly wrong in the recorded section when the guitarist's new effects pedal stopped working. Heaven 17 also messed up on their track, so we both had to re-film our segments. I asked the guitarist before the retake if his new pedal was essential to the song they were playing? The answer was no. Problem identified, targeted, and eliminated!

My last show with The Pierces was their opening performance at Elton John's show, outside in the gardens of Blenheim Palace, a country house in Oxfordshire. Instead of buying a road-hardened, flight-cased pedalboard, new guitarist 'Leggy' decided to put his guitar through his Apple Mac laptop and operate it in front of himself on stage. Inevitably, during the show it started raining so his computer filled with water. The guitar started to cut in and out as we struggled to find a dry area. Later, I wondered what Jimi Hendrix would've done if his laptop had gotten wet at the Monterey Pop Festival. Lighter fluid perhaps?

Medal of Honour

At check-in at Oslo Airport, Lissie was recognised, and the band were upgraded to executive class. During the flight I was enjoying my cattle-class seat when guitarist Eric came strolling down the aisle to explain that he felt embarrassed because I was a 'veteran guitar legend' and therefore should be taking his seat at the front of the plane since he was only a young pretender. To his amusement, I explained that he was now the new alpha male in the world of guitar rockin' and that I was now cast out, shunned by the females and doomed to spend my final years living alone on the fringes of the troop. Grunt!

The Last Post

Dad passed away on the 7th of March 2013.

Over time, I could tell his health was failing. He was walking slower and, when we shook hands, his hands were unusually cold, and his skin was becoming translucent. I had just got ready for bed one night and was lying on the sofa watching a movie when the phone rang at around 7pm. Mum was in tears, saying Dad had stopped breathing and an ambulance had just arrived. Rachael was already on her way to London with the car, so I jumped in a cab and high-tailed it over to Newhaven. When I arrived, the police were there but my father had gone.

At least Dad passed away in the comfort of his own bed, an ending I would certainly prefer rather than a cocaine-induced heart seizure on a cold muddy stage at a far-away festival.

As I entered their flat, I could see his bare feet sticking out through the bedroom door where the paramedics had placed him on the floor to try to revive him. Sat next to a young police officer, Mum looked up from the sofa with tears in her eyes and said:

"You can go see him if you like."

I declined. I wanted my last memory to be one of him laughing, joking and still breathing.

CHAPTER 38 – BILLY BUNTER'S FREE HOLIDAY

Not my department, mate.

Oh! The great British self-entitled, lazy working man. Surly and gruff, doing very little, swearing a lot and sitting around drinking tea.
School - the ideal training camp, where you learn to exert minimum effort for maximum reward in preparation for future employment, where you spend your days larking around and sitting in the toilet on your phone. That's how we defeated the might of the German Third Reich, by putting the kettle on, taking a cigarette break, and sticking some twigs on our helmets!

The Test Tubes continued this Great British tradition of idleness by only releasing nine official studio albums over 45 years, even out-lazying the Rolling Stones. I was reminded of our embarrassing legacy during lunch at a beach bar-café in Spain where the promoter's young girlfriend excitedly ran across the street to join us, exclaiming in broken English...

"I jus been in dat record store over de street, and dey got all your stuff in there ...shit ...cringe ...fart ...fuck and pissed."

Back in the Seventies when the Test Tubes first started rehearsing down in the vault of the old presbyterian church in Brighton, I would stuff my ears with large pieces of cotton wool in an attempt to try and preserve my hearing. Of course, I became the butt of all the jokes and was inevitably branded a 'wimp' for not braving the loud amplifiers that were all set to volume 10. Those soundwaves would deflect off the arched concrete rehearsal room ceilings and walls and then fire straight down your ear canal, stabbing you through the eardrum like a knitting needle. Peter eventually went deaf in one ear and had the hearing in the other reduced to just 30 per cent. Of course, this was all my fault for having my guitar too loud. I was also responsible for the shooting of JFK, 9/11, global warming and the downfall of the Mayan civilization.

The next lamb to be slaughtered at the Test Tube altar was chubby chancer Sam Griffin Fuller, a ginger Swindonian who played drums in his daddy Dermot's punk rock band Charred Hearts. At just 25, I soon realised I'd already made seven albums before he was even a twinkle in Dermot's ballbag. Being a fan of the band, it would make Sam's day when Caveman Dave handed over his drumsticks at live shows for him to play 'Banned From The Pubs' whenever he was in attendance. Sam later recounted his introduction to the band after Peter told him he needed to learn more of the set…

"*Back in 2009, my old band Charred Hearts were supporting the Test Tubes down in Brighton on New Year's Eve. I stupidly bought my then-girlfriend along with me and we were going to stay the night and drive back the next day so we could fully enjoy the night. About an hour or so before the gig some lad tried sticking his tongue down her throat and I went for him with a bottle. Security threw me out despite me telling them I was about to go on stage. Luckily, Peter got me in through the back door, so I managed to play. Since then, I became friends with the Test Tubes and would go to their shows whenever I could. Glastonwick 2015, we were once again playing with the Test Tubes and I drunkenly asked Peter and Dave if I could get up and play 'Banned From The Pubs', they both obliged and I sat side-stage waiting for my moment. I started it a bit too fast and threw Del for the intro, but it went ok, could've been worse! Afterwards, Peter told me to learn the set, I thought he was joking, but I later found out there were ulterior motives. Fast forward to Rebellion and Dave had fucked his foot up somehow, so legendary Empress Ballroom stage manager Beano jumped in and was playing instead and, once again, I asked to do 'Banned'. It was fucking amazing, a packed Empress Ballroom! Once again Chin told me to learn the set, but I still brushed it off thinking he was just being nice. On New Year's Day 2016 I got an e-mail from Peter asking me to fill in for a few shows; Reading, Watford, Stockholm and a two-week tour of the US. I couldn't believe my fucking luck!! I practised and learned some more and headed down to Brighton for my audition. The whole way down I had the set blaring from the speakers so I could get every bit right. The first song, you guessed it, 'Moped Lads', boom. We sat in the bar afterwards and I asked the guys how I did, and that was it, I was in the band! I guess it came full circle, from getting banned from the pub to playing 'Banned From The Pubs'! Brilliant.*"

Initially, Sam was full of excitement, running to breakfast and eager to soundcheck. On tour, he cheerily ate family packs of Haribo and crushed his tubes of Pringles so he could drink them like a pint. I felt it my duty to warn him that sooner rather than later all that enthusiasm and optimism would be crushed out of him just like his Pringles pint and, as predicted, within a year he had become a fully paid-up member of the fat and lazy losers club.

I listened with interest as young Sam explained to me how today's dating game works. It was news to me at the time but apparently phone apps allow users to anonymously swipe through to either like or dislike other people's profiles, based on their photos alone. As soon as you've been matched, you can exchange messages and choose the place where you want to meet (possibly the same pub you're already in). After that, you have sex. Wham Bam, no thank you, Maam! I wondered more about it and then asked…

"What if they like you and want to see you again?"

"Fuck 'em off and delete them," was sensitive lover Sam's reply.

In my adolescent years, the hunt for a partner or a casual encounter was a very different affair. You would take a shine to someone in a nightclub or at a gig, make eye contact, have a chat at the bar, and after a few weeks pluck up enough courage to ask for their home telephone number. Sunday night, you would nip down to the phone box with your bag of two pence pieces to find out if they'd like to go see a movie and maybe go for a drink afterwards.

After a few months of Sam being in the band, in contradiction to what I'd been told about the relative ease of being able to 'score' online, I noticed his distinct lack of female company. Did he even have a girlfriend? When we played at Bannerman's in Edinburgh, two of my old friends, twins Gemma and Tansy, came along to see the show. Gemma came to meet us for breakfast in the morning. Sam was staring and giggling and giving it the old nudge, nudge, wink, wink routine.

"We're just friends mate, and anyway, at least mine exist."

When H left the band to get his life back on track, we were in the middle of rehearsing songs for the long-awaited new album. Parisian harpist Christophe 'Croissant' Saunière drove over from Paris to take on bass guitar duties. However, he was already fully committed to a string of orchestral engagements so he was unable to perform live with us. To find a live-show bass player, Peter, Sam and I held auditions at Electric Studios in Brighton. Despite having four or five people lined up, only Andy Aggro and a guy named Nick Abnett showed up. Aggro had already played guitar and bass in the band at various points, so he knew all the songs. An hour later, after laboriously running through the set, Peter offered Aggro the position along with the list of upcoming shows.

"Can't do all of them mate. I've got a job."

Peter was irate…

"WHAT WAS THE POINT OF FUCKIN' AUDITIONING THEN?"

"Well, it's alright for you, you haven't got a mortgage or a family to support," Aggro replied.

Peter continued to get his knickers in a right old twist…

"I can't fucking believe it, it's everyone's boyhood dream to be in a rock 'n' roll band and go on tour around the world and you don't wanna do it. You'd rather go and work as a fuckin' plumber."

Next up at the audition was the aforementioned Mr Abnett, who looked the part, knew all of the songs and even re-introduced some of Trapper's lost notes that both H and Rum had let slip over the years. Nick was a perfect fit.

Nick and I had met before when he was in the dodgy Nineties Britpop band, Dodgy. I'd driven them to France to play John Otway's annual Dunkirk show, where he revealed to me that he was a Test Tubes fan and couldn't believe I was working for them, bemoaning the fact I was downstairs struggling to put his equipment away as he watched on from the comfort of the upstairs dressing room.

Nick recalled our first meeting:

"I first met Del in 2001 on the way to Dunkirk. I was playing bass for Britpop diamonds Dodgy at the time, and we were on the bill for John Otway's yearly Dunkirk weekender. Del was to be driving us there. I didn't find this out until the morning he was picking us up so, as a Test Tubes fan, I was excited and nervous about the prospect of meeting a major influence and a genuine British punk rock guitar legend. The rest of the band seemed bemused by my nervousness and excitement. On the way to Dunkirk, I remember rolling around in the back of the van with all of the equipment rather than sitting in the front of the van chewing Del's ear off. I can't remember if I was banished to the back to avoid embarrassing everyone through my inevitable attempts to be Del's new mate, or whether I hid through shyness. Either way, I managed to get through the weekend without embarrassing myself but also failed to become Del's new mate. Fast-forward 16 years and I find myself not only in the same van as Del once again, but also in the Test Tubes with him! Unfortunately, I am still rolling around in the back of the van with all the equipment. I understand that as a bass player I am to be treated with the contempt I deserve, but I have to say that on this occasion, it is worth it to be on tour with one of the funniest people and one of the best storytellers I have ever met. Viva Del!"

The rest of Dodgy wound him up in the bar on the boat home, implying that if he pulled his shirt up, he might have an Alan Partridge stalker-style 'Del' tattoo.

When they joined the band, both Nick and Sam sent us pictures of themselves dressed as women. Maybe this was one of Peter's secret band entry requirements?

As a classically trained musician, Christophe always played in time and in tune, while Nick had a more aggressive bass style. The plan was that Nick would now play all live shows, with Christophe taking care of the recording and helping out with some of the arrangements. Nick's style of playing better suited some of the newer songs, so I was racking my brains for a way to explain to Christophe we would now prefer Nick to play bass on some of the album tracks.

News filtered through from France that, in another strange quirk of fate, Christophe had been involved in a skiing accident and broken his shoulder. It was an unlucky break for him but a sort of lucky break for us as Nick had some great song ideas of his own, which he eagerly contributed to the collection of songs for the possible new album.

On a golf course in Germany, the Marquis de Henry was negotiating another egg-breaking, omelette-making record deal. This time he'd chanced upon Markus Staiger, from American thrash metal band Slayer's label Nuclear Blast. They were looking to sign alternative acts for a newly formed sub-label called Arising Empire. Henry told Markus that he was managing Peter and the Test Tube Babies in Europe. Marcus was surprised and said we were one of his favourite bands while he was growing up. He then asked what we were up to now?

In 2016 in Stuttgart, like a mother in agony during childbirth who swore she would 'never have another one', I decided to humiliate myself further by signing on the dotted line and committing myself to a new two-album recording deal with Arising Empire Records.

Writing songs has never been difficult for me. I would just come up with a funny idea, pick up a guitar, and then write the melody and riff. I wrote the song 'Up Yer Bum' in 45 seconds when I was sitting around a friend's house, after they asked me…

"How do you write a punk song?"

Quickly grabbing a guitar, I just shouted the first thing that came into my head...

...now where's my Ivor Novello award?

Finally, after nearly 15 years of dither and delay, I blew away the dust and cobwebs from the ancient song scrolls and we began recording 'That Shallot' at Perry Vale in South London, a recording studio run by ex-Vibrators' bassist Pat Collier, who came highly recommended.

Producing and recording a Test Tubes album was always problematic, with limited budgets, waning enthusiasm and little or no support. I would have to jump through hoops to get the reluctant troops on board, booking rehearsals and studio time around work and personal commitments. Adversity would be waiting around every corner to slap me in the face every time I suggested a start date. Peter rarely showed up, since there was always something more important to attend, such as a party or an England football match.

'None Of Your Fucking Business' and 'Crap Californian Punk Band' both became singles. Those tracks had been heavily derided by the rest of the band, so I was glad I stood my ground and they didn't end up on the scrap heap. The pUKEs accompanied me on 'Silicone Beergut', while Andy Aggro's wife Lynn Stenning sang 'Trampkiller'. We also acquired the services of our 'old friend' Olga, from the Toy Dolls. I took the lead vocal on '17 Red', a sad tale of a man who puts his whole life savings on a single number on the roulette table and, of course, loses. A few days later, bassist Nick WhatsApped me a photo of a roulette wheel along with a message...

'Sorry Del... 17 Red doesn't exist.'

'Even better,' I joyfully replied.

I also always try to choose the most obscure, non-punk cover versions for the band to attempt. This time my choice was 'Je t'aime', a song from 1967 written by French musician, singer-songwriter and filmmaker Serge Gainsbourg for iconic actress Brigitte Bardot. The best-known version was recorded by Gainsbourg and Jane Birkin. The duet reached number one in the UK but was banned in several countries due to its overtly sexual content. We were going to rename it 'Shit 'em!' Olga played a blistering solo on the sped-up middle section but the verses sounded pretty much the same as the original, so I suggested Peter record some Bardot/Birkin style real lovemaking. My suggestion had the desired effect as his enthusiasm for the track suddenly soared. He wanted to record himself having sex with his girlfriend on Pat Collier's grand piano right there and then, but Pat was having none of it. Peter's grunting and groaning was dubbed in later after he'd recorded a lovemaking session in his caravan.

Unfortunately, the track never made it on to the album, as Serge Gainsbourg's estate refused permission for the song to be used. Peter was furious, complaining the record label should never have bothered checking with them in the first place and we should have released the offending song anyway. In an ideal world that would be a good idea but unfortunately, we live in the real world and the distributors, Warner Brothers, weren't keen to have 5,000 unsellable CDs sitting in their warehouse due to an injunction.

There was an attempt to have 'Shit 'em' secretly released on benefit compilations and also as part of the Rebellion online festival during the pandemic, but Peter was afraid his girlfriend at the time would leave him if his ex's squelching ever made it onto the shelves of a record store.

In 2019 we returned to Perry Vale Studios to make the next record 'Fuctifano'. Over a six-month period, we recorded and mixed it a week at a time, giving us the time and space to reflect and ponder the mixes. I felt the results were excellent considering the limited budget.

These last two albums were particularly difficult to make due to Peter's constant delaying tactics, once again claiming that the songs weren't good enough and on both occasions trying to pull the plug at the last minute. I started to worry about his mental health when an e-mail arrived at the studio suggesting that we abandon the recording and pay the money back to the record company.

Peter: *"How much do we owe them?"*

Del: *"I'll have a look when I get home tonight. Probably around two thousand five hundred, although we would have to return the rest of the advance, the publishing and the money for the hearing moulds I bought for you."*

Peter: *"Pounds or euros?"*

Del: *"Pounds. Anyway, I'm off to catch the train home now. Nothing will go on the record if you're not happy with it. Simple as that."*

Eventually, after we'd finished the backing tracks, he arrived in the studio at 10.30am to replace my guides and sing his final vocal parts. He was back on the train home by 3pm, the same day! I tried in vain to get him to come back up and redo a few tracks, but he sadly wasn't interested.

Designing the sleeve became equally painful. Peter stubbornly disagreed with every suggestion, so we'd hit a creative brick wall. I had to get the unflappable, professional commercial artist Viki Vortex involved so she could rationalise with him. Even Viki became confused and worried when Peter came up with the idea of removing any trace of the band's name from the album artwork.

The reasoning behind this mystifying marketing decision?

"It worked for Pink Floyd on 'Dark Side Of The Moon'."

Nick succinctly described the idea as:

"Commercial suicide."

We then couldn't get a final tracklist decision out of him, so I printed and cut out all the song titles and spread them out on the dining room table of our chalet at the Butlin's Minehead punk weekender, so they could be easily rearranged like a nursery school word game. The timing had to be perfect because we were running dangerously close to the record company deadline, so we needed to catch Peter in the right mood. That 'right time', from weary experience, would be somewhere between asleep and belligerently unreasonable. Fortunately, we spotted him out of the chalet window, waddling along half-cut on his way back from the sports bar with a big smile on his face, where he'd witnessed a rare Brighton win. Two minutes later it was mission accomplished, the tracklist was finalised, and he took himself off to bed for a snooze.

The process of making a new record had now become like trying to push a mule up a hill. Whether it was the drink and drugs consumed over the years or the congratulatory pats on the back at the merchandise table, Peter now seemed to believe he was something more than just a shouter in a comedy troupe of alcoholics.

In the end I just put up with all the bluster and, although I've heard nothing since, he has got to admit he was wrong about the songs. The reviews for 'That Shallot' were excellent and for 'Fuctifano' even better…

Kerrang: *'Age may be just a number, but even so, punks Peter and the Test Tube Babies have no right to sound this fresh, energised and exuberant on their latest album. All bands should age as disgracefully as this.'*

Maximum Volume Music: *'The world is fuct. They know it, you know it. And in 32 minutes and 40 seconds, Peter and the Test Tube Babies have*

managed to take a swipe at just about everybody in proving why. Right now, that is all you need.'
Rating 9/10

Uber Rock: *'It is just wonderful classic punk and it is a lot of fun. I love that they also mix in a trumpet in a couple of tracks. It adds a little of a ska flair and breaks up the album a little. It is just wonderfully put together. Absolute fun.'*

Blabbermouth: *'Utterly irresistible and better than the new Green Day Album.'* *******

OX Magazine: *'This is the best punk rock of this band since the good old days of 'The Jinx' and 'Blown Out Again' except it has all been updated to take in modern life experiences.'*

With Nick and Sam now regulars in the band, drug-taking took a sharp upwards turn (or downward, depending on how you feel about drugs). Although they were arguably the most efficient rhythm section we ever had in the band, the entertainment and enjoyable drunken banter had now been replaced by coked-up gurning. Consequently, any disastrous shows due to daytime excess were dismissed and laughed off as Peter announced with insane coked-up confidence:

"Who fuckin' cares as long as we get paid."

When we toured France, Peter asked our French driver, Fred, to hook us up with his punk rock buddies around the country so we could have barbecues in their gardens on the way to the shows. The band would then spend the afternoon tucking into huge slabs of steak while guzzling copious amounts of red wine. We then headed to the venue where the priority was to score drugs so we wouldn't fall asleep during the show. It was no longer about the gigs or the equipment, but about filling your belly and getting sozzled for free. I nicknamed that tour...

'Billy Bunter's Free Holiday'.

To get my distinctive sound, I like to use a certain type of Marshall JCM 900 amplifier but, sadly, on that French tour, my hired equipment was wrong every single night. This, to me, was akin to asking Cristiano Ronaldo to play in a pair of wellington boots.

At one show, I was given an original 1950s VOX amplifier that Chuck Berry once used. I picked it up and threw it in a bin backstage, breaking the local promoter's heart as it was the love of his father's life. I ended up having to use a crappy old combo that Fred the driver had found in the back of his van. As long as the wine and meat juices were flowing, and the marching powder was on its way, problems like this were of no consequence. Peter just shrugged and said...

"Sounds ok to me..."

Said the deaf man…

"Looks good..."

Said the blind man.

The Test Tubes were booked to play in Poland, but Nick had already planned a vacation with his girlfriend so Andy Aggro once again stepped in. After the show, I took a taxi back to the hotel for an early night where I turned off my phone so I wouldn't be disturbed. The next morning, I awoke to a worrying number of missed calls and messages. Back in Brighton, Andy Aggros' wife, Lynn, had suffered a heart attack. His son, Dylan, was in tears as he told Ag over the phone Lynn probably wasn't going to make it. The doctors had to induce a coma so they could start the battle to save her heart – and her life.

We were due to fly back to Luton Airport that morning having been booked to play at a fashion show after-party in Leeds. At Luton Airport, we exchanged bass players. Peter had arranged with '13th choice' Paul H to get the train up from Brighton to meet us at the airport station while Aggro got picked up to be rushed to the hospital in Brighton by his friend, Gary. During Lynn's extensive surgery, on several occasions Ag was invited to come to the hospital to say his final goodbyes.

I then got a phone call from Walnut.

"Have you heard the bad news yet?"

"Oh no. Is it Lynn?"

"No. Tracy."

"What the fuck?"

Unbelievably, and devastating for all who knew and loved her, Mother Theracy had passed away in Dave's doorway. After a dinner party they had picked up the wrong jacket, couldn't find their keys, and decided to sleep on the porch. Dave couldn't wake her during the night. A blood clot had made its way into her lungs, causing acute pulmonary edema. Isn't it scary to think what could be happening inside any one of us right now?

Tracy June O'Brien was laid to rest at Worthing Crematorium on the 3rd of March 2018. The ceremony was packed with friends and family from all over Europe. She had made so many friends over the years and was one of the most popular, much-loved and nicest people that I ever had the pleasure to have known.

There's always hope, even in the darkest of places and, amazingly, after being in a coma for 20 days, Lynn managed to pull through.
Aggro didn't want her to find out about Tracy's passing just in case the shock was too much for her. However, when Lynn opened her first 'Get Well Soon Card' it was from Tracy, apparently sent the day before she died… Spooky!

At Tracy's wake, the now more than relieved Mr Aggro angrily offered me these words of wonder…

"What is it with your fucking band? Is it jinxed or something?"

CHAPTER 39 – GIVING UP DRINKING

'So you're giving up drinking, you've given up fun
You're staying at home now, and getting things done
So you've given up drinking, well that's up to you
You know too much thinking, it ain't good for you
Well, I'm not giving up drinking, I'm not giving up fun
I'm going out now, I'm gonna take lots of drugs...'

'Giving Up Drinking' (1995)

I confess that I am guilty of writing those once heartfelt, but now hypocritical lyrics.

During my teens and early twenties, I was on a constant daily mission to get mullered. It seemed like a fun way to escape the drudgery of everyday life and I loved those dark intoxicated days at party central, huddled in the corners of nightclubs, rolling spliffs and chopping out lines. Back then, the buzz phrases were 'party on', 'get 'em in', 'let's get wasted' etc... Tales of incompetence, losing it and walks of shame would get recounted loudly and triumphantly, viewed as subjects to laugh and brag about, like earning a medal or a badge of honour. After 45 years of drinking, the time had come when doing that, for me, was no longer enjoyable. I'd just had my fill. When the fun stops, stop.

There was no hitting rock bottom or sudden health emergency, I had just reached the Oliver Reed stage of my drinking, where my trousers would often inexplicably fall down and the next day's liveners were now being replaced by steadiers.

As well as becoming drivel intolerant, I had also been diagnosed with Type 2 diabetes (Type 2 is the one caused mainly by poor lifestyle choices, unlike Type 1 which you are born with). The doctor told me that you can control it with diet and exercise, which I later did.

Around me, people were dropping like flies. Every time I had a look at Facebook there was another friend or music business colleague in hospital wired up to a machine and one of my best friends, Paul 'H', was having heart problems and had unhappily lost part of his leg. In the past, I regularly attended weddings, birthday parties and christenings, but now it seemed like it was just funeral after funeral as my black suit hung permanently by the front door like Batman - RIP!

Rachael had quit several years earlier so we never had booze in the house and I only drank on rare visits to the pub. I'd already stopped drinking on tour as the so called 'partying' had become Groundhog

Day. I was now having to endure the same old conversations about the same old subjects at the same old venues. The magic had been sucked away and all that remained was a bunch of boring old blokes standing around in the dressing room, laughing at their own jokes and telling the same exaggerated stories.

Edge-of-your-seat-stuff!

Weighing up all these factors and taking into consideration the two to three-day nervous jangly hangovers made dispensing with the devil's dribble an easy decision. Maybe I could even squeeze a couple more years out of this sad old carcass?

I didn't need to join any groups, do any therapy or even rediscover myself by climbing Mount Everest or learning to knit. I'm quite strong-willed that way. I just made some lifestyle changes, like cutting down my time spent at social events. If I went to meet someone for a drink, it now felt unnecessary to stay there for six hours. I found attending gigs difficult at first. The music was just too ear-splittingly loud and without alcohol or drugs the shows seemed to go on forever. In order to escape I would pretend to go to the toilet and then slip out the nearest exit on to the street and go home. After my own shows in Germany, before the backstage drinking and repetitive story-telling commenced, I would announce that I was heading out to the tour bus to drop my stuff off and would be returning to the party shortly. Once onboard, the appeal of the party would quickly subside so I'd just watch a movie or do my accounts. The moment I heard the loud drunken hiccupping mob approaching from the venue, I would dive into my bunk and sew the curtains together.

On one tour, German punk rock band The Berlin Blackouts were travelling with us and Katja, the bass player came up to me and asked...

"Are you feeling better now?"

I asked her what she meant?

"Well, I haven't seen you for five days, so I thought, maybe you were ill?"

I shrugged and told her: *"I'm just boring now."*

I had given up drinking once before, for about a year, after my trip to Thailand in the 1990s. I'd been trying to save money to extend my stay there and, after a terrible bout of food poisoning, I'd lost quite a lot of weight and couldn't see the point of piling it all back on with loads of expensive fattening alcohol. On the Islands, a Singha beer or a quarter bottle of Mekhong Whisky would be more expensive than a whole day's food or the entire catch of the day.

When I returned to the UK, I was invited out on ex-Test Tube roadie Toot's birthday bash. The fact that I had stopped drinking was met with resentment and suspicion, I remember Toot turning around at one point looking me up and down before commenting…

"Shut up Greening, sitting there, trying to look all good."

On leaving the cosy comfort of the pub, Toot's party crew continued on to the neon guff of a nightclub. The horrifying realisation then hit me that I was going to be stuck in this miserable, dimly lit room for the next three hours. The sobering reality of the sticky floor, awful music, glazed expressions, clumsy dancing and terrible DJ with flashing traffic lights just didn't have the same appeal without mind-altering substances. Of course, everyone else was off their face so they all thought it was magical.

Despite my efforts to remain alcohol-free, there are only so many lime and sodas or blackcurrant and lemonades one can consume before your body starts overloading with sugar and so under severe social pressure, I folded and rejoined the merriment. Cheers!

Rocco from Flesh for Lulu and I once made a pact that we were never going to give up drinking. We pictured ourselves in our 70s in Hawaiian shirts with grey quiffs, sitting on deckchairs on a fishing pier in Jamaica with a spliff in one hand and a cold bottle of Red Stripe in the other. In more recent conversations, we agreed that the 'Keef Richards school of rock 'n' roll' is a total myth and, once you have kids, you need to stop elbowing everyone out of the way for that last seat in the party-bound taxi, step back and let the women and children go first.

It's fun to be drunk when you're young but there's nothing sexy about a 60-year-old man falling about in the street being sick. Maybe I have become a bore in the eyes of many, but I never preached or criticised anyone, I just moved along, did my own thing and paddled my own canoe.

As an artist, I still believe that drink and drugs expand your mind and enhance creativity, but as soon as dependency takes a hold that creativity soon turns to mush, and you become a deluded, self-righteous, grandiose cunt.

CHAPTER 40 – NEW FOUND FREEDOMS

Life's too long.

Everybody loves a happy ending but, if the truth be told, after all of life's trials and tribulations, when you die, all you've worked for and most of what you own ends up in a skip.

As that day of reckoning approaches, hypocrites cower in churches, moaning, groaning and hoping for redemption in fear of being cast down into the fiery pit. 'Live fast, die young' is a childish maxim that has never resonated with me. Personally, I like ageing and always looked forward to becoming that old grunter sitting in the corner of the pub in his slippers with half a mild and a Jack Russell.

In my mind, life's milestones were like levels on a computer game: turning 15, 16, leaving school, turning 18, getting served legally in bars and clubs, turning 21, getting my driver's licence. 30, 40, 50, 60, 67, bus pass, pension and death. Game over and peace at last. Hooray!

The phenomenon of FOMO (fear of missing out) has become increasingly common since the advent of social media, causing significant stress to people's lives. FOMO isn't just the feeling that there's something better you could be doing but the fear of missing out on something fundamentally important that others are experiencing.

I had started to develop the opposite – FOBI (fear of being included). Dreading party invitations, hoping not to be put on the guest list and praying with all my might for gigs to be cancelled.

The Punk Invasion 2K17 festival in Santa Ana, which brings together punk rockers from all over California, almost granted me my FOBI exclusion wish. On previous visits to the US the band had risked entering the country on holiday visas, so this time, Rachael, my son Sean and I flew in as a family via Texas a week earlier. We rented a car in LA, but it was so high-tech we couldn't work out how to turn the engine on, so we just sat on the forecourt of the car hire company too embarrassed to go back in to ask how to start it. We had booked an Airbnb in Hollywood, and during our stay there we decided to do the whole tourist thing, going to Universal Studios and Los Angeles Zoo to see the giant Galápagos tortoises.

During this trip, bassist Nick was planning to meet up with his estranged son, so Sam travelled with him pretending to be his stepson, coming to meet his half-brother for the first time. Peter was planning to say he was on a stag do (on his own?)

The three of them arrived in San Francisco together and headed up to the border checkpoint. Nick and his new son, Sam, were ahead in the queue but because Peter had been walking so slowly, he shouted ahead to *"meet in the bar"*. After Nick and Sam cleared immigration, they sat down to enjoy a beer and waited for Mr Slow Stride, but he never showed up. After a while, they had to leave so they could catch their connecting flight to LA.

While only Peter will ever know exactly what happened at immigration that day, we had encountered similar issues on previous trips...

In June 2000, the band had been invited to perform at the Promote Chaos festival in Atlanta, Georgia.

Peter had once again taken full advantage of the free transatlantic alcohol, to the point where the fed-up stewardesses had started to refuse to serve him. By the time we landed he had passed out. At passport control I noticed he wasn't behind us in the queue so I went back up the aircraft steps and saw him still fast asleep at the back of the plane. I woke him up but he couldn't find his passport. I finally located it for him between the pages of the in-flight magazine and then went on ahead to rejoin the line. By the time he'd got his stuff together another plane had arrived and now the queue was stretching out on to the airport tarmac. Every time I looked around, he was angrily rolling his eyes, shaking his head and mumbling about how much he hated America. The rest of us made it through with various tales of long-lost cousins and surprise birthday parties. The very last passenger to arrive at customs and immigration was Peter.

"Hello, sir. What is your reason for visiting the United States today?"

"What's it got to do with you?"
(Doing his very best to try to get deported.)

"Well, do you wish to enter the United States or not?"

"Not particularly."

You could see that the Atlanta immigration officer's patience was wearing thin, what with the arrival of three planes at once and the resulting long queues. The poor bloke just wanted to finish his shift and go home. He looked Peter up and down, sighed, stamped his passport, got his coat, closed the booth and walked away.

Peter wasn't so lucky this time around with even the BBC reporting on his latest arrival in the US:

'A British punk singer claims he was deported from the US because he once impersonated US President Donald Trump on stage. Peter Bywaters, of Peter and the Test Tube Babies, claims he was detained when he flew in for a festival. He said he was interrogated for six hours by border control staff and shown photos of himself dressed up as Donald Trump on tour in Germany last year. The band later posted a joke photo of Donald Trump saying he'd banned the band 'by executive order'. After being questioned by customs and border staff in San Francisco, Peter Bywaters says he had his phone and passport confiscated, had a DNA swab taken, was photographed and had to make an official statement before being escorted to a plane bound for London.

He was refused alcohol on the 11-hour United Airlines flight back to the UK and only had his mobile and passport returned when he'd landed. The rest of Peter and the Test Tube Babies performed at the Punk Invasion Festival in Orange County, California, with the help of several guest singers on Saturday. The band, who formed in 1978 in East Sussex, released their new album, 'That Shallot', in September.'

Peter later told the BBC:

"I had only been there 30 seconds when the border control guard swung his screen around and said, 'Is this you?' There in full view was a video from last year's German tour with me dressed as Donald Trump smoking a fake joint. From there it all went downhill. Six hours later I was forcibly escorted to my seat on the plane. I expect to still be the singer of Peter and the Test Tube Babies by the end of the year, but will Trump still be president by the end of the summer? A US tour or festival will never, ever happen again."

As a result of the BBC coverage, I was bombarded with calls from the tabloids seeking comments to add to their stories, and our social media platforms were flooded with questions about the incident.

The BBC also posted a live video of the band from the last German Christmas tour with Peter dressed as Donald Trump, which received 53,000 views on the BBC news page. Not surprisingly, our record label Nuclear Blast were over the moon with all the free publicity in the wake of the new album.

'Entertainment Weekly' in the US also ran with the story, interviewing US Customs and Border Protection official Jaime Ruiz:

"The claim that he was refused entry to the United States because he mocked the president of the United States, that is absolutely not true. That is false. The reason he was denied entry was because he came with the wrong visa. According to CBP, Bywaters presented himself as a visa waiver applicant, which would permit tourism but not paid work. He did not initially disclose to us that he intended to perform during his trip, which would require him to have a P1 visa."

To be fair, Peter never once said that he got deported for impersonating Trump. The press put two (the deportation) and two (discovery of the Trump picture) together... making five, which made for a fine headline-grabbing story.

Later that night, unaware of Peter's predicament and still expecting him to show up at any minute, we went out for dinner with an old school chum, Paul Mingham, and his new girlfriend Jennifer. We were all staying at a Motel 6 in Santa Ana so, after dinner, we went back to have some beers in Paul's room. I was laying on one of the beds when my phone rang. It was Peter, he had arrived back in London.
He sounded tearful and apologised profusely, but less than a week later any remnants of humility had been swept away as he bitterly announced:

"Fuck America! I'm never playing there again."

The next morning, I was enjoying my new-found freedom by doing some lengths of the hotel pool when a skinny spikey-haired guy came bounding down from his room and jumped in the pool to join me. It was Mike from Blanks 77, an American punk rock band who were also on the festival bill.

"Hey, Del. Where's Peter?"

I told him the story after which he made a helpful suggestion:

"Well, I know 'Banned From The Pubs'. I could sing that one."

I replied it was hardly worth getting on stage to play one song. Mike went on to mention that most of the other bands on the bill were also staying in the hotel and he could put the word out that we were looking for guest singers. That afternoon, a steady stream of weirdos began knocking on my hotel room door asking if they could sing songs from our back catalogue. The idea was starting to grow arms and legs. Could we possibly snatch a rare victory from the jaws of Peter's defeat?

The young girl working in the hotel lobby agreed to print out all the lyrics, so I e-mailed them across. On my way down to reception to collect the copies, I could see her through the glass reading them and chuckling to herself. As she accepted my tip and handed them over, she remarked:

"Some strange shit you got goin' on there, sir."

Upon arriving at the show, I distributed the lyric sheets to the relevant participants in their respective dressing rooms. Joey Bondage from Southern California's Narcoleptic Youth was so thrilled to be singing for one of his favourite bands that he spent the rest of the time pacing up and down, learning and practising them before the show. It really was a great honour to have all these guys getting into the spirit of things and helping to make the show happen. Rachael and Sean set up the merchandise stall outside in the sunlight of the band marketplace at 2pm, as The Observatory doors opened to concert-goers.

We started our set with the instrumental 'September', as the audience eagerly awaited Peter's entrance to the stage. Before the next song I took a moment to explain what had happened, as the crowd began chanting:

"FUCK TRUMP, FUCK TRUMP, FUCK TRUMP!"

I then introduced each guest vocalist as they came out to join the band. The whole theatre went crazy as a giant mixing bowl formed on the dance floor. Joey performed 'Moped Lads', 'The Jinx', and 'Run Like Hell'. 'Up Yer Bum' was joyously sung by Ron Conflict from Lower Class Brats before Gabe Zander from Oi Scouts smashed out a great rendition of 'Maniac'. Mike then sang 'Banned From The Pubs' as promised and Josh, a member of the Virus crew, attempted 'Blown Out Again'. It all went down fantastically well and as I was leaving the stage, the monitor and front of house engineers enthusiastically shook my hand.

As we sat in the sunshine outside after the show, Rachael thoughtfully observed...

"The day began at the Motel six as a complete disaster and quickly turned into one of the best gigs ever."

That morning's swim and my chance meeting with Mike Blank must have been written in the stars!

Fearing rejection again, Peter swore to us he would never return to the United States, which meant that this Peter-less resounding success of a show would be the last time the Test Tube Babies would perform in America, much to young Sam's disappointment, who'd absolutely loved it there. Every time a new tour offer was received Peter would resentfully declare:

"What do we wanna play there for? What's the fucking point?"

A week later, at the Rebellion Festival in Blackpool, I saw Peter in the Layton Rakes Wetherspoon pub. I gave him what remained of the US tour float but the paparazzi were still on his tail, snapping pictures of him at the bureau de change counter, changing his US dollars back into sterling.

2019 finished with a bang. The Test Tubes flew to Columbia to play a one-off festival with fellow British punkers Infa Riot and Zounds. The Del Strangefish Show reported on the punk scene in South America and we shot one of our best promo videos for 'The Queen Of Fuckin' Everything' with director Mark Richards. We also completed another successful German Christmas tour and, rather satisfyingly, saw pre-sale copies of our new record 'Fuctifano' receive rave reviews... but just around the corner, there was a devastating surprise in store for all of us…

One week before Europe was locked down, the Test Tubes played the 'Fuctifano' album launch party at Berlin's Quasimodo, an old worn-out jazz club with sticky carpets and decrepit furniture. In the taxi on the way back to the airport, Peter declared that the looming pandemic was nothing more than seasonal flu and that people should man up. A week later, all flights were grounded.

The death toll was tragic of course, but I am not ashamed to say that I really enjoyed the 2020/21 coronavirus lockdown. It felt like constantly being on holiday or Christmas without the stress, because, joy of joys, there was no intimidating list of gigs to prepare for. I could now take my time to get around to all those jobs that would have been chores beforehand but now seemed strangely therapeutic. I worked on my ukulele skills, improved my Spanish grammar and continued to write music and host my radio show from the comfort of my home studio. In addition to all that, I viewed it as a sort of preparation for early retirement.

While readjusting to a quieter way of life, I found that I slept really well but, on the down side, I'd started to experience vivid cheese dreams.

Not great ones involving Marilyn Monroe, a private yacht and an eight-ball of cocaine, more like a set of recurring chaotic night terrors. I would suddenly wake bolt upright, drenched in cold sweat, with the sound of a thousand alarm clocks filling the room – *"Noooooooo!"*

Brrring! – The van waking the neighbours by revving up outside at 4.00am as I'm whisked away to be delayed at some far-flung international airport.

Bzzzt! – Arriving and being squeezed into the local promoter's van to be force-fed loud unknown punk music.

Beeeep! – Praying for your life as the driver smokes cigarettes with one hand while texting with the other, all while steering with his knees at 140 kmph.

Dank! – With grim predictability, our hotel rooms aren't ready so we are forced to hang out at the dark, damp, venue, where you're immediately tracked down by the heat-seeking, evening spoiling, local nutter.

Dong! – Attempting to change guitar strings in an overcrowded dressing room full of wankers drinking your rider and then having to feign enthusiasm as you force your way through the hangers-on to get to the stage.

Thwack! – Henry, teeing-off at the first hole in Germany.

Nah. None of that shit was working for me.

Rock music now exists in a completely different sphere and mainstream radio has become dominated by pop, rap and dance. Even the biggest rock bands now struggle to crack the online stream-driven Top 20. Don't get me wrong, the demise of the rock star is a huge step forward in human evolution because, to me, people worshipping one another has always been a rather embarrassing way to behave.

Breaking a new artist now costs a lot of money and with the record industry on its knees due to downloading, it became increasingly impossible to put together a decent run of shows without any record company tour support. Management would now expect you to manage the tour, drive the bus, mix the music, sort out the merchandise, and provide mental health counselling.

I tried in vain to explain to artist management that cutting corners with an insufficient crew on a shoestring budget would cost more than they were trying to save. For example, after attempting to find somewhere to park, a box of merchandise would go missing or, if you stay in the venue to keep an eye on the equipment, the van would get towed. Plus, who would the band blame for all these budget cuts and distinct lack of hotels? Correct. The tour manager who has just closed down the backstage party and forced them to drive through the night back to London to unload the equipment as the sun comes up.

I got to learn a lot of money-saving tricks during my time on the road such as drinking the minibar dry, then filling the vodka and gin with water and the whiskey with tea. Then, when room service went to get some fresh towels, sneaking into the next room to make all your international calls. In those 'glory days' rock bands used to hurl TV sets from the window of their 20th-storey 5-star luxury hotel, now they just drop the remote control into a bush on the ground floor of the Travelodge.

(Tip: Keep the batteries!).

In addition to my disillusionment with the modern music scene, I started to notice more bands turning up for gigs with hard drive recorders containing keyboards, backing vocals and harmonies to mix in with their live sound, with the drummer playing along to percussion and a click track. Some artists dispensed with having a band completely and just blasted out the studio recordings in the concert hall while poncing around on stage shouting 'Let's go' or 'Come on' along to layers of vocal harmonies.

Lily Allen toured with a full live band in North America but, as we were about to cross the border to play in Buenos Aires, Mexico City and Santiago, Octave the bass player's South American visa never came through in time. Sound engineer John Delf just unmuted the bass channel on the hard drive. Problem solved!

In my opinion, live should be live. I don't want a band to sound like they do on their record, I can easily stay at home and get that. I want an artist to change the songs up a bit, do something different with the solos or sing it a little differently. What next for 'live' music? Digitally de-aged avatars of ABBA created by motion capture technology?

Oh, wait…

You're never too old to give up and by this stage I'd had enough of living out of suitcases, sitting in M6 traffic jams, changing rock stars' nappies, and tiptoeing around inflated egos. I must have spent a couple of years of my life hanging around in airports, therefore I made the decision to take myself out of the loop and no longer make myself available for touring. By coincidence, the coronavirus pandemic then totally destroyed live music and any income to be made from it, so I returned to civilian life and got a 'proper' job, working anonymously among the humans.

NHS workers had become the new rock stars, so I began driving for the local pharmacy. Helping out in my community and delivering medicine to little old ladies to relieve their arse pain now felt a lot more satisfying than being on tour with a pain in the arse.

This was only my third ever job. I had gone from waking up in strange places and struggling to find my clothes to now having them washed and ready after my bath on a Sunday evening.

Then one day I was talking to a staff colleague when a member of the public walked into the adjoining shop, spotted me and shouted:

"LOVE THE NEW ALBUM, DEL."

Jordan, who was working in the shop at the time, looked at me in bemusement and asked, *"You've got an album?"*

One of the young female assistants chipped in…

"Are you famous then?"

This was followed by…

"Oh! I'll bring a guitar in, and you can give us a song."

A little later, after viewing one of our gigs on YouTube, one of the older ladies commented:

"Not my cup of tea at all. I prefer Lionel Ritchie…"

Despite losing out to Lionel, my riotous punk rock adventures had allowed me to see the four corners of the globe, although mostly through steamed-up, rain-soaked tour bus windows between drink and drug-induced naps.

Would I go back and do it all again?

Absofknlutely…

...NOT

AFTERWORD

Firstly, thanks for buying this second edition! I was shocked and of course grateful that this book's first edition sold out within a month. In the wake of reading it, people started approaching me to ask...

"What inspired you to write the book?"

The idea probably came to me subconsciously over 40 years ago on a beach in Koh Phangan. After recording an album in Australia, I decided to break my journey home by visiting the Thai islands. Upon arrival at Haad Rin pier, a few Thais were desperately seeking customers for their bungalow resorts so I was quickly bundled onto the back of a pickup truck driven by a young Thai boy who couldn't have been more than 18 years old and spoke no English. Handing me a machete, we sped off into the jungle, ducking and chopping at branches before they sprang back to smack us in the face. Finally, we emerged at his 'beach resort', which turned out to be a small alcove with a couple of rickety huts he'd built himself. Full of enthusiasm, the lad pulled a couple of chairs out from his 'restaurant' – two lopsided wooden tables under a palm tree – proceeding to place them on the sand, facing the sea. He then ran inside one of his homemade huts, before scuttling back down the beach holding a large chillum pipe filled with opium. I puffed away and watched the sun go down in slow motion...

As it dipped over the horizon, I started to wonder where I was and where I was going to sleep. There was nobody around so I wandered back up to the rickety huts and got settled into a hammock. Within reach was a 'bookcase' – a plank resting between two beer crates – which contained a few old books left behind by previous guests. I selected a tatty copy of Bob Geldof's autobiography 'Is That It?' Flicking through, early promise fizzled out and in one particularly uninteresting development, he talks about Catholic guilt, discovering how to wank, and then having his first shag. I became disinterested and started to flick forward until I got to the world-famous benefit gig... 'Live Aid', where I came across one priceless story which stood out above all the dross...

The B-side of the accompanying charity single 'Do They Know It's Christmas?' was the song's backing track with some interspersed spoken messages from the likes of Paul McCartney, Bono and David Bowie urging everyone to donate money to the starving people of Ethiopia.

Bowie appealed *"It's Christmas 1984 and there are more starving people on the planet than ever before. Please give a thought to them this season and give whatever you can, however small, to help them live."*

Among the other participants was Steve Norman, the dimwitted saxophonist for Spandau Ballet, who'd unfortunately misinterpreted the purpose of these taped messages and recorded his as follows...

"I'd like to say hi to all our fans in Ethiopia. Sorry we won't be able to make it over there to tour this year but, we're going to try again for next year."

BANG! - That was it!

This was the kind of wince-inducing faux-pas which would inspire me to start recording, reporting, and writing down any ludicrous rock 'n' roll mishaps that crossed my path during my travels.

Fast forward 40 years and the Covid-19 pandemic had struck. All tours had been cancelled, and the radio studio was closed so, with no gigs to review, no guests and no co-presenters, my radio programme now consisted of me on my own talking to a concrete wall in my garage. Enthralling!

I put the show on hold which, along with the lack of gigs, freed up a lot of time so I started compiling my collection of rock 'n' roll anecdotes. Then those dastardly T&M publishers began twisting my arm to add a bit of personal history and... Voilà!
'JINXED - How not to Rock 'n' Roll' was born. No guilt, no wanking, no first shags and absolutely no baby in the bath photo.

The events in this book take place from the year of my birth until the Coronavirus cruelly slammed the door in the face of live music and life in general. I am now working on the follow-up, 'JINXED AGAIN - Back on the Road' which will cover the post-Covid-19 era until we begin our descent into inescapable death, either my own, the band's or the whole planet, whichever comes first.

Until the next time, I hope you enjoy this second edition and I look forward to seeing you... on the other side.

Ha ha ha! (...evil echoey laugh!)

DEL - February 2023

APPENDIX 1 – DEL GREENING DISCOGRAPHY

All releases listed chronologically.
UK release listed first, unless indicated after record label.

ALBUMS

1978: Peter and the Test Tube Babies
'Elvis Is Dead' (1 song contribution)
'Vaultage 78' Compilation LP (Attrix Records)

1980: Peter and the Test Tube Babies
'Rob A Bank (Wanna)' / 'Intensive Care' (2 song contribution)
'Oi! The Album' Compilation LP (EMI)

1982: Peter and the Test Tube Babies
'Pissed And Proud'
(No Future)

1983: Peter and the Test Tube Babies
'The Mating Sounds Of South American Frogs'
(Trapper Records)

1985: Peter and the Test Tube Babies
'The Loud Blaring Punk Rock Album'
(Hairy Pie/Red Rhino)

1986: Peter and the Test Tube Babies
'Soberphobia'
(Jungle Records)

1987: Flesh for Lulu
'Long Live The New Flesh'
(Beggars Banquet)

1989: Flesh for Lulu
'Plastic Fantastic'
(Beggars Banquet)

1990: Peter and the Test Tube Babies
'The Shit Factory'
(SPV)

1991: Peter and the Test Tube Babies
'Cringe'
(SPV)

1995: Peter and the Test Tube Babies
'Supermodels'
(We Bite Records)

1996: Peter and the Test Tube Babies
'Schwein Lake Live'
(We Bite Records)

1998: Peter and the Test Tube Babies
'Alien Pubduction'
(We Bite Records)

2006: Peter and the Test Tube Babies
'A Foot Full Of Bullets'
(Locomotive)

2012: Peter and the Test Tube Babies
'Piss Ups'
(Randale)

2019: Peter and the Test Tube Babies
'That Shallot'
(Arising Empire)

2020: Peter and the Test Tube Babies
'Fuctifano'
(Arising Empire)

SINGLES & EPs

1982: Peter and the Test Tube Babies
7" Single: 'Banned From The Pubs'
(No Future)

1982: Peter and the Test Tube Babies
7" Single: 'Run Like Hell'
(No Future)

1983: Peter and the Test Tube Babies
7" Single: 'The Jinx'
(Trapper Records)

1983: Peter and the Test Tube Babies
7" Single: 'Zombie Creeping Flesh'
(Trapper Records)

1984: Peter and the Test Tube Babies
7" Single: 'Wimpeez'
(Trapper Records)

1984: Peter and the Test Tube Babies
12" Single: 'Blown Out Again'
(Trapper Records)

1985: Peter and the Test Tube Babies
12" Single: 'Rotting In The Fart Sack' EP
(Jungle Records)

1986: Peter and the Test Tube Babies
7" Single: 'Key To The City'
(Jungle Records)

1987: Peter and the Test Tube Babies
7" Single: 'Louise Wouldn't Like It'
(Profile Records - US)

1990: Flesh for Lulu
7" & 12" Single: 'Time And Space'
(Capitol Records - US)

1990: Flesh for Lulu
7" & 12" Single: 'Every Little Word'
(Capitol Records - US)

1990: Peter and the Test Tube Babies
7" Single: 'When I Fall In Love / Toy Boy'
(SPV)

1995: Peter and the Test Tube Babies
7" Single: 'Supermodels'
(Dr Strange - US)

2017: Peter and the Test Tube Babies
7" Single: 'Crap Californian Punk Band'
(Arising Empire)

APPENDIX 2 – DEL GREENING
SELECT SOUNDTRACK AND FILMOGRAPHY

Film: Uncle Buck - Universal Pictures 1989
Track: 'Slide' - Flesh for Lulu

Film: Flashback - Paramount Pictures 1990
Track: 'Next Time (I'll Dream of You)' - Flesh for Lulu

Film: The Next Karate Kid - Columbia 1994
Track: 'Mystic Trader' - Flesh for Lulu

Film: You're Dead - Atlantic 1999
Track: 'Rob A Bank (Wanna)' - Peter and the Test Tube Babies

Film: Bones Brigade - Nonfiction Unlimited 2012
Track: 'Blown Out Again' - Peter and the Test Tube Babies

Film: Little Feather - Uvadeji Film 2016
Track: 'Banned From The Pubs' - Peter and the Test Tube Babies

Film: I'm Not OK With This - 21 Laps 2020
Track: 'Pissed Punks (Go For It)' - Peter and the Test Tube Babies

Film: For All Mankind - Sony Pictures - 2022
Track: 'Every Little Word' - Flesh for Lulu

Film: Until The Wheels Fall Off - Duplass Brothers 2022
Track: 'Blown Out Again' - Peter and the Test Tube Babies

Film: For All Mankind - Sony Pictures 2022
Track: 'Time And Space' - Flesh for Lulu

DVDs

1983: Peter and the Test Tube Babies
DVD: 'Cattle And Bum'
(Cherry Red Films)

2005: Peter and the Test Tube Babies
DVD: 'Paralitico'
(Locomotive Records)

Tome[1] & Metre[2] [3] Publishing[4] - 2022

---

[1] A book, especially a large, heavy, scholarly one.
[2] The rhythm of a piece of poetry.
[3] The basic rhythmic pattern of beats in a piece of music.
[4] To make information available to people, especially in a book.

Here we go again…

The lawyers take us to DEFCON 6, as we head towards oblivion with the further (How Not To...) rock 'n' roll adventures of Del Greening aka Del Strangefish.

His new collection of unbeliev҉   ҉ extraordinary backstage shenanigans retold by loɳɡ ҉ ...ɘrɪng colleagues, fresh hilarious encounters and nightmare flashbacks that were simply too risque for this book.

Grimace and snigger along as the free-thinkers of the music world unite in the struggle against the new Brexit restrictions and battle to overcome the deadly grip of the Covid-19 pandemic.

Witness the death and demise of punk rock legends Peter and the Test Tube Babies with Del continues to giggle in the face of adversity as the long-running police operation draws to its close, with officers beginning to surround and close in...

What goes on tour... stays in the next book!